Library of
Davidson College

International Law
and the
Independent State

To my daughter Paola

International Law and the Independent State

INGRID DELUPIS

Crane, Russak & Company, Inc.
New York

First published in Great Britain by Gower Press Limited, Epping, Essex 1974

© Ingrid Delupis, 1974

Published in the United States by
Crane, Russak & Company, Inc.
347 Madison Avenue
New York, N.Y. 10017

Library of Congress Catalog Card No. 73-94048

ISBN 0-8448-0317-0

Printed in Great Britain

Contents

Preface   ix

PART ONE   INTRODUCTION

1   *Sovereignty and Self-determination*   3
    1 : 1   Sovereignty and its aspects   3
    1 : 2   Territorial independence and self-determination   4

2   *Sovereignty and its Limitations*   21
    2 : 1   Types of restrictions of territorial sovereignty   21
    2 : 2   Presumption in favour of the competence of the territorial state   23

PART TWO   RESTRICTIONS OF SOVEREIGNTY OVER TERRITORY

3   *Passage Through Water*   29
    3 : 1   Territorial waters and adjacent zones   29
    3 : 2   Passage through straits and artificial canals   41
    3 : 3   Rights of navigation on international rivers   44
    3 : 4   Internal waters   45

4   *Passage Over Land*   59
    4 : 1   Requirement of treaty regulation or consent *in casu* for fixed installations   60

4:2	Transit by road	65

5 *Passage Through Air* — 79
   5:1 Historical background — 79
   5:2 ICAO regulations — 80
   5:3 Limits of the airspace — 82
   5:4 A general right of transit? — 84

6 *Other Restrictions of Sovereignty Relating to Territory* — 91
   6:1 Questions of pollution — 91
   6:2 Equitable use of water — 95

PART THREE   RESTRICTIONS OF SOVEREIGNTY OVER INDIVIDUALS AND PROPERTY

7 *General Rules on Immunity for State Activities* — 101
   7:1 State agency trading and private acts of heads of state — 102
   7:2 Jurisdiction over foreign ships — 103
   7:3 Jurisdiction over visiting forces and foreign military bases — 105
   7:4 Immunity of foreign state property? — 107

8 *Immunity of Diplomats and Consuls* — 115
   8:1 Immunity of diplomats — 115
   8:2 Immunity of consuls — 119
   8:3 Immunity of state delegates and international civil servants — 121

9 *Treatment of Individuals* — 125
   9:1 Treatment of aliens — 125
   9:2 Treatment of a state's own nationals — 129
   9:3 Derogation from sovereignty by extraterritorial asylum — 134

PART FOUR   COERCION AND CONSENT

10 *Coercion of a State to Conclude Treaties* — 141
   10:1 Developing countries' need for safeguards — 141
   10:2 Coercion and its historical background — 143
   10:3 Types of illegal force — 148

11	*Expression of a State's Consent*		*165*
	11:1	Force against whom?	165
	11:2	The requirement of consent and the problem of state succesion	173
12	*The Problem of Unequal Treaties*		*195*
	12:1	Identification of unequal treaties	195
	12:2	Agreements restricting territorial sovereignty and the theory of continuous consent	197
	12:3	Potentially unequal treaties: agreements on military bases	200
	12:4	'Sovereign' rights over foreign military bases	214
	12:5	Legal characteristics of military base agreements	216

PART FIVE   CONCLUSIONS

Conclusions   227

Index of Cases   233
Index of Treaties   237
Index of Subjects   243

Preface

Problems relating to independence are becoming of increasing importance in the modern international community, particularly to developing nations. In this work I shall analyse the meaning of independence and self-determination and their practical implications: the right to secede from colonial rule, the right to organize a community as a state sees fit, and the right to remain free from foreign interference.

In particular, I shall concentrate on the power a state exercises in its own territory. Here, a state has, by tradition, been the 'supreme power' and entitled to enact whatever laws or regulations it deemed necessary in its own domain. However, I shall show how this 'supreme' power has diminished to allow for certain prerogatives of other states under general international law or under special treaties. Second, I shall establish that states, especially developing nations, enjoy some protection against undue foreign interference under modern international law.

A state may bind itself by treaties to allow restrictions of its territorial sovereignty. But its power in its own territory may also be restricted under general international law—that is, whether or not the state has concluded a treaty on the matter. A state's territorial sovereignty may be restricted in two ways under general international law: there are restrictions which relate to the territory itself, or to the environment—for example, certain rights of transit and a duty to refrain from pollution—and there are restrictions which relate to individuals residing in the territory, for example immunity of state agents and human rights. Contrary to the old concept that a state could enact any laws in its own territory, a modern state is bound by international law to respect such restrictions, whether or not it has adhered to any treaty on these matters. According to the traditional view, the rules protecting diplomats and other state agents were one of the few exceptions where a state, in its own territory, had its own power reduced under international law— on the basis of reciprocity. But I shall establish that in this sphere the power of the territorial state is actually growing: state agents no longer enjoy absolute immunity and their prerogatives are gradually diminishing as their role as the sole medium of international cooperation has decreased. Nowadays, many of the functions formerly carried out by state agents are, for example, transferred to international organizations.

On the other hand, there are other matters in which a state formerly had complete power in its own territory and where modern international law has introduced restrictions. I shall establish that, contrary to what most traditional works on international law indicate, rules on transit, pollution and human rights have greatly changed in recent years. These changes show that the international community has adopted other standards and has introduced new priorities. Modern rules, for example, take more notice of the interrelationship of states in the contemporary community of nations, and, on the basis of reciprocity, allow for far-reaching restrictions of a state's sovereignty as to how it uses its own territory, or as to how it treats individuals, aliens or nationals, in its own land. In other words, international law is gradually breaking through the walls of a state, and the so-called 'reserved domain' which used to grant complete freedom to a state to handle its 'internal affairs' is being continually reduced.

The 'reserved domain' has thus been decreased by new rules of general international law which bind a state whether or not it has adhered to an agreement or treaty on the matter. But a state may also wish to restrict its territorial supremacy further by special treaties, for example to allow another state to use its territory for a certain purpose. Such territorial restrictions by treaty merit some special attention. Here, states are nowadays protected by new rules on coercion and by certain rules requiring the full and free consent of states when they enter into treaties. These rules are of particular importance to developing nations: such states may need special guarantees under international law to make sure that they do not suffer undue pressure in treaty negotiations where, because of their lack of strength, they may find it difficult to make their voices heard.

Treaties allowing for territorial restrictions are of particular importance to the problems of independence. It appears that some of these treaties constitute a new category of agreements which states by certain mechanisms may even denounce. I shall advance a new theory by which the rule of *pacta sunt servanda,* or the rule on sanctity of treaties, may be safeguarded although a state, in certain specific circumstances, may exercise a right to denounce treaties on territorial restrictions under the rules of self-determination.

I shall analyse in detail certain treaties relating to military bases. Such treaties reduce effectively important sovereign functions of a state in its own territory. Treaties by which a state allows its territory to be used for military bases have sometimes been called agreements on 'military servitudes'. But lawyers who have written on such 'servitudes' have not paid much attention to the type of coercion under which some of these agreements were concluded, nor have they analysed the character and function of such alleged 'servitudes' under international law. On the other hand, writers who have dealt with state succession have often claimed that treaties on military bases, being *in rem*—that is, relating to the territory—are 'inherited' by newly independent states. These writers have avoided discussing the problem of consent, the problem of 'unequal treaties', as well as the problem of whether a treaty concerning military bases can become unequal and burdensome to a successor state. Conversely, recent writers on unequal treaties have not noticed that the problem has a bearing on state succession and on the problems relating to independence.

It is the purpose of this work to cast some light on the intricate relationship between the host of questions mentioned above in order to present a systematic view of new problems of international law.

Acknowledgement

I wish to thank the Swedish State Council for Research for a research post and a grant which made the present study possible.

PART ONE

INTRODUCTION

Chapter 1

Sovereignty and Self-determination

1:1 SOVEREIGNTY AND ITS ASPECTS

Sovereignty has traditionally been used as a term to denote the collection of functions exercised by a state. Initially, it implied the supremacy enjoyed by a prince over his subjects—that is, it was a term concerned with the powers *within* a state. Later it came to be used to describe both internal powers and certain external relations. Jean Bodin perceived in his *Six livres de la république,* published in 1577, that sovereignty has a double aspect: it means that the state, or the prince, is the supreme power over subjects in a particular territory; second, it also signifies that the state enjoys freedom from interference by other states. Thus, there are both internal and external aspects of sovereignty. However, the external aspects only became important after the rise of the nation-states in the sixteenth and seventeenth centuries: after this time when there were several states in Europe, it became vital to examine the relationship between states and sovereigns.

Certain incidents of sovereignty gradually crystallized mainly because of the formation of several new states. The concept was used to cover three important rights of a state under international law: the right of equality, the right of independence and the right of self-determination. The first of these incidents appears to be mostly concerned with the external relations of a state whereas the rule of independence is concerned both with external aspects and with the power of a state in its own territory. In other words

> Sovereignty in the relations between states signifies independence. Independence in regard to a portion of the globe is the right to exercise therein, to the exclusion of any other state, the functions of a state.[1]

There appears to exist a certain causality between the concept of equality and the rule of independence: *because* all states are equal under international law they all enjoy the rights of independence. Furthermore, self-determination appears to be part of the rule of independence concerned mainly with the powers within the territory itself. It could also be pointed out that the rule of independence represents the negative aspects (the right to remain free from foreign interference) whereas the rule of self-determination represents the positive elements (the right to exercise the supreme power in the territory).

This book concentrates on the actual power of a state in its own territory under modern international law and analyses the practical implications of independence and self-determination.

1:2 TERRITORIAL INDEPENDENCE AND SELF-DETERMINATION

The territory of a state is the framework within which the state exercises its competence; the territory could even be said to furnish the very title of that competence. To have a territory is, in fact, one of the conditions of statehood and one of the main differences between a state and an international organization. Some international organizations nowadays exercise functions remarkably similar to those of a state: a law-making function, as well as executive and judiciary functions.[2] In the past many international organizations specialized in a certain field and were endowed with specific and limited powers. Now there are organizations, such as the European Economic Community, that enjoy a general legislative power, which is one of the corollaries of a state. The EEC also has 'subjects' over which it can exercise judiciary and executive functions. These subjects are not only the civil servants of the organization itself but also the member states and their citizens. But one important condition for statehood is not fulfilled by the European Community: it cannot be said to have a territory of its own within which it exercises general functions.

The territory of a state furnishes the title for the competence of the state: it is mainly within this territory that the state exercises its functions. However, this does not mean that the limits of the territory impose boundaries on the competence of the state. There are numerous functions which are extraterritorial or which have extraterritorial effects. For example the jurisdiction of a state extends for certain purposes beyond territorial waters to the contiguous zone which does not come within the limits of its territory. Some states may further claim jurisdiction over their subjects abroad or even over the subjects of other states for crimes committed abroad if the consequences of the crime extend to their own territory. But this book is not concerned with problems related to so-called 'objective' jurisdiction or other functions that a state may justly or unfoundedly claim outside its own territory. We are here concerned more with the actual exercise of power within the territory itself.

A state has been said to have *exclusive* competence within its own territory,[3] and *general* competence to legislate on all matters.[4] However, since international law regulates the behaviour between members of the society of nations there must necessarily exist some rules, based on reciprocity, which restrain the power of a state within its own territory in the interest of the community. A state cannot enjoy its exclusive and general rights within its territory under international law without at the same time assuming corresponding obligations. Max Huber, arbitrator in the *Island of Palmas* case formulated this rule as follows:

> Territorial sovereignty . . . involves the exclusive right to display the activities of a state. This right has as corollary a duty: the obligation to protect within the territory the rights of other states, in particular their right to integrity and inviolability in peace and in war, together with the rights which each state may claim for its nationals in foreign territory. Without manifesting its sovereignty in a manner corresponding to circumstances, the state cannot fulfil this duty. Territorial sovereignty cannot limit

itself to its negative side, i.e. to excluding the activities of other states; for it serves to divide between nations the space upon which human activities are employed, in order to assure them at all points the minimum of protection of which international law is the guardian.[5]

Most writers have assumed that the obligations that a state has to respect in its own territory mostly concern the treatment of aliens. A state would be bound to give aliens some minimum standard of treatment to comply with its obligations under international law. Rather than invent some artificial 'minimum standard' for aliens as writers have attempted in the past, I wish to suggest that obligations concerning aliens could be related to general rules on human rights.[6] Indeed, it is not only aliens who have such rights under international law: the state's own nationals also enjoy some basic human rights. The rule that a state can legislate 'as it pleases' for its own nationals —a view which is still held by many writers of today[7]—cannot be reconciled with emerging rules on human rights. The current view that rules on human rights have no effect 'inside' a state unless that state has adhered to a specific treaty on the matter can hardly be justified after the Second World War and the Nürnberg trials. Of course, a state can reserve a host of other matters for itself and it cannot be claimed that the whole cobweb of human rights applies to a state that has not adhered to the binding conventions on such rights: it is submitted merely that the state's power to legislate for aliens *and* its own subjects is limited by a few fundamental human rights, as I shall proceed to show.

1:2:1 Historical Background of the Rule of Self-determination

On 19 November 1792 the French National Assembly issued the following declaration:

> In the name of the French people the National Assembly declares that it will give help and support to all peoples wanting to recall their freedom. Therefore, the Assembly considers the French authorities responsible to give orders to grant all means of assistance to those peoples to protect and compensate

the citizens who might be injured during their fight for the case of liberty.

The Assembly furthermore declared that it would not interfere in the affairs of other states. Numerous declarations by states have repeated these principles of self-determination. But it is only during the last few decades that the rule of self-determination has assumed real importance for nations under colonial rule aspiring to acquire their independence.[8]

Article 1(2) of the Charter of the United Nations, which deals with the purposes of the organization, states that one aim of the UN shall be

> to develop friendly relations among nations based on respect for the principle of equal rights and self-determination of peoples and to take other appropriate measures to strengthen universal peace.

Furthermore, article 55 of the Charter provides that

> With a view to the creation of conditions of stability and well-being which are necessary for peaceful and friendly relations among nations based on respect for the principle of equal rights and self-determination of peoples, the United Nations shall promote higher standards of living, full employment, and conditions of economic and social progress and development.

Apart from these general articles there is nothing in the Charter which specifies the right of developing countries to acquire independence and self-determination and no rules which safeguard the independence of new developing nations once they have emerged as states.

It could be argued that chapters 11, 12 and 13 of the Charter, which concern the administration of non-self-governing territories and trust territories, reflect the international concern for such territories. Under article 73, members of the UN which administer non-self-governing territories undertake to 'develop' self-government and to 'take due account of the political aspirations of the peoples, and to assist them in the progressive development of their free political institutions'. States that administer trust territories have similar obligations under article 76. Although there is an obligation to report to the UN on the developments in such territories there are no safeguards to ensure that peoples of such territories actually do attain independence. Chapter 11 was presumably devised to replace colonial aspirations with the concept of self-government of territories under the administration of members of the UN; but the Charter failed to provide the UN with a machinery to deal with most postwar colonial crises. The Indonesian struggle for independence, and those of Morocco, Tunisia, Algeria and Cyprus have all come to the attention of the United Nations, not under chapters 11, 12 or 13, but either under the general powers of discussion of the General Assembly under articles 10, 11 or 14 or under the aegis of the Security Council under chapter 6 on pacific settlement of disputes, or under chapter 7, which concerns threats to the peace.

The San Francisco negotiators did not foresee such complications in colonial evolution as subsequently occurred—otherwise they might have enabled the United Nations to take other action under chapter 11 where the powers of the organization are limited as soon as a country has emerged as 'sovereign'.

1:2:2 Instruments dealing with Self-determination

(a) Resolutions of the General Assembly
The rudimentary rules on self-determination found in the UN Charter have been partly supplemented by resolutions adopted by the General Assembly on these and related matters. Article 21 of the Universal Declaration of Human Rights thus provides that

> (1) Everyone has the right to take part in the government of his country directly or through freely chosen representatives . . .
> (2) The will of the people shall be the basis of the authority of government; this will shall be expressed in periodic and genuine elections which shall be by universal and equal suffrage and shall be held by secret vote or by equivalent free voting procedures.

And resolution 637(VII) of 1952 provided that the 'State members of the United Nations shall uphold the principle of self-determination of all peoples and nations.'

The now-historic Declaration on the Granting of Independence to Colonial Countries and Peoples—resolution 1514(XV) of 1960—has had much impact on the attitudes of the Great Powers. The resolution which was adopted by a vote of 89 to 0 with 9 abstentions provides that:

1. The subjection of peoples to alien subjugation, domination and exploitation constitutes a denial of fundamental human rights, is contrary to the Charter of the United Nations and is an impediment to the promotion of world peace and cooperation.
2. All peoples have the right to self-determination; by virtue of that right they freely determine their political status and freely pursue their economic, social and cultural development.
3. Inadequacy of political, economic, social or educational preparedness should never serve as a pretext for delaying independence.
4. All armed action or repressive measures of all kinds directed against dependent peoples shall cease in order to enable them to exercise peacefully and freely their right to complete independence, and the integrity of their national territory shall be respected.
5. Immediate steps shall be taken, in Trust and Non-Self-Governing Territories or all other territories which have not yet attained independence, to transfer all powers to the peoples of those territories, without any conditions or reservations, in accordance with their freely expressed will and desire, without any distinction as to race, creed or colour, in order to enable them to enjoy complete independence and freedom.
6. Any attempt aimed at the partial or total disruption of the national unity and the territorial integrity of a country is incompatible with the purposes and principles of the Charter of the United Nations.
7. All states shall observe faithfully and strictly the provisions of the Charter of the United Nations, the Universal Declaration of Human Rights and the present Declaration on the basis of equality, non-interference in the internal affairs of all states. and respect for the sovereign rights of all peoples and their territorial integrity.

To implement the resolution the General Assembly established a special committee in 1961 by resolution 1654(XVI). This committee was empowered to make recommendations and suggestions to the General Assembly. The committee has been receiving petitions and has held hearings with petitioners. The Fourth Committee of the General Assembly has also in recent years developed a practice of receiving petitions from non-self-governing territories and has also granted hearings to petitioners. This new practice constitutes an important departure from the former policy of the United Nations that no organ of the organization should consider human rights petitions.

Other resolutions on equality and on natural resources—such as General Assembly resolutions 626(VIII), 1236(XII), 1301 (XIII), 1495(XV), 1505(XV), 1686(XVI), 1803(XVII), 1815(XVII), 1904(XVIII), 1966(XVIII) and 2158(XXI)—are also of great importance to the position of developing nations under international law and to their right of self-determination. For the few rules laid down in the Charter on equality, self-determination and independence reflect the view of only a comparatively small number of states. The United Nations now comprises almost three times as many states as in 1945—and nearly all developing nations became members of the UN after that date.[9]

In 1970 the General Assembly took an important resolution called 'The Declaration on Principles of International Law concerning Friendly Relations and Cooperation among States in Accordance with the Charter of the United Nations' adopted as resolution 2625(XXV) on 24 October, the twenty-fifth anniversary of the United Nations. Here, the General Assembly elaborated further what aspects of self-determination it considers necessary to guarantee in order to implement the Charter and to secure international peace and security: for, said the General Assembly, the subjection of peoples to alien subjugation, domination and exploitation constitutes a major threat to the promotion of international peace and security. The resolution provides that

> By virtue of the principles of equal rights and self-determination of peoples enshrined in the Charter of the United Nations, all peoples have the right freely to determine, without external

interference, their political status and to pursue their economic, social and cultural development, and every state has the duty to respect this right in accordance with the provisions of the Charter.

But self-determination does not, under this resolution, involve only the right to remain free from foreign domination; it also involves a right of the citizens to elect a government representing 'the whole people'. However, the General Assembly's opinion that this aspect also forms part of the rule of self-determination was only made evident by the concluding negative paragraph:

> Nothing in the foregoing paragraphs shall be construed as authorizing or encouraging any action which would dismember or impair, totally or in part, the territorial integrity or political unity and independent states conducting themselves in compliance with the principle of equal rights and self-determination of peoples as described above and thus possessed of a government representing the whole people belonging to the territory, without distinction as to race, creed, or colour.

(b) Conventions on Self-determination
In 1948 the General Assembly directed the Economic and Social Council to prepare recommendations on human rights including certain rules on collective supervision and guarantees which the Universal Declaration had omitted. It was agreed that civil and political freedoms and economic, social and cultural rights are interconnected and interdependent. They cannot always be easily divided into different categories nor can they be arranged in any hierarchical order: they are all equally vital. Without economic, social and cultural rights, political and civil rights become merely nominal: without civil and political rights, economic, social and cultural rights cannot survive. Still, as the two groups are basically different in nature it was decided to have two instruments laying down rules for each group. The General Assembly then directed the Commission on Human Rights to draw up draft covenants to ensure international respect for self-determination of people by resolution 545 on the basis that

> Member states shall in their relation with one another give due respect to the right of self-determination . . .

The Commission submitted two draft covenants in 1954: one on civil and political rights and another one on economic, social and cultural rights. In both draft covenants the Commission had included an article on self-determination which read:

> A. All peoples and all nations shall have the right of self-determination namely the right freely to determine their political, economic and cultural status.
> B. All states including those having responsibility for the administration of non-self-governing territories and those controlling in whatsoever manner the exercise of that right by another people, shall promote the realization of that right in all their territories and shall respect the maintenance of that right in other states in conformity with the provisions of the United Nations Charter.
> C. The right of people to self-determination shall also include permanent sovereignty over their natural resources. In no case a people may be deprived of its own means on the grounds of any rights that may be claimed by other states.

From these articles of the two covenants—which still have not entered into force as international conventions—it becomes clear that the covenants deal with different incidents of self-determination. The paragraphs concern different specific rights of states and their citizens and it is on these aspects of self-determination that this book will concentrate. The third paragraph was hotly opposed by the United States as it claimed it would endanger its investments in Latin America and other areas of the world. The United States delegate held that

> if we give the right of sovereignty over natural wealth and resources in the form of permanence it will be contradicting the principle which says that every state could limit at her own will at any time its sovereignty over its natural wealth and resources and also it will give to such state the authority to confiscate or nationalize foreign capital or break international treaties.

The sponsors of the article replied that the intention behind the third paragraph was not to 'threaten' foreign capital but to warn the owner of such capital that he should not misuse other nations' resources.[10]

By June 1973 each of the two covenants had been signed or acceded to by 52 states.[11]

1 : 2 : 3 Legal Value of the Rules of Independence and Self-determination under International Law

Independence and self-determination involve various rights under modern international law. It may be convenient to group the negative aspects together under the heading independence (the right to remain free from foreign interference and to denounce certain unequal treaties) whereas the positive elements can be referred to the rule of self-determination (the right to secede from colonial rule, the right to exercise the supreme power in the territory, the right to adopt a new constitution and the right to a representative government).

Thus self-determination entails not only a right of a country to attain independence, rid itself of foreign domination and remain free from foreign interference, but also certain human rights of the *citizens* of its territory. The Universal Declaration of Human Rights (see pp. 129-34) emphasizes the right of a nation's people to organize its government according to their wishes as expressed in free elections.

As a resolution of the General Assembly, the Universal Declaration does not, technically, have binding force. Nevertheless, the Assembly's resolutions reflect the attitude of a majority of nations on important matters. In some cases resolutions are more important than the loose provisions of the United Nations Charter, although the Charter, as a treaty, is endowed with 'binding force'. It is true that resolutions of the General Assembly are binding when they repeat rules which exist in customary international law or rules which on some other ground may be binding, for example rules embodied in other treaties.[12] In such cases, resolutions of the Assembly are not binding on their own merit but only because they reflect rules, the obligatory nature of which derives from some other underlying document or from international customary law. Still, the importance of the resolutions is paramount as they reflect the attitude of an overwhelming majority of states. At a time when new rules are emerging the resolutions may be the first instruments to crystallize them into clearly defined norms. In such cases, a resolution contributes not to law-making, as the Assembly is not competent to do that, but to the formulation of laws: it is the states themselves who are the authors of the underlying rules.[13]

It appears that the various aspects of self-determination have been secured under international law to different degrees. For example, the right to decide on a representative government through free elections is a rule which appears to be widely accepted. The right of secession, on the other hand, is highly controversial, whereas the right to remain free of foreign domination *after* independence is, at least in theory, less questionable.

To allow a people the right to organize their political entity as they wish may seem reasonable enough. Still, it is quite a change in international law to allow for this as a legal rule. International law has traditionally never interfered with such matters and has never granted any political rights to the citizens of a country unless there was a treaty with that effect. But international law is changing: the right to self-government, which thus involves the internal aspects of self-determination, is emerging as a new rule of international law and it will gradually crystallize so as to oblige states to respect the political will of citizens.

It was mentioned earlier that certain human rights apply to citizens of a state and bind the state even if there is no treaty embodying such obligations: this will be elaborated later. At this stage it may be emphasized that such binding rules on human rights include only certain fundamental rights (see p. 129). It is suggested that the right to elect a representative government—that is, the right of peoples to majority rule—is emerging as such a fundamental right. In spite of difficulties in overcoming the argument that some peoples are 'not yet ready' for such rights, and in spite of difficulties in ensuring that the new international legal rule is respected, political realities still seem to prove the thesis: for example, to the United Kingdom Investigating Commissions in Rhodesia the will of the people has been of paramount importance. However, it has been claimed that, for example, article 1(2) of the Charter of the United Nations refers to the relationship between states and that therefore self-determination of 'peoples' really refers to a right of states.[14]

The International Court of Justice went further than many traditional writers on international law when it gave its advisory opinion in 1971 on the legal consequences for states of the continued presence of South Africa in Namibia (South-West Africa): the Court treated the inhabitants of Namibia as having rights under international law and said the *people* was a 'jural' and an injured 'entity'. The *people* of that territory have a right, under international law, to progress towards independence and, the Court said, South Africa had violated this right by failing to comply with its obligations to submit to the supervision of the United Nations.[15] In May 1973 South Africa told the UN that independence could come to the territory within ten years and promised to respect the wishes of 'the whole population' in achieving 'self-determination and independence'.[16]

It is, however, often claimed that the rule of self-determination is a 'principle' and not a 'right'.[17] Or that even if it is a 'right' it is 'of a second order', or is a 'political' rather than a 'legal' right.[18] It has even been said that self-determination should have been excluded from the Human Rights Covenants[19] as it is concerned with the rights of peoples and not of individuals and, as such, rather than being directly enforceable it is a precondition for the exercise of other human rights.[20] However, there seems to be no reason why the right of self-determination could not be thought of as a human right of *collectivities*,[21] and this view is compatible with the opinion of the International Court in the *Namibia* case.

On the other hand, the rule of self-determination is not merely concerned with the rights of the citizens in one country to organize their government as they wish. It also implies the right of secession from colonial rule, a question which is more complex than the human rights aspects just discussed.

The right of secession may be willingly subscribed to by all colonial powers as long as they do not bind themselves to any time-schedule: here, again, the argument that certain people are 'not ready' for independent rule is put forward.

It has been claimed that the principle of independent rule has relevance only when *'foreign'* domination is the issue: that does not apply in cases of dissident citizens as such dissent would only cause territorial disintegration.[22] The commission established by the League of Nations to make recommendations in the Åland islands dispute held that the people of the islands did not have the right to secede from Finland by any principle of self-determination in spite of the fact that a referendum showed that there was almost unanimity that the islands should obtain an association with Sweden. The islanders are all of Swedish origin and Swedish is their mother tongue. But the commission of the League of Nations recommended that the islands remained under Finnish rule, although their Swedish traditions and language should be safeguarded by certain provisions for limited autonomy (see p. 184). The reasoning behind the recommendations was that any rule to secede under international law would result in complete 'anarchy' in the international community and would lead to serious territorial disintegration and rupture of political unity.[23]

It has also been claimed that the principle of self-determination, in so far as it involves the right to secede, is designed to safeguard non-self-governing territories against 'saltwater colonialism'.[24] This implies that a community may have a general right to form its own government if it is subjugated by an 'overseas' government. Recent developments in Pakistan and Bangladesh should show amply enough that the right to secede does not apply only to such 'saltwater colonialism' and that it may also operate in a number of other circumstances when a portion of a state secedes to form its own independent state in the same geographical area. To determine when such an emerging territory achieves statehood one still has to apply the classic conditions of international law: when there is a population within a specific delimited territory effectively controlled by their own proper political organs.

The colonial powers adhere to all provisions of the United Nations Charter having signed that instrument, which is both a treaty and a constitution for the United Nations. But the colonial powers have persistently denied that article 1 of the Charter, which among other things deals with self-determination, entails any 'legal right' for peoples to attain such self-determination.[25] In the debates on the Human Rights Covenants colonial powers refused to adhere to any provision on self-determination, and they have made clear that they will not sign a convention without reservations concerning such a clause.

Even if colonial powers did admit a legal right to secede it would be of little consequence for territories aspiring to independence. There is no way to safeguard such a right. There is no international tribunal available to peoples who seek judicial confirmation of their right to exercise self-determination: and there is no authority, apart from the colonial powers, to decide *when* such a right shall be *exercised* by a dependent territory.

Furthermore, problems arise over what entities should enjoy such a right of secession. It has been claimed that each 'nation' has a right to constitute an independent state and to determine its own government.[26] But what is a 'nation'? Is it a group of people of the same ethnic background? Or a group of people within some delimited geographical area, separated from the 'metropolitan' state? It is obviously difficult to define at what stage there is a 'nation' and at what stage the right to secession is bestowed on such an entity. It may, at least in theory, be easier in international law to decide that a new state has come into being (that is, when there is a territory with a population that is ruled effectively by centralized political organs). But once there is an actual state under international law there is no further problem about secession. A right to secession must be enjoyed *before* independence is reached. But if any 'group' is allowed such a right of secession then the coherence of many states may be disrupted by increasing fragmentation and this cannot be in the interests of either industrialized or developing nations. The right to secede must therefore be enjoyed only by certain fairly consolidated groups of people which to themselves and to the world appear to be emerging 'nations'. Although this may be clear in the case of 'colonies' that are geographically detached from the metropolitan country, in other cases a right of secession is less apparent.

It has been claimed that self-determination involves mainly a right to secession. Supporters of this view note that this aspect of self-determination has developed into a 'legal right'[27] and is no longer an essentially domestic matter: the General Assembly may not prescribe the exact time for the granting of independence but only urge that this occurs 'speedily'. But this is not all there is to self-determination. As shown above, other important aspects concern the right to decide on a representative government, the right to amend a state's own constitution and the human rights enjoyed under modern international law by the *citizens,* and not by the territory as such, to majority rule as well as the right to be free from foreign interference.

One aspect of self-determination, on which this book will concentrate, is the right to self-government once a country has established itself as a state. This aspect of self-determination is naturally closely linked to political issues such as foreign policy and to sociological issues such as the aptitude of a country for a certain socio-economic system. However, this book will concentrate on the questions which concern legal problems and, by examining a state's competence within its own territory, the limitations of this competence, and the problems of independence and foreign domination, will seek to establish rules which may form part of a new international law.

NOTES

1 Permanent Court of Arbitration (1928), *Reports of International Arbitral Awards*, vol. 2, p. 829.
2 See further I. Detter, *Law Making by International Organizations* (Stockholm: Norstedts, 1965), pp. 216 et seq.
3 *Savarkar* case (1911), J. B. Scott (ed.), *The Hague Court Reports*, vol. 1 (New York: Oxford University Press, 1916), p. 275.
4 *Free Zones of Upper Savoy and the District of Gex, Judgment, 1932, P. C. I. J., Series A/B, No. 46*, p. 96 and *Legal Status of Eastern Greenland, Judgment, 1933, P. C. I. J., Series A/B, No. 53*, p. 22.
5 Permanent Court of Arbitration (1928), *Reports of International Arbitral Awards*, vol. 2, p. 829.
6 See further infra, pp. 129 et seq.
7 For example, H. Kelsen, *Principles of International Law* (New York: Rinehart & Winston, 1952), p. 242, 'General international law does not impose upon the state any obligations concerning the treatment of its own nationals.'
8 On the history of self-determination, see A. Cobban, *National Self-determination* (London, 1945).
9 See Detter, 'The problem of unequal treaties', *International and Comparative Law Quarterly* (1966), p. 1071. In the same

article, references are given to numerous resolutions outside the UN framework on equality, independence and self-determination.
10   Cf. *US Department of State Bulletin*, vol. 28 (1953), p. 579 for the announcement that the United States could not, at that time, become party to any multilateral treaties like the two draft covenants on human rights. On nationalization of natural resources, see I. Delupis, *Finance and Protection of Investments in Developing Countries* (Gower Press, 1973), pp. 54 et seq.
11   The following states have signed or acceded: Algeria, Argentina, Australia, *Barbados*, Belgium, *Bulgaria*, Byelorussia, *Chile*, China (Taiwan), *Colombia*, Costa Rica, Cyprus, Czechoslovakia, Denmark, *Ecuador*, Egypt, *El Salvador*, Finland, Germany (Federal Republic), Germany (Democratic Republic), Guinea, Guyana, Honduras, Hungary, Iceland, Iran, Iraq, Israel, Italy, Jamaica, Jordan, *Kenya*, Liberia, *Libya, Malagasy Republic, Malta* (not the Civil Rights Covenant), Mongolia, Netherlands, New Zealand, *Norway*, Philippines, Poland, Romania, Senegal, *Sweden, Syria, Tunisia,* Ukraine, USSR, United Kingdom, Uruguay, Venezuela, *Yugoslavia*. Those in italics are bound by the covenants.
12   See Detter, *Law Making by International Organizations*, pp. 207 et seq.
13   It has been claimed that the Declaration on the Granting of Independence to Colonial Countries and Peoples (resolution 1514(XV) of 1960) is not even a 'recommendation' but constitutes an authoritative interpretation of the Charter—see Sir Humphrey Waldock in *Académie de droit international. Recueil des cours* (1962), ii, p. 33.
14   For example, H. Kelsen, *The Law of the United Nations* (London: Stevens & Sons, 1950), p. 52.
15   *I.C.J. Reports 1971*, p. 16 at p. 56.
16   UN press release. Cf. *Sunday Times*, 6 May 1973. Cf. infra p. 166.
17   Capotorti discussing Fawcett's paper. 'The role of the UN in the protection of human rights', in *International Protection of Human Rights: Proceedings of the Seventh Nobel Symposium, Oslo, September 25-27, 1967* edited by A. Eide and A. Schou (New York/Chichester: Interscience, 1968), p. 283.

18 Fawcett, in *International Protection of Human Rights*, p. 284
19 See infra, pp. 129 et seq.
20 Fawcett, in *International Protection of Human Rights*, pp. 96-8. Cf. Jenks at p. 285.
21 Scheuner, in *International Protection of Human Rights*, p. 283.
22 Statement of the Kenya delegation on the Somali question at the African summit conference in Addis Ababa 1963; see further, R. Emerson, *Self-determination Revisited in the Era of Decolonization* (Cambridge, Mass.: Harvard University Center for International Affairs, 1964).
23 League of Nations, *Journal Officiel* (1920), supp. 3; Toynbee, *Survey of International Affairs 1920-1923*, pp. 234 et seq. Cf. infra, pp. 183 et seq.
24 G. Schwarzenberger, *Foreign Investments and International Law* (London: Stevens, 1969), p. 6.
25 Cf. Eagleton, 'Self-determination in the UN', *American Journal of International Law* (1953), pp. 88 et seq.
26 Cf. Cobban, *National Self-determination*, p. 4.
27 See Shukri, *The Concept of Self-determination in the United Nations* (London, 1963); Emerson, 'Political development and the United Nations', *International Organization*, vol. 19 (1965), p. 484; see also American Society of International Law, *Proceedings* (1966), p. 129.
28 For example, Rosalyn Higgins, *The Development of International Law through the Political Organs of the United Nations* (London: Oxford University Press, 1963), pp. 104-5.

Chapter 2

Sovereignty and its Limitations

A state enjoys full sovereignty and self-determination over its territory and over persons and property in that territory unless international law contains specific rules to the contrary. As sovereignty implies a totality of power this means that legislative, judicial and executive functions in the territory can be carried out without foreign interference. In what ways, then, may international law restrict this exercise of sovereignty by a state in its own territory?

2:1 TYPES OF RESTRICTIONS OF TERRITORIAL SOVEREIGNTY

There might be a treaty concluded by the state by which it delegates certain sovereign functions to another state: in China the 'capitulation treaties' provided that certain *judicial* functions would be exercised by the consuls of foreign powers;[1] treaties between European states provide that certain *legislative* functions shall be exercised by the European Communities;[2] the same treaties allow the European Communities to exercise *sanctions* against individuals in the territory of the member states;[3] other treaties may allow foreign states to keep *armed forces* in the territory of a state.[4]

Such delegation of sovereign functions implies *positive* restrictions of sovereignty. Because of their importance, such restrictions are invariably granted by explicit treaties. Other positive restrictions may involve rights deprived of sovereign character, for example, rights of passage or grazing rights; in this category restrictions are commonly granted by treaty but occasionally, as far as transit is concerned, they are conceded under general international law or local custom. Finally, restrictions could, in some cases, appropriately be called *negative*, in so far as they imply that the state must refrain from certain action, such as pollution or misuse of common waters, or refrain from jurisdiction because certain persons are exempt, or 'immune' from territorial jurisdiction. In these cases restrictions of sovereignty are normally imposed by general international law, even if states have sometimes found it convenient to 'codify' rules in treaties.

The *subject-matter* of restrictions of territorial sovereignty thus ranges from delegation of important sovereign functions to a mere waiver of jurisdiction. The *method* by which territorial sovereignty may be restricted is not merely through the conclusion of treaties: there may be rules of general international law or local custom that impose limitations on the action of a state in its own territory.

The present work concerns *continuing* relations between *law-abiding* nations. Therefore, questions of use of a state's territory without its consent in war, or for enforcement action under chapter 7 of the Charter of the United Nations, or for self-defence purposes, will not be relevant. Nor will questions of self-help be discussed as such measures are, by definition, used in emergencies and are of an exceptional and temporary character, and not constituting any principle which is susceptible of continuous and recurring application, as the rules on which I shall concentrate.

Rules restricting territorial sovereignty may either concern the *territory as such* (the sea, land or airspace of a state) or the *persons and property* in that territory. I shall first examine restrictions concerning the territory itself and investigate what restrictions are imposed on a state even when it has not concluded a treaty on this matter, in other words I shall establish what restrictions exist under general international law. Right of transit may, for example, be claimed over sea, land or air, and it is important to examine whether rules of *general international law* allow for such passage. Other topical questions related to the territory as such concern the duty under general international law to refrain from pollution or misuse of common waters.

I shall then examine rules of *general international law* which concern restriction of sovereignty over persons and property in a state's territory, in the absence of treaties.

Finally, I shall show that when states restrict their territorial sovereignty further by *treaties*—further than general international law stipulates—special rules govern such agreements to protect the territorial sovereignty of states.

2:2 PRESUMPTION IN FAVOUR OF THE COMPETENCE OF THE TERRITORIAL STATE

There is a presumption in favour of the full sovereignty of a state over its territory unless a title or a rule can be shown under which international law would restrict the sovereignty. Thus for both a treaty and a customary or general rule of law there must be unequivocal proof that such a title to restrict the sovereignty exists. The legal implications of this statement are obvious in proceedings before an international court: it then becomes a question of *burden of proof*. The onus is on the one who claims restrictions of sovereignty to show a legal title, either by treaty or by customary international law or by general principles of law.

The rule that the burden of proof rests on the party who claims that the territorial sovereignty of a state has been restricted was clearly laid down in the *Lotus* case.[5] The case concerned a right of jurisdiction. A French ship had collided with a Turkish ship and considerable damage was caused to the Turkish ship and its crew on the high seas. When the French ship came to a Turkish port for repair the master of the ship was arrested, prosecuted and convicted for manslaughter. France argued before the Permanent Court of International Justice that since it was a French vessel and since the incident had taken place on the high seas, jurisdiction belonged to France under the normal rules of international law. The Permanent Court, however, held that since it was not possible to show any customary rules of international law restricting the jurisdiction of a state over ships in its ports, Turkey had not violated international law by exercising its jurisdiction.

The same principle, both as far as a presumption in favour of the territorial state and as a rule concerning burden of proof, was applied in the *Right of Passage* case.[6] Portugal claimed right of passage from a Portuguese enclave across Indian territory. India invoked *The SS Lotus* case and claimed that the burden of proof lay on Portugal to establish unambiguous evidence of a legal rule that there was a right to pass over Indian territory in derogation of India's exclusive sovereignty. Portugal referred to a number of treaties concluded with Indian princes in the eighteenth century as well as to customary international law and to general principles of law concerning the right of passage to enclaves. The International Court of Justice held that Portugal's claims were justified by customary international law but that the right of transit was limited to private persons and goods and that it could not possibly extend to military personnel and arms. The Court did not discuss general rules on the right of passage to enclaves and it did not rely on previous treaties to establish that Portugal had a right of way: its title to passage in derogation of Indian territorial sovereignty was derived from bilateral customary law.

Similarly, the right of asylum which excludes a person from the sovereign jurisdiction of a state must be unequivocally proved in each individual case. Or as the ICJ formulated it in the *Asylum* case[7] between Colombia and Peru:

> A decision to grant diplomatic asylum involves a derogation from the sovereignty of that state. It withdraws the defendant from the jurisdiction of that state and constitutes an intervention in matters which are exclusively within the competence of that state. Such a derogation from territorial sovereignty cannot be recognized unless its legal basis is established in each individual case.

A state which claims a title to derogate from the territorial sovereignty of another state thus always retains the burden of proof. When there is a treaty a claimant might find little difficulty in proving his title.[8] However, as will be seen, the situation may be more complex where a claimant state relies on customary international law and general principles of law as a basis for its title to derogate from the sovereignty of a territorial state.

Other complications arise, as will be seen, if a state wishes to denounce a treaty concerning restrictions of sovereignty.⁹

NOTES

1. See Detter, 'The problem of unequal treaties', *International and Comparative Law Quarterly* (1966), pp. 1073 et seq. and infra, pp. 141 and 199.
2. See I. Detter, *Law Making by International Organizations* (Stockholm: Norstedts, 1965), pp. 271 et seq. and infra, pp. 141 and 198-9.
3. Detter, *Law Making by International Organizations*, pp. 311 et seq.
4. See, infra, pp. 195-219.
5. 'Lotus', *Judgment No. 9, 1927, P.C.I.J., Series A, No. 10*.
6. *I.C.J. Reports 1960*, p. 6.
7. *I.C.J. Reports 1950*, p. 394.
8. But note the difficulties of Portugal in the *Right of Passage* case when the treaties dated from the eighteenth century and their provisions were not clear cut. Here, there was also the problem of state succession to treaties, a problem which the Court avoided, cf. infra, pp. 168-88.
9. See infra, pp. 197 et seq.

PART TWO

RESTRICTIONS OF SOVEREIGNTY OVER TERRITORY

Chapter 3

Passage Through Water

3:1 TERRITORIAL WATERS AND ADJACENT ZONES

3:1:1 Passage Through the Territorial Sea and Adjacent Zones

The territorial sea comes within the full sovereignty of a state:[1] for it is not just selected sovereign functions which a state is entitled to exercise over this stretch of water. Article 1 of the Geneva Convention on the Territorial Sea and the Contiguous Zone of 1958 states that

> The sovereignty of a state extends, beyond its land territory and its internal waters, to a belt of sea adjacent to its coast, described as the territorial sea.

This sovereignty is, however, limited by the traditional right of innocent passage of ships from other nations, a right which can be derived not only from the Geneva convention, other treaties or customary international law, but from general principles of law.[2]

Several writers have found difficulties in reconciling the concept of sovereignty with this right of innocent passage and some have suggested that territorial waters are not subject to sovereignty but only to some sort of servitude by the coastal state;[3] others suggested that territorial waters are really 'territoire submergé' and form a true part of the territory of a state although international law allows free passage in territorial waters.[4] The same controversy is reflected in some cases where municipal courts have refused jurisdiction for incidents in territorial waters. The *Archimedes* case before a Swedish court in 1869 indicates that a court may hesitate to exercise jurisdiction in territorial waters, claiming that the flag state should enjoy jurisdiction as the ship is 'part of the territory of the flag state'.[5]

In *The Franconia* case[6] in 1876, a British court similarly refrained from jurisdiction on the ground that

> by the principles of international law the power of a nation over the sea within three miles of its coast is only for certain limited purposes and Parliament could not consistently with those principles apply English criminal law within those limits.

Two years later the Territorial Waters Jurisdiction Act 1878 was passed, mainly as a result of the *Franconia* decision. The Act clearly lays down that British courts have full sovereignty over British territorial waters. However, a British court may choose not to exercise that right.[7]

Although the Geneva convention provides that the coastal state enjoys sovereignty over territorial waters, it clearly limits the right of jurisdiction in territorial waters and introduces several conditions which must be fulfilled before the coastal state can assume jurisdiction: the consequences of a crime on board a ship must extend to the coastal state, disturb its peace and good order, or concern crimes like illicit trafficking in drugs. A fourth exception provides that the coastal state is always competent to adjudicate if it is expressly requested to do so by the captain of the ship. These restrictions are not founded on general international law but form, at least as far as Anglo-Saxon practice is concerned, a noticeable deviation from customary international law.[8] Therefore, if a state is not a party to the Geneva convention it can probably still claim full jurisdiction over its territorial waters. But the right to innocent passage, which has consistently been granted by all nations, is not a right which relies only on the Geneva convention. If a state has not adhered to the Geneva convention it still has to accord innocent passage according to general principles of law.[9]

It is of little avail to assert that a state enjoys 'sovereignty' and not a 'bundle of servitudes' over territorial waters without knowing how far this marginal stretch of water extends. Lawyers disagree about the breadth of territorial waters.

The width of territorial waters was originally assessed by sight: the marginal stretch of water extended as far as one could see. Later, the cannon shot measured the stretch of waters that states could claim but for reasons of neutrality 12 miles were often allowed, or two 'lieues'.[10] States often used different limits for different purposes: under the Spanish–French treaty on customs limits of 1774, six miles was the limit for fishing and customs; but, by special decree, Spain adopted a three-mile limit for the purpose of neutrality in 1914. Some states applied six miles in relation to certain states under a treaty, and based their claims *vis-à-vis* other states on reciprocity: this was, for example, the case with Portugal under its treaty with Spain of 1885. The four-mile limit was, in particular, adopted by the Scandinavian states in the eighteenth century: they all used a 'German mile' (or a Swedish, Norwegian or geographical mile) which is equal to four nautical miles.[11] The three-mile limit was first applied by the United States in 1793 when it declared a three-mile neutrality limit during the naval war between Britain and France. In Britain the three-mile limit was originally applied at the beginning of the nineteenth century.

It is sometimes claimed that a three-mile limit is the 'proper limit' of territorial waters.[12] But four- to twelve-mile limits are widely claimed and accepted.[13] Some lawyers insist that 'any limit over 12 miles is invalid.'[14] However, state practice shows that many claims beyond 12 miles are made and, at least in some cases, the lack of protests from other states indicates that such claims may be allowed. El Salvador declared in 1950 that it claims a 200-mile limit for its territorial waters. By the Santiago declaration of 1952, Chile, Peru and Ecuador[15] claimed 200 miles. Similar 200-mile claims have come from Argentina (1966), Panama (1967), Uruguay (1969), Brazil (1970) and Sierra Leone (1971). Guinea claims 130 miles (1967), Nigeria, Ghana and Mauritania 30 miles (1972) and Iceland 50 miles (1972). The rights of coastal states in adjacent waters were confirmed by the Montevideo and Lima declarations of 1970[16] and by the Santo Domingo and Yaoundé declarations of 1972.[17]

The baseline from which territorial waters are measured is the mean low-water mark of spring tides following the shape of the coast and not a straight line drawn from point to point. Following the decision of the International Court of Justice in the Anglo-Norwegian *Fisheries* case,[18] article 4 of the Geneva Convention on the

Territorial Sea and the Contiguous Zone allows, in certain cases, for straight baselines, namely where there is a deeply indented coast or a coast with a fringe of islands. As will be seen from the discussion on internal waters, it may be a subjective decision of states whether a straight baseline is justified in an individual case.

The Geneva Conferences on the Law of the Sea of 1958 and 1960 failed to reach an agreement on the width of the territorial sea. However, article 24 of the Convention on the Territorial Sea and the Contiguous Zone specified that, within a stretch of water outside the territorial sea a coastal state may exercise certain sovereign functions to prevent and punish infringements of its customs, fiscal, immigration or public health regulations: but this stretch of water, the so-called 'contiguous zone', is not to extend beyond twelve miles from the coast, or, more accurately, from the baseline from which the territorial sea is measured.

This article may be interpreted to mean that the territorial sea itself may not, at least for the parties to the convention, extend beyond twelve miles. In other words, it would preclude any further extension of fishery zones or zones for other purposes.[19] But developments since 1958 show that states have not considered themselves precluded from claiming further zones, especially for fishing purposes. Such zones have been claimed by states which are bound by the Geneva convention as well as by states which have not adhered to this treaty. The convention may not be declaratory of existing international law[20] and therefore states that did not sign the Geneva convention remained free to claim such zones. But even states that did adhere to the convention appear to have retained their freedom to assess the width of their territorial sea at or beyond twelve miles, as well as to claim special zones adjacent to the territorial sea. Article 24 is in need of revision as it no longer reflects realities: far from precluding states from claiming adjacent zones it appears to have encouraged a number of countries to claim exclusive fishery zones. At the time of the Geneva Conferences only a few states made any claims to special zones; by 1973 at least 79 states had put forward such claims. There is a similar tendency to apply a wider limit for the territorial sea; in 1951 only three states claimed 12 nautical miles but 22 years later 51 states applied this wide limit and quite a few even more.

The idea of extending zones adjacent to territorial waters has been recurring in recent state practice. In June 1972 a number of African states declared in the so-called Yaoundé recommendations that—although their claims to a territorial sea would be limited to 12 miles—they would claim a further zone, the 'patrimonial sea' comprising a further 200 miles off the shores of coastal states. In this zone the coastal state (and African landlocked states) would have the right to exploit both the seabed *and* the superjacent waters: in other words African states would, among other things, have privileged fishing rights in this zone. On the other hand, the continental shelf should not, in the opinion of these states, be exploited exclusively by the coastal state further than the 'patrimonial sea'. Beyond the 200 miles it would be preferable to subject resources of the seabed, whether continental shelf or ocean floor, to international control, preferably under United Nations auspices. The Yaoundé recommendations were adhered to by Algeria, Cameroon, Dahomey, Egypt, Equatorial Guinea, Ethopia, Ivory Coast, Kenya, Mauritius, Nigeria, Sierra Leone, Tanzania, Togo and Zaïre.[21]

Similar suggestions were made in the Santo Domingo declaration of July 1972 and here the states attending the conference did not even find it necessary to restrict the exploitation of the continental shelf to any specific distance from the shores. The declaration was issued by Latin American and Caribbean states: Colombia, Costa Rica, Dominican Republic, Guatemala, Haiti, Honduras, Mexico, Nicaragua, Trinidad and Tobago, and Venezuela.[22]

In March–April 1973 talks were going on in New York in preparation for the UN conference on the law of the sea. Then, Australia took the initiative of forming a cohesive group consisting of Argentina, Brazil, Canada, Chile, Iceland, India, Indonesia, Kenya, Mexico, New Zealand, Norway, Peru, Sri Lanka, Trinidad and Tobago, Tunisia and Venezuela. These states would all like to see the exclusive privileges of the coastal state affirmed by a patrimonial sea of 200 miles. For example, Australia is ready to limit territorial waters at 12 miles but would claim a further 200 miles as 'patrimonial sea' where it would enjoy the right to exploit all reserves above and below the seabed, and retain existing rights to explore the continental shelf even beyond the 200 miles.[23] Some states forming part of the 'New York group' have even previously claimed territorial waters up to 200 miles, for example Argentina and Brazil (see p. 31). Others claim more limited territorial waters but have declared a fishery zone of 200 miles, as for example Costa Rica (since 1955), or oil protection and fishery zones at 100 and 200 miles, like Canada (since 1970). Some of the 'New York group' have, like Kenya, adhered to the Yaoundé recommendations (see p. 33). Finally, others, like Indonesia, have expressed their concern for extended privileges of the coastal state in the archipelagic principles (see p. 42).

There has, in fact, been a gradual erosion of the limits of the territorial sea and other 'zones': what matters most of all to so many nations of the world is fishing and consequently the fishery zones have become of the greatest importance even if, technically, the coastal states only exercise 'some' functions in such zones and not full sovereignty as in the territorial sea. The width of territorial waters has become important in modern international law partly because of the increased importance of fishing: it mattered little in the Middle Ages if states claimed 80 nautical miles for *jurisdiction* but agreed to let the waters be *used by all*.[24] Nowadays, states may be more willing to relinquish their claims to, say, criminal jurisdiction than their fishing rights.

In most cases, extensive claims to territorial waters are coupled with express provisions for *freedom of navigation*: beyond a certain moderate limit not only *innocent* passage is allowed but all ships, warships and submarines may pass as on the high seas.[25] Conversely, all recent claims for extensive fishing zones or for a 'patrimonial sea' have provided for full freedom of navigation.[26] There is then little difference from the point of view of *passage* between the 'patrimonial sea' and 'territorial waters'.

The unilateral extension of territorial waters and fishing zones adjacent to the territorial sea has caused some international disputes. For example, the United Kingdom has filed a suit against Iceland before the International Court of Justice; Iceland declared, by unilateral resolution, that it would extend its exclusive fishery zone to 50 miles as from 1 September 1972, in spite of protests by the United Kingdom. This case is particularly interesting as the United Kingdom had entered into an agreement in 1961[27] with Iceland. Under this agreement the United Kingdom government declared that it would 'no longer object to a twelve-mile fishery zone' around Iceland. In certain areas and during certain periods British fishing vessels would be allowed to fish in the outer six miles of this zone. But another provision stipulated that the Icelandic government would continue to 'work for the implementation' of a resolution of the Icelandic parliament regarding further extension of the fishery zone to the whole of the continental shelf—some 50 miles off shore; Britain would be given six months' notice of any such further extension. This wording may well imply that Britain knew about, and was agreeing to,[28] a further extension of the fishery zone claimed by Iceland.

On 17 August 1972 the International Court of Justice made an order for interim measures of protection in this case on the application of the United Kingdom. The Court ordered Iceland to refrain from applying administrative, judicial or other measures against British ships, or their crews, fishing outside the twelve-mile limit. On the other hand, the Court took into consideration that Iceland is economically dependent on fishing and decided that the annual catch by British ships should be limited in size. Iceland, which was not represented at the hearing of the Court, has declared that the International Court did not have jurisdiction to proceed to an injunction because the sole basis for jurisdiction was embodied in the 1961 exchange of notes which was no longer in force when the United Kingdom made its application.[29] Furthermore, the 1961 agreement had been concluded 'when the British Royal Navy had been using force to oppose the twelve-mile fishery limit'.[30] Finally, Iceland has contested the jurisdiction of the Court for the purpose of an interim order because 'negotiations' were proceeding and therefore any injunction would disrupt such talks.[31]

The interim order of the International Court is naturally in no way prejudicial to the substantive questions to be dealt with by the Court after it declared itself competent in January 1973. However, it is interesting to note that the Court does recognize that *economic* dependence of a coastal state on fishing may warrant limitations on the catch of other states; in other words, the coastal state appears to enjoy some priority. To take such economic dependence into consideration appears to be a new approach in international law, although the special interest of a coastal state in fishing in adjacent waters has been recognized, for example, in the 1958 Convention on the High Seas.[32]

It may still be true that states can extend their territorial waters and fishery zones by unilateral decisions as long as they allow for *free navigation* for all beyond some reasonable limit. There have been protests in the past, both by the United States in the case of South American extensions[33] and by Britain and Germany in the case of Iceland. The extending states have, however, made clear that they were prepared to safeguard their new limits, by force if necessary. In 1954 Peru effectively enforced its 200-mile claim: Peruvian naval and air units seized two whaling vessels owned by Onassis 160 miles off the Peruvian coast.[34] In 1971, 17 United States fishing vessels were seized 50 miles off the coast of Ecuador and heavily fined. In 'retaliation' the United States announced that it would reconsider the question of economic aid to Ecuador.[35] In the Icelandic additional zone British vessels are said to be 'harassed'. It has been claimed that in the case of South America regional customary law has already developed.[36] However, it is difficult to justify the status of customary law for a rule that has been the subject of constant protests by interested states: for customary rules are, by definition, based on some *initial* consensus between nations about what is to be regarded as 'law'. On the other hand, once such law has developed a state cannot by later protests reverse the established rules.

It is, therefore, submitted that the initial consent—perhaps in the form of acquiescence—of other interested states is necessary to allow for any changes of the width of territorial waters and fishing zones. Furthermore, even if such consent is given by 'interested' states it can only, beyond a certain 'reasonable' limit, allow for the *temporary* use of such waters for there may come a time when other nations may become 'interested parties' and the states which happen to be geographically near cannot waive the rights of the international community as a whole.

The principle of the freedom of the sea undoubtedly forms part of international law. It cannot be possible for states to extend by unilateral decisions, or even by joint or collective decisions, their territorial waters or fishery zones up to *any* limit. There must come a stage when such extended limits infringe upon the freedom of the seas, in other words when these limits are no longer 'reasonable'.

But what is reasonable? I should like to submit that this must be assessed *in casu,* as each individual case must be judged on its own merits. But the main criterion is, I submit, a geographical one: if a state is situated in an isolated position, it may not be unreasonable to allow that state a comparatively larger portion of territorial waters and adjacent fishing zones. A state's dependence on fishing for national economic reasons must also be taken into account. This may also be one case where developing nations must enjoy special priorities under international law if this legal system is to promote their economic growth.

However the width of the territorial sea and adjacent zones is assessed, a coastal state is in all circumstances bound to allow for the innocent passage of ships of other nations. The same also applies to the waters above the continental shelf: here, as within fishery zones, free transit must be allowed and here 'free transit' implies far more than innocent passage, for the waters above the shelf are high seas through which all ships, submarines and warships, have the right to pass.[37] Some South American states do claim all the epicontinental sea as territorial waters. In such cases they are naturally obliged to allow for innocent passage. However, these states invariably allow free transit even for warships beyond a certain limit.[38]

Under the 1958 Convention on the Continental Shelf the 200-metre depth contour is the decisive limit of the portion of the shelf that may normally be claimed by the coastal state: but the convention allows states to exploit the shelf beyond this limit where exploitation is possible. In 1958 it did not appear likely that states would be able to exploit the shelf at any greater depth than 200 metres but because of subsequent technical developments it is now possible to exploit resources at a much greater depth. The provision allowing the coastal state to exploit the shelf up to the limit where the depth admits such exploitation, was included in the convention to safeguard the interests of countries like Norway where a deep trench outside the coast would otherwise unduly reduce its rights.

It soon became important to consider the effects of excessive claims by states to the continental shelf. By resolution 2340 (XXII) of 1967 the UN General Assembly sought to establish certain principles governing the seabed and the ocean floor and subsoil thereof. By resolution 2750 C (XXV) of 1970 the General Assembly recommended a general conference to be convened in 1973 to review regimes on the high sea, territorial sea and contiguous zone—including the breadth of such zones—fisheries—including the preferential rights of coastal states—and problems concerning conservation of the living resources of the high seas, preservation of the marine environment—including pollution—and scientific research.[39]

According to a proposal by Britain made during the preparation for this conference on the law of the sea, the whole ocean floor could be 'carved up' and allotted in blocks to various nations of the world.[40]

However, at present the regime applicable to the continental shelf is embodied in the 1958 convention. This convention stipulates that the rights of a coastal state to the continental shelf do not affect the legal status of the superjacent waters as high seas. In other words, although a state's territory could be said to extend to the continental shelf, it is only the resources in the seabed itself to which the state has priority: those resources include minerals and oil as well as the living organisms that retain constant contact with the seabed. Other fish and crustaceans are not included among the 'resources' of the continental shelf that the coastal state has the exclusive right to exploit but belong to the resources of the high seas.

But the continental shelf cannot be exploited without installations and pipelines, which might interfere with both navigation and fishing in the superjacent waters: the 1958 convention provides that inconveniences caused shall not be 'unjustifiable' which appears to be rather a weak safeguard. Contracting states must also 'notify' each other about relevant installations.

The International Court of Justice held in the *North Sea Continental Shelf* cases[41] that in so far as the convention concerns the equidistance principle for division of a continental shelf common to several states, it does not lay down any general principle of international law; in other words, a state that has not adhered to the Convention on the Continental Shelf is not bound to apply this principle as the convention goes beyond what general international law demands. Several agreements have now been concluded between states which have a common continental shelf—for example in the Persian Gulf[42] and in the North Sea[43]—and under these agreements the shelf has been divided to allow for prospecting of oil and gas by individual countries.

Provisions in these agreements attempt to safeguard competitive drilling if a gas or oil field extends across the dividing line.[44] Although some agreements mention other resources, such as gravel,[45] they are mostly concerned with division of the shelf for the purpose of exploiting oil and gas. The national areas of the continental shelf in the North Sea are divided into blocks. Prospecting licences may be obtained from the state that 'owns' the block. The size of each block is usually 100 square miles which could well encompass the whole of an oil or gas field. The famous Masjid-i-Suleiman Field in Persia is twelve by four miles; the gas field at Groningen covers several hundred square miles but is thought to be exceptional in size.[46]

Even if the Convention on the Continental Shelf is not declaratory of general international law in so far as it concerns the equidistance principle, it does appear to possess such declaratory force as far as certain other rules are concerned: a state which has not signed the convention is still bound to allow for innocent passage in its territorial sea above the shelf; and it is bound to allow for free transit in the waters above the shelf outside such territorial waters. The provision of the Convention on the Continental Shelf that the 'sovereign rights' a coastal state enjoys to the resources of the shelf will not alter the legal status of superjacent waters is thus declaratory of general international law, as it embodies a rule which binds all states whether or not they have adhered to this convention.

3:1:2 What Constitutes Innocent Passage?

Article 14(1) of the Geneva Convention on the Territorial Sea and the Contiguous Zone lays down that

> ... ships of all states, whether coastal or not, shall enjoy the right of innocent passage through the territorial sea.

Such passage may, according to paragraph 2, involve navigation for the purpose of traversing the territorial sea without entering into internal waters or of proceeding to internal waters or, finally, making for the high sea from internal waters. According to article 14(4) the right of innocent passage includes stopping and anchoring but only in so far as these are incidental to ordinary navigation or are rendered necessary by *force majeure* or by distress. No charges may be levied except as payment for specific services rendered to a ship.[47]

The right of innocent passage is, according to the Geneva convention, specifically accorded to 'all ships', and article 14(6) provides that submarines are required to navigate on the surface and to show their flag

which indicates that the right of free passage is also enjoyed by warships. The draft submitted by the International Law Commission, on which the Geneva convention was based, had suggested that passage of warships would require previous authorization of the coastal state. The convention is silent on this point but by referring to 'all ships' it is hardly reasonable to assume that warships should be excluded from the right of innocent passage.[48] This, however, appears to exceed the obligations of a coastal state under general international law and a state which has not signed the Geneva convention therefore retains the sovereign right to refuse passage to warships but is obliged to let merchant ships pass through its territorial waters.[49]

The fact that a number of nations require previous notification of passage of warships and that they choose to 'authorize'[50] such passage in each individual case confirms the view that no general right of innocent passage of warships exists under general international law.[51] Authorization should not be withheld unreasonably in times of peace.[52] Passage by oil tankers or nuclear-powered merchant ships is presumably to be considered as 'innocent' in spite of potential danger to the coastal state in case of an accident.[53]

On the other hand, the right of a coastal state under the Geneva convention to interfere with the passage of foreign ships including warships through its waters has been slightly enlarged. In accordance with general rules on innocent passage the International Law Commission had suggested that

> passage is innocent so long as a ship does not use the territorial sea for committing any acts prejudicial to security of the coastal state or contrary to the present rules or to other rules of international law.

Instead of adopting this draft article which laid down present rules of international law the Conference adopted article 14(4) which provides that

> passage is innocent so long as it is not prejudicial to the peace, good order or security of the coastal state. Such passage shall

take place in conformity with these articles and with other rules of international law.

This implies that the coastal state can interfere not only when acts committed within the territorial sea endanger its security but also when the coastal state feels threatened by acts that occurred before the ship reached territorial waters.[54] The very presence of warships in the territorial sea could well constitute such a threat.[55] And the very reasons why international law once granted ships a right of innocent passage—to facilitate international trade—could hardly concern warships.[56]

It has been claimed[57] that this aspect of the Geneva convention is based on the *Corfu Channel* case[58] where the International Court of Justice held that a warship enjoys a right of innocent passage through the territorial waters of another state in time of peace, even if it has not obtained previous authorization. But this right of innocent passage concerned only a special type of territorial water: namely territorial waters that form part of *straits*. Straits are subjected to a special regime.

3:2 PASSAGE THROUGH STRAITS AND ARTIFICIAL CANALS

If the land on both sides of straits belongs to the same state and the width of the entrance of the straits does not exceed six miles then the waters are internal and subject to the same rules as national waters.[59] There is one exception to this rule: if the straits connect open seas they must be open to all ships of all states at least in time of peace. In other words, warships enjoy a right of innocent passage through straits connecting two high seas if the land on the sides of the straits belongs to one state or if it belongs to two different states and the ship has to pass through their territorial waters in the straits.

The reasons for this exception to the rule that warships can be denied innocent passage in territorial waters and, even more validly, denied passage through national waters, is that straits connecting two portions of the high seas form part of the 'highway' for international traffic where foreign warships can hardly be denied innocent passage.[60]

In the *Corfu Channel* case[61] it was made clear that straits do not have to be 'essential' for maritime communications. It would suffice if they were 'normally used',[62] a formulation which was also adopted by the Geneva Convention on the Territorial Sea and the Contiguous Zone which declares that straits used in international navigation are 'open' to all vessels.[63]

It appears, then, from the words used by the International Court, as well as those in the Geneva convention, that the rule allowing innocent passage to 'all ships', even warships, through national or international straits connecting two large areas of the high seas is based on the *use* of such waters, in other words on *custom*. A right to pass through straits must therefore be more clearly established than a right of innocent passage through ordinary territorial waters, a right which exists independently of any custom: a merchant ship can claim a right of innocent passage through territorial waters even if it is the first ship ever to do so. If straits have always been closed to foreign ships, for example national straits where neither merchant vessels nor warships have attempted to enter, it is difficult to substantiate a claim that they should be entitled to innocent passage.

If a stretch of water has been *used,* over a period of time, by foreign vessels then a legal right will have emerged through custom and other nations will have come to rely on that right. It is indeed questionable whether a coastal state may later interfere with such rights established by custom.

In the case of the Straits of Malacca and Singapore both Malaysia and Indonesia have declared that the waters concerned are not international straits although the two governments fully recognized 'their use for international shipping in accordance with the principle of innocent passage'.[64] Singapore, on the other hand, did not concur in this view but 'took note' of the position of the other two states on this point.[65]

Some states concerned with passage through straits which they wish to de-internationalize declared in 1972 in the 'archipelagic principles', that high sea passage would no longer be permitted in such straits without the consent of and on certain conditions laid down by the coastal state. The states making this declaration were Indonesia, the Philippines, Fiji and Mauritius.

However, it is doubtful whether straits can, in this way, be 'de-internationalized' if, for a considerable time, they have been used by ships of all nations. One reason for attempting such action may be that a coastal state intends to impose a national toll on passing ships allegedly to cover pollution risks caused mainly by oil tankers. But this cannot be permissible if the right of transit has already been established by firm custom although charges for specific services rendered may be levied.[66] Therefore, the only way in which a coastal state may interfere with a right of transit through international straits is in case of national emergencies when certain temporary restrictions may be allowed under international law.

The same rules as for straits apply to international and national canals. Merchant ships enjoy a right of innocent passage, *even in the absence of treaties,* but a right of passage for warships may be more difficult to sustain.

An example of a national artificial canal which through custom has been open to foreign merchant ships, even if not to foreign warships, is the Corinth Canal, which, since it was opened in 1883, has been consistently used by foreign merchant vessels.[67] The canal is entirely within Greek territory but the right of free navigation is so firmly established by custom that it can hardly now be closed to foreign vessels by Greece.

The great interoceanic canals of Panama, Kiel and Suez were regulated by international conventions that opened them to all ships of all nations. In the case of Panama there were two relevant treaties, one concluded between the United States and the United Kingdom —the Hay–Pauncefote treaty in 1901—and one concluded between Panama and United States—the Hay–Bunau-Varilla treaty of 1903. Under the first treaty the United States agreed that the canal, which was to be built between the Atlantic and the Pacific, would be open to all ships at all times. Under the second treaty, by which Panama granted a concession of land to the United States for the construction of the canal, Panama was bound to let the canal be open at all times to vessels of all nations and this right *erga omnes* is now part of general international law and subsists irrespective of the treaty.[68]

Navigation through the Suez Canal was regulated by the convention of Constantinople of 1888 which opened the canal to all ships; and even after the nationalization of the canal[69] Egypt declared that it considered itself bound by the convention and that it was 'determined to afford and maintain free and uninterrupted navigation of all nations'.[70] As a result of the war in which Egypt has been involved the canal was, however, closed in 1967.

The Kiel Canal was constructed in 1896 and lies wholly within German territory. By article 380 of the treaty of Versailles it was opened to all nations. Its status was reconfirmed by the important *Wimbledon* case before the Permanent Court of International Justice.[71] The Court held that the Kiel Canal was 'an international waterway intended to provide under treaty guarantee easier access to the Baltic for the benefit of all nations'; even warships used the canal. The Kiel Canal shows what right of transit can be claimed by foreign ships in the absence of treaties. Hitler emphatically denounced the Versailles treaty but even if there were no treaty in force regulating the Kiel Canal it would still be open to vessels by force of customary international law,[72] at least as far as merchant ships are concerned as such vessels *use* the canal and rely on the right *erga omnes*.

3:3 RIGHTS OF NAVIGATION ON INTERNATIONAL RIVERS

By a famous declaration of 16 November 1792 the French provisional executive ordered the French commander-in-chief in Belgium to ensure that the rivers Meuse and Escaut were subjected to a regime of free navigation. International treaties regulating these rivers were concluded in 1795 and in 1804 a convention on the Rhine was adopted. The legal status of the Rhine was further elaborated at the Congress of Vienna in 1815. Treaties were concluded concerning the Elbe (treaty of Dresden 1821), the Rhine (treaty of Mainz 1831 and convention of Mannheim 1868), the Escaut and Meuse (treaty of London 1839), the Danube (treaty of Paris 1856, treaty of Berlin 1878 and treaty of London 1883) and for the Congo and the Niger (general act of the Berlin conference 1885).

Other treaties regulated navigation on rivers in South America: agreements were concluded in 1850 to grant free navigation to all on the Rio Grande, Amazonas and Río de la Plata; another treaty of 1853 granted the right of free navigation to all nations on the Paraguay and Paraná. In North America the St Lawrence river was opened to all nations by a treaty of 1854.

Thus by the end of the nineteenth century a number of international rivers were subjected to elaborate treaty regimes, all based on the principle of free navigation. The peace treaties of 1919 and the Barcelona convention of 1921 reconfirmed the right of free navigation on principal European rivers. Some international rivers, for example the Danube, were governed by river commissions which, as forerunners of international organizations even exercised a law-making function.[73] These regimes were highly detailed, but it can be established that even without treaty regulation a legal right of free navigation for merchant ships on international rivers has crystallized. The view is nowadays generally admitted that rivers whose navigable waters pass through the territory of more than one state, or which form a boundary between two states,[74] and thus are 'international' are open to merchant ships of all nations.[75]

3:4 INTERNAL WATERS

Internal or national waters are those which entirely lie within the baseline of the territorial waters—that is, bays and gulfs, ports and harbours, landlocked seas, straits and rivers.

3:4:1 Access to Bays

Inland bays are now defined by article 7 of the Geneva Convention of 1958 on the Territorial Sea and the Contiguous Zone. The convention stipulates that if the distance between the low-water marks of the natural entrance points of a bay does not exceed 24 miles then a straight baseline may be drawn to enclose the bay as internal waters. If, on the other hand the points are wider apart than 24 miles then a straight line should be drawn further inside the bay to enclose as internal waters what is nearer to the coast along that line. This artificial formula is different from the solution adopted by the International Court of Justice in the Anglo-Norwegian *Fisheries* case[76] where the Court allowed certain straight lines drawn by Norway to delimit internal waters on the ground that a fringe of islands formed 'a whole' with the mainland and that the territorial sea must follow the 'general direction' of the coast; straight lines may then be called for if a coast is deeply indented. The formula of the Court might prove somewhat ambiguous particularly if the map of a sea coast is examined at different scales. However, it appears that the Geneva convention also complicates the definition of 'internal waters' by introducing the questionable criteria employed by the Court in the *Fisheries* case. Article 4 introduces the principles laid down by the Court and provides that straight baselines may be used in localities where the coastline is deeply indented and cut into, or if there is a fringe of islands along the coast in its immediate vicinity; in such case the above mentioned formula for bays no longer applies.[77]

By using straight baselines, a considerable portion of what were previously territorial waters or the high seas may be claimed as internal waters by states. To safeguard established rights of transit in such cases article 5(2) of the Geneva convention provides that:

> Where the establishment of a straight baseline in accordance with article 4 has the effect of enclosing as internal waters areas which previously had been considered as part of the territorial sea or of the high seas, a right of innocent passage, as provided in articles 14 to 23, shall exist in those waters.

Although this restriction of a state's sovereignty over internal waters is imposed by a treaty, the Geneva convention, it is submitted that even without a treaty states could probably claim a right of passage under customary international law over waters which have only recently become 'internal' by virtue of the formulae enunciated by the Geneva convention. A right of prescription could possibly be claimed even over internal waters that have not undergone any change of status in the case of unequivocal custom.

3:4:2 Rights of Navigation on National Rivers

Although national rivers, according to the traditional view of international lawyers, are the concern only of the territorial state there is reason to believe that a right of navigation on such internal rivers is emerging as a rule of international law.[78]

However, as described earlier in the case of internal canals there is, in my opinion, probably no general right of navigation as in the case of an international river but a right which has to be reinforced by custom and use tolerated by the territorial state. The eminent Dr Colombos went as far as to suggest that the award of Duffield, umpire in the arbitration between Germany and Venezuela in *The Faber* case, was 'wrong': the umpire had held that Venezuela possessed the right to prohibit altogether navigation in the Catatumbo and Zulia rivers, two internal rivers, even to seagoing vessels carrying oceanic commerce.[79]

But even allowing for such free navigation if reinforced by custom and tolerated by the territorial state, there is naturally still a right for the territorial state to exclude any vessel that might endanger the state's security—for example, warships. The territorial state is also entitled to impose fiscal and police regulations on merchant vessels provided such regulations do not restrict free navigation.

There are several instances in which free navigation on national rivers may be a right to be enjoyed under international law: if rivers are navigable from the open sea and if they are indispensable to international commerce; if a navigable river is convenient for a landlocked state that has no other access to the sea. As will be seen in the discussion of transit over land the rule of equal right to the high seas for all nations becomes purely illusory if landlocked states are denied access by being refused all rights of transit.

3:4:3 Access to Ports

Ports and roadsteads are under the full territorial sovereignty of a state. Such a state consequently enjoys full jurisdiction over merchant ships in its ports although, as a gesture of 'international courtesy', many states may not exercise jurisdiction.[80] English courts, and courts in some other states, following the French leading cases *The Sally* and *The Newton*[81] which came before the Conseil d'Etat in 1806, tend to decline jurisdiction in cases of crimes committed by one member of the crew against another or which concern the internal discipline on board. They may claim jurisdiction if a foreigner of the flag state is involved, if a crime is committed ashore, if the general order of the coastal state has been disturbed, or, if jurisdiction is specially requested.[82] Warships, on the other hand, are commonly held to enjoy immunity from jurisdiction.[83] At least English courts also grant immunity to public ships although such privileges appear increasingly unjustified in the case of trading vessels.[84] However, even if a coastal state enjoys full sovereignty over its ports and consequently enjoys full *jurisdiction* (see pp. 103-5), it does not follow that it can close its ports to foreign merchant vessels.

Although ports come within the full sovereignty of a state merchant vessels of other states thus enjoy a general right of access to ports.[85] A state can refuse access to ports only if this does not infringe rights established by custom or by treaty or if the state finds itself in danger.[86] But, unless a state gives special authorization, only merchant ships enjoy this right of access and they can only expect to be admitted to commercial—but naturally not to military—ports. If a ship is in distress it is probably the duty of a coastal state to allow her into any port.[87]

The right of access to ports may be incidental to other rights of transit: if there is to be free navigation on international rivers, for example, there must also be some minimum access to a port at the mouth of the river. It was also held by the Permanent Court of International Justice, in line with this argument, in the *Jurisdiction of the European Commission of the Danube*[88] that the freedom of navigation of a river includes freedom of movement for vessels going to and from the sea and also extends to ships coming into or leaving a port.

The Permanent Court confirmed the same view in the later *Oscar Chinn* case.[89] This case concerned, inter alia, certain privileges granted by Belgium to the Belgian company 'Unatra' of the Belgian Congo. The Court decided with respect to the right of access to ports that it is

> universally accepted [that] freedom of navigation referred to by the Convention comprises freedom of movement for vessels, freedom to enter ports and to make use of plants and docks, and to load and unload goods and to transport passengers.

The right of access to ports that merchant vessels enjoy under international law merely involves certain *minimum rights*. It does not, for example, include the right to trade along the coast (cabotage). If any more extensive rights are demanded the coastal state must give its express consent. The rights to be described shortly that are enjoyed by the Agence belge de l'Afrique de l'Est in the port of Dar es Salaam clearly exceed such minimum rights and unless Tanzania gave its consent to these rights they could not subsist. This consent must not be construed as following from any rule of state succession.⁹⁰ The background of the rights in the dock of Dar es Salaam is as follows.

In 1921 Belgium concluded the Belbase agreement with the United Kingdom by which Belgium acquired right of transit for persons and goods coming from and going to the territories of the Belgian Congo and of Ruanda-Urundi. Belgium acquired, under the same agreement, a lease in perpetuity at one franc a year for sites at Dar and at Kigoma for the construction of port facilities. The leased sites were to be immune from British customs control.⁹¹ In 1951 a supplementary agreement provided that the leased sites would be moved to enable the construction of a deep-water quay.⁹² The operation of facilities was granted to the Antwerp company, Agence belge de l'Afrique de l'Est. In 1962 Tanganyika, as a newly independent state, asked Belgium to evacuate the sites. But, in 1960, the Belgian Congo had become independent, as the Republic of the Congo, and it was the Republic that had paid the one franc rent and so Belgium passed on the diplomatic request to them and declared by a note to Tanganyika that Belgium only remained interested in the matter in so far as Ruanda-Urundi was concerned; but shortly afterwards, on 1 July 1962, these territories emerged as the independent Rwanda and Burundi and Belgium declared that it no longer had any interest in the matter. At its independence Tanganyika had announced in connexion with the leased sites that it

> would not object to the enjoyment by a foreign state of special facilities in our territory if such facilities had been granted in a manner fully compatible with our sovereign rights and our new status of complete independence.

On the other hand, Belgium had invested a large sum of money in the construction of a deep-water quay and would consequently be entitled to some compensation if its facilities were discontinued. These claims were now passed on to the Republic of the Congo and to Rwanda and Burundi. The three states were willing to ascertain among themselves their proportionate share of compensation. However, Tanganyika, by now Tanzania, decided to tolerate the continued operation of the Agence belge in the port of Dar es Salaam and the concession was not revoked.

Thus, express consent either by a new treaty or by clear acquiescence appears to be necessary to expand the minimum rights of access to a port as elaborated earlier. Such minimum rights of access merely imply that a state is not entitled under international law to close its ports to merchant ships without warning and without cause. Merchant vessels enjoy a right of access and minimum facilities for loading and unloading. The territorial state may prescribe any rules for overloading or other matters, and can subject all foreign ships to public health or police regulations. Foreign merchant ships are also subjected to the jurisdiction of the territorial sovereign. There is no obligation on the coast state for the upkeep of port installations to be used by foreign merchant traffic. All that can be required is that the state does not abuse its right of sovereignty by unfairly excluding such traffic. A state may extend its obligations under international law in this respect by adhering to an international convention imposing further restrictions on its sovereignty, for example, by ratifying the Geneva convention of 1923 relating to international regulation of maritime ports.

The right of access to commercial ports enjoyed by merchant ships is also granted for the purpose of transit from landlocked states. Unless such access exists the freedom of the high seas becomes utterly meaningless.

NOTES

1. C. J. Colombos, *The International Law of the Sea,* 6th edition (London: Longmans, 1967), p. 87; L. Oppenheim, *International Law,* vol. 1, 8th edition, edited by H. Lauterpacht (London: Longmans Green, 1955), p. 442; J. L. Brierly, *The Law of Nations,* 6th edition, edited by Sir Humphrey Waldock (Oxford: Clarendon Press, 1963), p. 237.
2. Cf. Colombos, *The International Law of the Sea,* p. 132.
3. de Lapradelle, *Revue générale de droit international public* (1891), p. 264; P. Fauchille, *Traité de droit international public,* 8th edition (Paris: Rosseau, 1925), vol. 1, p. 133.
4. Gidel, *Le Droit international public de la mer* (Paris, 1934), vol. 3, pp. 168 et seq.
5. Gihl, *Statens Offentliga Utredningar,* 1930: 6, p. 288.

6   R. v Keyn (*The Franconia*) (1876), 2 Ex. D. 63.
7   See Brierly, *The Law of Nations*, p. 240. See further infra, pp. 103-5.
8   Brierly, *The Law of Nations*, p. 240.
9   Cf. P. C. Jessup, *The Law of Territorial Waters and Maritime Jurisdiction* (New York, 1927) p. 120, for older practice.
10 Gihl, in *SOU*, 1930: 6, p. 21; such a shot would normally reach about three nautical miles, Galiani, *De Doveri de principi neutrali* (1782).
11 Gihl, in *SOU*, 1930: 6, p. 20.
12 Colombos, *The International Law of the Sea*, p. 101.
13 This has been established practice for many years, see Gihl, in *SOU*, 1930: 6, p. 27.
14 I. Brownlie, *Principles of Public International Law*, second edition (Oxford: Clarendon Press, 1973), p. 197.
15 Chile and Peru have claimed 'sovereignty' over 'protection zones' since 1947—see, for Chile, Presidential Declaration 23 June 1947 and, for Peru, Supreme Decree 781, 1 August 1947. These two countries do not formally claim all the sea within the 200-mile limit as 'territorial waters' but claim appertaining sovereign functions. Chile, at least, allows free transit for all ships—see infra, pp. 34 and 37. Ecuador made a formal claim to a 200-mile territorial limit in 1966. In substance, Ecuador appears to have exercised identical functions over the 'protection zone' before that date. There is thus very little difference between 'protection zones' and 'territorial waters'.
16 The Montevideo declaration was signed by Argentina, Brazil, Chile, Ecuador, El Salvador, Nicaragua, Peru and Uruguay. The Lima declaration was signed by these states and by Mexico, Colombia, Honduras, Guatemala and the Dominican Republic. Neither of the declarations mentioned any specific limit for territorial waters.
17 See infra, p. 33.
18 *I.C.J. Reports 1951*, p. 116.
19 Eek, Världshavens frihet (Stockholm, 1971), p. 60. On various zones, see Brownlie, *Principles of Public International Law*, pp. 211 et seq. and Burke, *Contemporary Legal Problems in Ocean Development* (Uppsala, 1969), p. 62. The 1964 European Fishery Convention allows for a six-mile exclusive fishing zone,

and another outer zone of six miles where contracting parties are allowed fishing on the basis of reciprocity. The 1967 Convention on Fishing in the North Atlantic also provides for special fishing zones. Cf. the United Kingdom Fishery Limits Act of 1964 under which the United Kingdom claims a twelve-mile fishery zone. Cf. infra, pp. 32-6. For other zones relating to pollution, see infra, p. 93, and for air identification zones, see infra, p. 82.
20 Cf. supra, p. 30.
21 Under article 4 there would be incidental travel over land—cf. infra, p. 74.
22 But territorial waters would be limited to 12 miles—see article 2.
23 Cf. Australia's statements in the UN Seabed Committee, A/AC.138/SC II/SR51 at 9 (1973).
24 Nys, *Le Droit international,* vol. 1, p. 541. As under Roman law, the sea was 'commune quoad usum, sed proprietas est nullius . . . jurisdictio est Caesaris, et sic ista tria sunt diversa: proprietas, usus, jurisdiction et protectio.' These views were, for example, put forward by Bartolus a Saxoferrato in the fourteenth century, and later, by Baldus, see Gihl, in *SOU* 1930: 6, p. 16.
25 Uruguay and Argentina allow free navigation beyond 12 miles and Chile beyond three miles. Cf. supra, p. 31 and note 15, and infra, p. 37 and note 38.
26 See article 6 of the Montevideo declaration, article 3 of the Lima declaration, article 3 of the Yaoundé recommendations and article 5 of the Santo Domingo declaration; see supra, pp. 29 and 31 and notes 16, 21 and 22.
27 Agreement on the Settlement of the Fisheries Dispute with the British, 11 March 1961, Agreement No. 194, 1961.
28 Cf. the dissenting opinion by Judge Padilla Nervo to the Interim Order of the International Court of Justice of 17 August 1972, p. 4.
29 Letter from Iceland to the I.C.J. dated 29 May 1972.
30 Ibid.; cf. infra, pp. 141 et seq. on agreements concluded under force.
31 *Iceland's New Fishing Limits, The Facts* (London, 1972), p. 2.
32 See articles 6 and 8. This convention came into force in 1966 after 22 ratifications.

33 See, Colombos, *The International Law of the Sea,* pp. 97 et seq., for protests by the United States; cf. B. Johnson, *Suveränitet i havet och luftrummet* (Stockholm: Norstedt, 1972), p. 154.
34 See Colombos, *The International Law of the Sea,* pp. 98-9.
35 OAS, Off. rec., SER. G.C.P./Doc. 81/71 (1971). See further, infra, p. 158.
36 Cf. Johnson, *Suveränitet i havet och luftrummet,* p. 198.
37 Cf. supra, p. 34 and note 25.
38 For example, Argentina (since 1946) and Uruguay (since 1969). Cf. supra, p. 32.
39 Cf. resolution 2564 (XXIV) of 1969.
40 Report of the Committee on the Peaceful Uses of the Sea-Bed and the Ocean Floor Beyond the Limits of National Jurisdiction, 1970, A/8021, Annex VI, Working Paper submitted by the United Kingdom, p. 180.
41 *I.C.J. Reports, 1969,* p. 3.
42 On the agreement between Saudi Arabia and Iran, see Finlay, 'Equitable solutions for offshore boundaries', *American Journal of International Law* (1970), p. 154.
43 Apart from agreements between the parties to the North Sea continental shelf dispute concluded in 1971 to give effect to the pronouncements of the International Court, there are agreements for the delimitation of the continental shelf between the United Kingdom and Norway of 1965, Cmnd. 2626 and Cmnd. 2757; between the United Kingdom and the Netherlands of 1965, Cmnd. 2830 and Cmnd. 3253 as amended in 1971, Cmnd. 4875; between United Kingdom and Denmark of 1966, Cmnd. 2973 and Cmnd. 3278; between United Kingdom and Germany of 1971, Cmnd. 4881. Cf. agreements between Sweden and Norway, 24 July 1968, *SÖ* 1969, No. 3; and between Sweden and Finland, 29 September 1972, *SÖ* 1973, No. 1.
44 There are provisions for 'consultations' in case of a dispute about which side of the dividing line an installation is situated, see the agreement between the United Kingdom and Germany of 1971, Cmnd. 4881. Other agreements provide for an obligation to 'seek to reach agreement' in case a field extends across the dividing line, see the agreements between the United Kingdom and the Netherlands of 1965, Cmnd. 2830 and Cmnd. 3253, as amended in 1971, Cmnd. 4875. But not all these agree-

ments provide for arbitration if the parties fail to reach an understanding: of the abovementioned agreements only the one concluded in 1971 between Germany and the United Kingdom provides for arbitration.

45 For example, the agreement concluded in 1966 between the United Kingdom and Denmark, Cmnd. 2973 and Cmnd. 3278, which mentions 'gravel and sand'.
46 See, B. Cooper and T. F. Gaskell, *North Sea Oil—the Great Gamble* (London: Heinemann, 1966), p. 52; cf. P. Hinde, *Fortune in the North Sea* (London: Foulis, 1966). On the question of constitutional authority for legislation outside territorial waters see Lumb, 'Jurisdiction over the Mineral Resources of the Australian Continental Shelf', AULSA Conference Papers 1966, p. 22.
47 See article 18. On exercise of jurisdiction, see infra, pp. 103-5.
48 According to a draft convention elaborated by the International Law Association in Vienna in 1926 on laws of maritime jurisdiction in time of peace, warships would also be allowed innocent passage subject to 'regulations' of the coastal state, see ILA, 34th Report, 1926, p. 102.
49 Cf. W. E. Hall, *A Treatise on International Law*, 8th edition by A. P. Higgins (Oxford: Clarendon Press, 1924), p. 198; cf. Resolutions of the Institute of International Law, *Annuaire*, 1928, vol. 34, p. 757.
50 See Brownlie, *Principles of Public International Law*, p. 206 for a list of countries which demand previous authorization.
51 Contra, Johnson, *Suveränitet i havet och luftrummet*, p. 249 who alleges that the 'Western world' has adopted a principle of innocent passage of warships in territorial waters. This view does not take account of actual state practice; numerous states require authorization, see the previous note.
52 Cf. Fauchille, *Traité de droit international public*, vol. 1, p. 156.
53 Cf. M. Sørensen, 'Principes de droit international public', *Académie de droit international. Recueil des cours*, vol. 101 (1960), iii, p. 188.
54 Sir Gerald Fitzmaurice, 'Some remarks on the Geneva conference on the law of the sea', *International and Comparative Law Quarterly*, vol. 8 (1959), p. 95.

55 Colombos, *The International Law of the Sea*, p. 261.
56 Colombos, *The International Law of the Sea*, p. 261 and note numerous reservations to the Geneva convention in this respect, Brownlie, *Principles of Public International Law*, p. 206. Cf. resolution of the Institute of International Law, *Annuaire*, vol. 13 (1894), pp. 325 et seq., and the draft convention of the International Law Association on laws of maritime jurisdiction in time of peace, Vienna 1926, 34th report, p. 102.
57 Brierly, *The Law of Nations*, p. 237.
58 *I.C.J. Reports 1949*, p. 4.
59 Colombos, *The International Law of the Sea*, p. 197.
60 Oppenheim, *International Law*, vol. 1, p. 511; Colombos, *The International Law of the Sea*, p. 260.
61 *I.C.J. Reports 1949*, p.4.
62 Cf. criticism by Brühl, 'Some observations concerning the legal position of international straits', in *Festschrift Laun* (1953), p. 273, who considers that the Corfu Channel is not sufficiently *important* to be called an international strait. Cf. E. Brühl, *International Straits* (Copenhagen: Nyt Nordisk Forlag Arnold Busck, 1947), vol. 1, p. 42.
63 Article 16(4) of the Geneva Convention on the Territorial Sea and the Contiguous Zone.
64 Straits of Malacca and Singapore, Joint Statement, 16 November 1971, *Foreign Affairs Malaysia*, vol. 4 (4) (December 1971), p. 54. Cf. *Official Gazette of Indonesia*, no. 16 (1971), on the treaty with Malaysia. Cf. second joint statement, March 1972, claiming the right to control passage.
65 *Foreign Affairs Malaysia*, vol. 4 (4), p. 54.
66 Cf. R. R. Baxter, *The Law of International Waterways* (Cambridge, Mass.: Harvard University Press, 1964), p. 247. On pollution, see infra, pp. 91-5.
67 Colombos, *The International Law of the Sea*, p. 222.
68 See infra pp. 164-5 and p. 200. This is an example of a treaty in favour of a third party; cf. I. Detter, *Essays on the Law of Treaties* (London: Sweet & Maxwell, 1967), p. 113.
69 See I. Delupis, *Finance and Protection of Investments in Developing Countries* (Gower Press, 1973), pp. 103-4.
70 Declaration of 24 April 1957, *United Nations Review*, vol. 3, no. 12 (June 1957).

71 S. S. *'Wimbledon'*, Judgments, *1923*, P.C.I.J., Series A, No. *1*.
72 Cf. Brierly, *The Law of Nations*, p. 236.
73 But 'approval' was necessary at times, see I. Detter, *Law Making by International Organizations* (Stockholm: Norstedts, 1965), p. 214.
74 For the method of apportioning a joint river to two states and on the division of the *Talweg* or channel, see Colombos, *The International Law of the Sea*, p. 224 et seq.
75 See, Colombos, *The International Law of the Sea*, pp. 236-7 and a number of authorities quoted by him to this effect. But Brownlie, *Principles of Public International Law*, pp. 264-6 is hesitant about whether such a rule exists.
76 *I.C.J. Reports 1951*, p. 16.
77 For a critical discussion, see Brierly, *The Law of Nations*, pp. 199 et seq. On 'historic bays' see Colombos, *The International Law of the Sea*, pp. 180-8. On off-coast islands enclosed by straight lines by the Philippines, see *Yearbook of the International Law Commission 1956*, vol. 2 (New York: United Nations, 1956), pp. 69-70.
78 Colombos, *The International Law of the Sea*, p. 236.
79 Colombos, *The International Law of the Sea*, p. 236.
80 See, further, infra p. 103.
81 Bulletin des lois, 1806, no. 126, p. 602. See further infra, p. 105. For Italian practice see, e.g. *The Albissola* (1930), AD 1929-1930, p. 105 to a similar effect. For French practice see, Crim., 12 June 1952, S.1953.1.79; Crim. 25 February 1859, S.1859.1.183; Rouen, 21 January 1916, D.P.1917.2.62; Trib. corr. de Nantes, 2 April 1937, D.H. 1937.2.63.
82 See infra, p. 105.
83 See infra, pp. 103 and 105 for exceptions.
84 See infra, pp. 104-5.
85 Cf. Resolution of the Institute of International Law, *Annuaire*, vol. 47 (1957), paragraph 2.
86 Colombos, *The International Law of the Sea*, p. 176.
87 Colombos, *The International Law of the Sea*, p. 177.
88 *Jurisdiction of the European Commission of the Danube Advisory Opinion*, *1927*, P.C.I.J., Series B, No. *14*.
89 *Oscar Chinn*, Judgment, *1934*, P.C.I.J., Series A/B, No. *63*, p. 65.

90 See, further infra, pp. 173 et seq. But see commentary by Sir Humphrey Waldock to article 30 of the draft convention on state succession, UN Doc. A/8710, 1972, p. 212.
91 *LNTS*, vol. 5, p. 319; *BFSP*, vol. 114, p. 182.
92 *UNTS*, vol. 110, p. 3.

Chapter 4

Passage over Land

In the seventeenth century Grotius claimed that there exists a general right of transit across the territory of another state in the interest of the community of nations.[1] But a number of writers have subsequently rejected this idea and denied, most categorically, that any such right exists.[2] It is possible to enjoy such a right of way only, it has been claimed, if there is a treaty to that effect. Some writers have gone as far as to say that there exists an obligation under general international law to enter into treaties to regulate rights of transit.[3]

There appear to be two types of states which have particular interest in claiming a right of transit under general international law: those which are completely cut off from the sea, the so-called landlocked states, and states which, because of their geographical position, are cut off from the main international trade routes.

It has been suggested that the fact that the United States has not claimed any right of transit to Alaska would indicate that no such rights of passage exist under international law.[4] However, that example is very different from a claim by a state which has no access to the sea *at all*. It is not unreasonable to assume that a landlocked state must be allowed some minimum access to the sea. The position of such a state is similar to that of an enclave[5] which, in order to survive, must be granted certain rights of transit to international trade routes.

Developing nations have a particular interest in establishing what right of transit exists under general international law because they are newly independent states which have rarely taken part in such extensive regulation of transit rights by treaty as, for example, European states have. The position of the problem is thus: what right does a landlocked state, or a state cut off from international trade routes, have to transit to obtain access to the sea or to trade routes? The problem presents itself with some acuteness to developing states: would Zambia, in the absence of treaties, not have any right of access to the sea? Or would a lorry going from Malawi to Kenya not have the right to use the main roads through Tanzania?

4:1 REQUIREMENT OF TREATY REGULATION OR EXPRESS CONSENT *IN CASU* FOR FIXED INSTALLATIONS

Article 23 of the Covenant of the League of Nations stipulated that

> Members of the League ...
> will make provisions to secure and maintain freedom of communications and of transit and equitable treatment for the commerce of all members of the League.

A subsequent conference in Barcelona in 1921 elaborated a Convention on Communication and Transport and established a Permanent Advisory and Technical Committee under the supervision of the League of Nations. There was to be a new conference every fourth year. Three conventions were elaborated, one dealing with transit, one with international waterways and one with the right to flags of ships of landlocked states. Most European states adhered to the transit convention which, however, only dealt with water and rail transport.

Other conventions dealt with further questions relating to transport by rail (the Geneva convention of 1923) and with related matters such as the transmission of electric power.

4:1:1 Transit by Rail

The express consent of the territorial state is required both for the construction and for the operation of fixed installations. In the case of railways, numerous bilateral treaties regulate these aspects. Railway routes between two states may, as a result of boundary changes, cross the territory of a third state without serving its economy. Similarly, railway routes essentially serving one state only may, as a result of boundary changes, cross the territory of another state. The main railway route between Schaffhausen and Zürich, for example, crosses a stretch of the territory of the Federal Republic of Germany. The route is operated by the Swiss Federal Railways and trains not stopping on German territory are exempt from all customs regulations.[6] There are similar arrangements regarding Czechoslovak and Polish railways which cross over short stretches of the other state's territory.[7] Similarly, treaties have been concluded for a railway between Aleppo in Syria and Mosul in Iraq, which crosses and recrosses the Syrian-Turkish border. Traffic between Svilengrad in Bulgaria and Istanbul is regulated by treaty as the railway crosses short stretches of Greek territory.[8]

It appears that there is no general right of transit for railway transport. The consent of the territorial state is required both to construct and to operate railways. States have usually arrived at some understanding in the form of a treaty to regulate the right of transit by rail to enable a state to transport, in particular, natural resources or their derivatives as the following examples may show.

The vast copper deposits of Zaïre lie in the Katanga region in the southern part of the territory. Zaïre has a seaport at Matadi, on the northwest coast, but this is several thousand miles away from the copper mines and to transport the copper there would require transshipment from river vessel to railway at Kinshasa. However, the seaport of Lobito in Portuguese Angola is only some 1,200 miles away from the copper mines. In 1927 Belgium and Portugal concluded an agreement regarding the traffic from Katanga (which was then part of the Belgian Congo) through the port of Lobito by the Benguela railway. Portugal granted Belgium transit through Angola for all persons, mails, goods and rolling stock, free of all transit fees, delays, restrictions, or pecuniary guarantees. Belgian vessels embarking or disembarking goods and passengers to and from the Belgian Congo were guaranteed treatment equal to that accorded to Portuguese vessels.[9] When the Belgian Congo became independent there was a new 'understanding' between Portugal and the government of the Republic of the Congo as well as an agreement with the Union

Minière which operated the copper mines.[10] It may be interesting to note that the Benguela railway which was to take care of the transport is owned by a British-Portuguese company in which the majority shareholding is British. This company was granted a renewed railway concession for 99 years in 1903 which entitles it to operate in Portuguese Angola.

Sir Robert Williams was granted this concession in 1903 to build and operate a railway from Lobito to the Katanga frontier, a distance of 838 miles. A Portuguese company, Companhia do Caminho de Ferro de Benguela, was established; the new company was financed by Tanganyika Concessions Ltd, of which Sir Robert was managing director. Tanganyika Concessions subscribed the initial capital of £3,000,000 and became one of the principal shareholders of Union Minière. Construction was completed in 1928 and through traffic started in 1931. The principal shareholder in the railway company is still the Tanganyika Concessions Group which has now invested some £52,000,000 in the Benguela railway.[11]

In 1967 Union Minière's assets in Katanga were nationalized;[12] the company eventually received 'adequate' compensation and the Benguela railway, which was dependent on Union Minière, continued to serve the Katangan copper belt.

After the unilateral declaration of independence by Southern Rhodesia (now known as Rhodesia) the Benguela railway also took over a large portion of transport of Zambian copper which Zambia would no longer allow to be taken through Rhodesia to Beira, on the east coast, in Moçambique.[13]

There were transit agreements between the United Kingdom and Portugal to allow for the transport of copper from Northern Rhodesia through Southern Rhodesia to the ports of Beira and Lourenço Marques in Moçambique. When Northern Rhodesia became independent as Zambia there were new agreements between the governments of Zambia and Portugal.[14] However, in January 1973 the rail link between Zambia and Beira was closed by Rhodesia as retaliation against Zambia's alleged harbouring of guerrillas infiltrating Rhodesia. Initially copper exports were exempted from the ban; but Zambia decided to divert all copper shipments as well.[15]

Between industrialized states there is a host of agreements regulating transit by rail. One example is the important treaty for transport of Swedish iron ore through Norway.

Under an agreement between Sweden and Norway, Swedish iron ore can be transported to Narvik in Norway for further shipment. The Swedish iron-ore deposits lie roughly halfway between the Swedish port of Luleå, on the Gulf of Bothnia, and the Norwegian seaport of Narvik. Luleå, however, is icebound in winter whereas Narvik is open to navigation all year on the Atlantic. Free transit over this railway line is granted under a convention on transit traffic which formed part of the general treaties and convention regarding the dissolution of the Swedish-Norwegian Union in 1905. The convention confirms the contract for the transport of minerals of 1898 between the Norwegian state and Luossavaara-Kiirunavaara AB establishing freight rates for a contractual quantity of ore to be transported on the railway line to Narvik.[16]

4:1:2 Transmission of Electric Power

As mentioned earlier, certain conventions allowing for transit of railway traffic also stipulate a regime for transmission of electric power. This was, for example, the case with the Geneva convention of 1923 which dealt with both these interrelated matters. Previous conventions had regulated questions relating to telephone and telegraph installations within the framework of the International Telecommunications Union.[17]

A state does not have to tolerate the erection of pylons or other installations in its territory without giving its express consent; such consent, when it is granted, is usually given in the form of a treaty. A state is, however, very often party to multilateral conventions for international cooperation in these and related matters for its own benefit and therefore often does give such consent because, on the basis of reciprocity, it can enjoy the advantages of international technical cooperation.[18]

4:1:3 International Pipelines

The international transport of resources by pipeline equally requires the consent of the territorial state either in the form of a treaty or by express concession. In some cases pipeline regimes are governed by national common carrier legislation in which case the pipeline is treated as a national common carrier of the state in which the actual section is situated.[19] Concession regimes apply especially in the Middle East where the pipeline is usually the property of an affiliate of a petroleum company and exclusively carries that company's products.

Numerous bilateral treaties govern the construction and operation of petroleum pipelines which cross national boundaries; there is also a multilateral agreement on international pipelines in the making.[20]

One example of a bilateral treaty is an agreement concluded between Brazil and Bolivia under which both parties are to cooperate in the preliminary work of surveying, prospecting and drilling with a view to determine the true industrial value of the petroleum deposits in Bolivia. Operations are carried out by a joint undertaking of the two states, constituted according to the legislation in force in the two states. The petroleum supplies shall, in the first instance, satisfy the domestic needs of Bolivia and only in the second place go to the market of Brazil. Where oil production warrants it, Bolivia undertakes to grant to joint undertakings of the two states, to the exclusion of others, concessions for the construction and surveying of petroleum pipelines. Brazil has agreed to extend every facility for the construction of these pipelines and allow them to pass freely through its territory. Furthermore, petroleum and petroleum derivatives originating in one of the two states and which are exported through the other shall enjoy the fullest facilities of free transit in accordance with accepted international practice and the treaties in force between the two countries.[21]

Another agreement concluded between Chile and Bolivia in 1957 provides for the construction of an oil pipeline from Bolivia to the Chilean port of Arica, along the La Paz/Arica railway. The construction, operation and maintenance of the line was put into the hands of the Yacimientos Petroliferos Fiscales Bolivianos (YPFB), a Bolivian government organization. The agreement provides for the free movement of construction material and equipment for the line between the two countries and also for the permanent stationing of maintenance equipment and personnel on Chilean territory. Chilean land rights for the line are conceded to YPFB for the duration of the line's operation and Chile is entitled to authorize YPFB to purchase land for the pipeline terminal, storage tanks and other installations, as well as housing for its personnel, in the Arica department. Chile may also request YPFB to establish junction points for branch pipelines at points to be determined.[22]

Other agreements on pipelines concern general defence purposes. The United States and Canada have concluded a treaty for such purposes under which the United States undertook to construct, own and operate oil pipelines passing through the territory of Canada. Under the agreement all land required for the construction of pipelines would remain in the title of Canada. Canada would grant to the United States an easement for and the use of access roads to the pipelines. The ownership of the pipelines and auxiliary installations belongs to the United States, which is under obligation to remove pipelines and restore the original right of way at the termination of the arrangement. Any contractor awarded a contract for the construction of pipelines was required to give preference to qualified labour from Canada; and nothing in the agreement derogates from the application of the domestic law of Canada in its own territory.[23]

In one case the construction of a pipeline was caused by a country's refusal to allow for other transit traffic. When Rhodesia closed the border to certain traffic in 1965 Zambia constructed an oil pipeline in conjunction with Tanzania and the Italian company AGIP.[24]

4:2 TRANSIT BY ROAD

If a state does not wish to construct railways or pipelines or other installations or operate such facilities in the territory of another state but merely to use existing roads for 'innocent' transit, that is to say transit for civilians and ordinary goods, the position is slightly different. If landlocked states are to be allowed access to the sea so that they can share equal right to the high seas, and if states in general are to be allowed access to international trade routes, it may be possible to suggest that a minimum right of transit for 'innocent traffic' exists across existing roads in other states.

When international lawyers refuse to accept that such a general right of transit exists, they are making only an academic claim since there are hardly any states that are not bound by treaties and conventional agreements which allow for such transit. International lawyers often seem to ignore that treaty regulation is of such immense extent that it is almost pointless to discuss whether any right of transit exists outside the framework of such comprehensive agreements.

4:2:1 GATT Regulations

Article 5 of the General Agreement on Tariffs and Trade provides that

> 1. Goods (including baggage) and also vessels and other means of transport shall be deemed to be in transit across the territory of a contracting party when the passage across such territory, with or without trans-shipment, warehousing, breaking bulk or change in the mode of transport, is only a portion of a complete journey beginning and terminating beyond the frontier of the contracting party across whose territory the traffic passes. Traffic of this nature is termed in this article 'traffic in transit'.
> 2. There shall be freedom of transit through the territory of each contracting party, via the routes most convenient for international transit, for traffic to or from the territory of other contracting parties. No distinction shall be made which is based on the flag of vessels, the place of origin, departure, entry, exit or destination, or on any circumstances relating to the ownership of goods, of vessels or of other means of transport.
> 3. Any contracting party may require that traffic in transit through its territory be entered at the proper customs house, but, except in cases of failure to comply with applicable customs laws and regulations, such traffic coming from or going to the territory of other contracting parties shall not be subject to any unnecessary delays or restrictions and shall be exempt from customs duties and from all transit duties or other charges imposed in respect of transit, except charges for transportation or those commensurate with administrative expenses entailed by transit or with the cost of services rendered.
> 4. All charges and regulations imposed by contracting parties on traffic in transit to or from the territories of other contracting parties shall be reasonable, having regard to the conditions of the traffic.
> 5. With respect to all charges, regulations and formalities in connexion with transit, each contracting party shall accord to traffic in transit to or from the territory of any other contracting party treatment no less favourable than the treatment accorded to traffic in transit to or from any third country.

6. Each contracting party shall accord to products which have been in transit through the territory of any other contracting party treatment no less favourable than that which would have been accorded to such products had they been transported from their place of origin to their destination without going through the territory of such other contracting party. Any contracting party shall, however, be free to maintain its requirements of direct consignment existing on the date of this agreement in respect of any goods in regard to which such direct consignment is a requisite condition of eligibility for entry of the goods at preferential rates of duty or has relation to the contracting party's prescribed method of valuation for duty purposes.

7. The provisions of this article shall not apply to the operation of aircraft in transit, but shall apply to air transit of goods (including baggage).

Thus, under GATT there does exist a general right of transit for all goods: the members of GATT undertake to grant each other free transit on roads which are internationally best suited and not to apply any discrimination based on origin of goods or their destination. Members are to be treated as most-favoured nations and fees must not be imposed to cover administrative costs unless they are actually incurred by the transit traffic and, in such case, fees must always be 'reasonable'.

The General Agreement entered into force on 1 January 1948 pursuant to a Protocol of Provisional Application of GATT signed on 10 October 1947. A number of subsequent GATT instruments in the form of protocols have been deposited with the Secretary-General of the United Nations. In June 1973 no less than 78 states had adhered to GATT; among them numerous developing states.[25] In spite of the fact that GATT itself is only 'provisionally' in force,[26] some states have announced their *de facto* application of GATT.[27]

GATT is not merely a 'framework' agreement which does not involve any legal obligations for the parties. Although it is technically only 'provisionally' in force the parties to it have undertaken and are bound by a series of specific legal obligations.

4:2:2 1949 Road Convention

The United States had wished an International Trade Organization (ITO) to be established under the auspices of the United Nations and at the preliminary negotiations at Havana in 1948 the principles of GATT were repeated in a draft document for this organization. However, ITO never came into being largely because of the opposition of the Soviet Union which insisted that the functions of the proposed organization were better taken over by the Economic Commission of the UN for Europe (ECE). Consequently ECE did take care of a number of these functions and prepared a number of conventions on various matters. Among these conventions are numerous agreements restricted to European transport but also the important Road Traffic Convention of 1949 which was intended to have worldwide application.

This convention prescribes that contracting states shall allow international transit traffic of goods and civilians on their roads, provided vehicles and drivers fulfil certain conditions. No less than 85 states are bound by this convention, including the whole of the Eastern bloc.[28] The convention will, gradually, be replaced by a new convention which contains the same rules on free transit, signed in 1968, and which has not yet entered into force.

4:2:3 Bilateral Agreements

Bilateral agreements on transit exist largely between states where at least one of the parties is not a member of GATT or has not signed the 1949 Road Traffic Convention. For example, under an agreement concluded in 1958, Pakistan and Afghanistan grant each other free transit to and from their territories, without distinction as to flag of vessels, place of origin, departure, etc. Transit traffic is exempted from all charges other than transport charges and costs of services rendered.

Under another agreement dated 1955 Afghanistan and the USSR grant each other free transit of goods under the conditions governing the transit of goods of any third country through the territory of the party concerned, free of duties, taxes or any charges other than those relating to the handling and forwarding of goods in transit.[29]

Similar agreements have been made with their neighbours by Bolivia, Laos, Mali, Nepal, Niger, Paraguay and Upper Volta.

4:2:4 Convention on Landlocked States

In the negotiations for a transit convention to safeguard the rights of landlocked states most proposals emanated from states which were not members of GATT nor signatories of the 1949 Road Traffic Convention, such as Afghanistan, Nepal, Laos and Bolivia. The background of this transit convention is as follows.

A resolution by the United Nations in 1956—1028 (XI)—provided that the need of landlocked states of a right of transit should be 'recognized'; a similar encouragement to conclude further treaties was embodied in a resolution of the Organization of American States in 1957 in which members were asked to conclude agreements on transit to counterweigh the drawbacks of the geographical position of some states. Article 3 of the Geneva Convention on the High Seas of 1958 also concerns such *pacta de contrahendo*: states having a sea coast and those lacking one shall by *common agreement* accord free transit to landlocked states, and settle all matters relating to such transit and equal treatment in ports.

The question was also discussed when UNCTAD met in Geneva in 1964: there Afghanistan, Laos and Nepal presented a draft resolution based on previous discussion in ECAFE. UNCTAD adopted several 'principles' on transit which included all means of transport, obligation for the transit state to keep up transport capacity to correspond to transit needs, and free bunkering of goods if delays caused without fault; assembly of cars and vehicles and of large goods consignments were to be considered part of the transit operation.

The United Nations Conference on Transit of Landlocked States in 1965 based itself on UNCTAD I which had stated the desirability of a right of transit for landlocked states. Afghanistan attempted to have recognized a general right of transit at the conference but failed to get sufficient support. A compromise solution suggested by Bolivia and Paraguay also failed: according to this alternative drafting the right of transit would be admitted while, at the same time 'admitting' the sovereignty of the transit state. The convention adopted, however, as a 'principle' the rule that a landlocked state shall have a right of transit although the transit must not infringe the legitimate interests of the territorial state; there must be no customs or other fees not connected with immediate costs incurred because of the transit. The convention encourages states to conclude *regional agreements* for detailed regulation of the right of transit and thus mainly provides a framework for future more specific conventions. There are also several provisions of material interest based on the earlier Barcelona Statute. But the extent of the convention is seriously hampered by a number of reservations; several states have now adhered to the convention.[30] The convention provides that right of transit shall be granted on acceptable routes; that there may only be fees for immediate administration costs; that goods handling shall be on the basis of equal treatment as to national goods; that restriction of these rights of transit must be avoided and may only be allowed in case of *force majeure;* that benefits under the conventions are exempted from provisions on most-favoured-nation treatment on the basis of reciprocity; that, finally, there will be arbitration in case of disputes under the convention.

4:2:5 Trans-African Highway

The plans for a trans-African Highway from Mombasa in Kenya to Lagos in Nigeria are likely to be the subject of an international convention between all countries concerned regarding the right of transit of the highway.[31]

4:2:6 EEC Treaties

In customs unions, such as the EEC, states may be granted a general right of transit for goods and workers either by becoming full members or by association agreements. The EEC is founded on the principle of free circulation of goods, capital and manpower and these are principles which form the basis of the customs union and, as such, are accepted by full members and by some associated states.[32] Associated states now include Greece, Turkey, Malta, Yugoslavia, eighteen African francophone states as well as Nigeria, Kenya, Uganda and Tanzania.[33]

Right of movement goes further than a mere right of transit: it implies the right to enter and reside in other EEC states for the purpose of working. However, association agreements do not provide for the immediate implementation of the rights of movement of workers. Most such agreements merely stipulate that the right of free circulation will 'gradually' be secured.[34] For example, under the agreement with Greece free circulation will be guaranteed after a certain transitional period.[35]

It has been argued that any association under article 238 of the treaty of Rome would 'by necessity' cover free movement of workers. On the other hand, such claims have been accompanied with the assertion that only fully developed states 'such as Greece' could be associated under this article—other states could only obtain association with the EEC under part 4 of the treaty of Rome which provides neither for nor against the free circulation of workers.[36] This view has subsequently been proved inaccurate: numerous nations, both industrialized and developing states, have obtained association agreements with the EEC explicitly concluded under article 238,[37] and the principle of free movement of workers is covered by most such agreements at least as an ultimate aim.

Not only freedom of movement of workers is envisaged by the association agreements. A 'right of establishment' is guaranteed under, for example, the agreements with Greece and Turkey. It is sometimes difficult to delimit this right from the above mentioned right to circulate but the right of establishment would usually be enjoyed by persons having their own enterprises and not working as employees.[38]

4:2:7 Investment Guarantee Agreements

A 'right of establishment' is also granted under another group of treaties. Numerous industrialized states have concluded investment guarantee agreements with developing nations; other such agreements have been concluded between industrialized states.[39] Under these agreements citizens of both parties are usually granted a right of entry into the other state as well as permission to enter into business in certain fields.[40]

4:2:8 A General Right of Transit?

There are few states which, by one convention or another, have not bound themselves to allow transit traffic. Traditional international law insists on the distinction between treaty regulation and general international law: but when regulation by agreement has become as complex and intense as the arrangements described in this section then it may be suggested that this indicates the existence of a minimum rule which exists apart from treaties, at least in some cases.

This 'minimum right of transit' may be *reinforced* by custom. The International Court of Justice confirmed in the *Right of Passage* case[41] that a right of way across foreign territory can exist if the exercise of this right is reinforced by consistent use and custom: the Court left open whether there was any general right of transit to, in this case, Portuguese enclaves in India. Portugal had invoked some ancient treaties with Indian princes, as well as custom and the existence of a general right. The Court, however, based its findings only on custom and, in particular, declined to discuss whether there exists any general right of transit to and from enclaves. It may be interesting to note that, at least for the transit of civilian goods, Portugal's counsel could also have invoked the GATT provision on transit (see pp. 66-7) by which both India and Portugal were bound at the time of the dispute, although there appears to have been no reference to this agreement.

It is clear that if custom is firmly developed then a right of transit across foreign territory may exist. However, such customary right can only develop into an established legal right if the custom is tolerated by the territorial state over a period of time. Also the right can only extend to civilians and goods and not, as the Court remarked in the *Right of Passage* case, to military personnel and arms unless such traffic is specially authorized by the territorial state.

But if there is no custom? Is there then no right of transit to enclaves? Most existing enclaves like Baarle-Duc, Baarle-Nassau, Büsingen, Llivia and Campione have a right of transit to them guaranteed under various treaties.[42] The position of certain states is analogous to such enclaves. There must exist a general right of transit from landlocked states to the sea—a rule which can be deduced from the maxims on freedom of the seas and the equality of states. There must also be a minimum right of transit for states which, because of their geographical position, would otherwise be cut off from international trade routes. This right must also exist under general international law for otherwise such states could not survive. Permission for transit traffic cannot then depend on a discretionary decision by another state.[43] A minimum right of transit on existing roads for civilians and goods in these two cases exists under general international law for reasons of necessity; for general international law must provide sufficient authorizing norms to guarantee the survival of sovereign states. Even so, few states are not bound by one of the general conventions on this matter.

In this context it is important to emphasize that the USSR, and later the DDR, have never denied the transit right *as such* to West Berlin. What they have disputed has been the right of the Western Powers *to be in West Berlin at all*.[44] Consequently, they have contested the transit right incidental to this presence. However, even this dispute is being solved and the parties concerned have agreed on a treaty guaranteeing access to Berlin, both for civilians and for military personnel.[45]

This suggested minimum right of transit must not be confused with the power of a state to admit aliens. Diplomats may enjoy a right of transit 'along the shortest route'.[46] Such a route would, nowadays, rarely be overland. As shown in cases before English courts such as *Musgrove v Chun Teeong Toy*[47] and American cases such as *Nishimura Ekiu v US*,[48] the right to refuse entry of other aliens is an incident of territorial sovereignty. But these cases did not concern the *right of transit for a state*. In other words, a state need only admit *some* citizens from a landlocked state, or from a state cut off from international trade routes, for the purpose of *transit*. The state that allows its territory to be crossed may select at its own discretion which aliens are to be granted a right of transit and may impose any restriction on their journey or length of stay, or may require advance permission in the form of a visa. The same power of selection may not arise with respect to transit of unaccompanied civilian goods and there are few cases where such transport has caused difficulties in the international community.[49]

4:2:9 Innocent Passage Overland

There exist then a number of conventions or bilateral agreements by which states bind themselves to allow free transit for civilians and goods. In the absence of such treaties there may still exist a right of transit established by custom, with the consent of the territorial state, but such consent is presumed to cover only civilians and goods and does not extend to military personnel and arms, unless specifically authorized. Finally, in the absence of such a custom one can still deduce a minimum right of transit for landlocked states which otherwise would not be able to share in the equal right of all sovereign states to the high seas as codified by the 1958 Geneva convention. A similar right is enjoyed by states that require transit for access to international trade routes. That such a right of transit exists is corroborated by political realities: when Rhodesia, for example, closed its border to Zambia in January 1973 many states hastened to provide or to finance alternative routes. Zambia claimed that the international community should bear the increased costs incurred when it was cut off from the shortest transit route to the sea.[49] On 21 May 1973 the Secretary-General of the UN gave assurances on a programme for developing alternative trade routes.[51] The Yaoundé recommendations also recognize a right of transit for land locked states.[52]

The 'minimum right of transit' which, it is suggested, exists under general international law must fulfil certain conditions:

1 It must concern civilians and goods.
2 It must be limited to existing roads.
3 Transit must be innocent and peaceful.

In the interests of the commerce of the community of nations all states should, on the basis of sovereign equality, be able to share international communications. If then a minimum right of transit overland were not acknowledged, a state which, for example, can reach the sea by using an international river would be unduly privileged. On the other hand, the territorial state is always entitled to restrict transit traffic for reasons of security and, in particular, may allocate special roads for this purpose and validly close others. But complete restrictions of transit traffic must be imposed for serious, specific reasons, such as when the security or other vital interests of the territorial state are threatened. It is within the discretionary competence of the territorial state to decide that such interests are in peril. Such a right to refuse transit also exists under the above-mentioned agreements on international traffic and transit but it is invariably limited to cases of danger to the vital interests of the territorial state—dangers which that state may have to demonstrate to other parties.

NOTES

1. Grotius, *De jure belli ac pacis,* bk. 2, ch. 2, para. 13. Cf. Vitoria, *De Indis,* iii, 1.
2. A. Verdross, *Völkerrecht,* 5th edition (Vienna: Springer, 1965), p. 292; Klimenka, *Pravo proshoda cherez inostrannuyu territoriyu* (Moscow, 1967), p. 1034.
3. G. Dahm, *Völkerrecht* (Stuttgart: Kohlhammer, 1958), vol. 1, pp. 617 et seq.
4. Dahm, *Völkerrecht,* vol. 1, pp. 617 et seq.
5. UN Secretariat, Memo, UN Doc. A/Conf. 13/29 (1958).
6. Treaty between Germany and Switzerland of 1895.
7. See, for example, *UNTS,* vol. 84, p. 34.
8. *LNTS,* vol. 145, p. 138.
9. *LNTS,* vol. 71, p. 430.
10. Information obtained from the Portuguese Embassy, Stockholm, 6 February 1972.
11. *The Geographical Magazine* (1967), p. 261; see further d'Almada, *An Historical Outline of the Benguela Railway* (n.p., n.d.); R. Hutchinson and G. Martelli, *Robert's People: The Life of Sir Robert Williams, Bart, 1860-1938* (London: Chatto, 1971).
12. See further, I. Delupis, *Finance and Protection of Investments in Developing Countries* (Gower Press, 1973), pp. 162 et seq.
13. Hutchinson and Martelli, *Robert's People,* p. 244.
14. See, Northern Rhodesia Chamber of Mines, *Yearbook,* 1958.
15. *Sunday Times,* 14 January 1973.
16. G. F. de Martens, *Nouveau Receuil des traités* (Göttingen, 1817-42), vol. 34, p. 708.
17. See I. Detter, *Law Making by International Organizations* (Stockholm: Norstedts, 1965), pp. 223 et seq.
18. Detter, *Law Making by International Organizations,* pp. 206 et seq.

19 Legal Provisions for the Supply of Natural Gas through International Pipelines, ECE. GAS/Working Paper No. 43, 23 February 1959.
20 See M. O. Hudson, *International Legislation* (Washington: Carnegie Endowment for International Peace, 1931-50), vol. 8, p. 623.
21 *UNTS*, vol. 51, p. 256.
22 Tratados, Convenciones y Arreglos Internacionales de Chile, Acuerdo sobre el Oleoducto de YPFB de Sicasica-Arica a su paso por Territorio Chileno, 24 April 1957.
23 *UNTS*, vol. 206, p. 93. Cf. *UNTS*, vol. 99, p. 223 and *UNTS*, vol. 11, p. 325.
24 Cf. statement by the High Commissioner of Zambia in London, *The Times*, 28 February 1973.
25 Argentina, Australia, Austria, Barbados, Belgium, Brazil, Burma, Burundi, Cameroon, Canada, Central African Republic, Chad, Chile, Congo (People's Republic), Cuba, Cyprus, Czechoslovakia, Dahomey, Denmark, Dominican Republic, Egypt, EEC and ECSC (member states), Finland, France, Gabon, Gambia, Federal Republic of Germany, Ghana, Greece, Guyana, Haiti, Iceland, India, Indonesia, Ireland, Israel, Italy, Ivory Coast, Jamaica, Japan, Kenya, Korea, Kuwait, Luxembourg, Malagasy Republic, Malawi, Malaysia, Malta, Mauritania, Mauritius, Netherlands, New Zealand, Nicaragua, Niger, Nigeria, Norway, Pakistan, Peru, Poland, Portugal, Rhodesia, Rwanda, Senegal, Sierra Leone, South Africa, Spain, Sri Lanka, Sweden, Switzerland, Tanzania, Togo, Trinidad and Tobago, Turkey, Uganda, UK, USA, Upper Volta, Uruguay, Yugoslavia.
26 See, the Protocol on Provisional Entry into Force, supra p. 67.
27 Algeria, Botswana, Equatorial Guinea, Khmer Republic, Lesotho, Maldives, Mali, People's Democratic Republic of Yemen, Singapore, Swaziland, Tonga, Tunisia, Zambia.
28 By June 1973 the following states had adhered to the convention: Albania, Algeria, Argentina, Australia, Austria, Barbados, Belgium, Botswana, Bulgaria, Canada, Central African Republic, Chile, China (Taiwan), Congo (People's Republic), Cuba, Cyprus, Czechoslovakia, Dahomey, Denmark, Dominican Republic, Ecuador, Egypt, Finland, France, Ghana, Greece, Guatemala, Haiti, Hungary, India, Ireland, Israel, Italy, Ivory

Coast, Jamaica, Japan, Jordan, Khmer Republic, Korea (South), Laos, Lebanon, Luxembourg, Malagasy Republic, Malawi, Malaysia, Mali, Malta, Monaco, Morocco, Netherlands, New Zealand, Niger, Norway, Paraguay, Peru, Philippines, Poland, Portugal, Vietnam (South), Romania, Rwanda, San Marino, Senegal, Sierra Leone, Singapore, South Africa, Spain, Sri Lanka, Sweden, Switzerland (signature only), Syria, Thailand, Togo, Trinidad and Tobago, Tunisia, Turkey, Uganda, USSR, UK, USA, Vatican City, Venezuela, Yugoslavia, Zaïre.

29 *UNTS*, vol. 240, p. 254.
30 By January 1972 23 states had signed the convention, among them Laos, Lesotho, Malawi, Mali, Nepal, Niger, Nigeria, Sudan, Swaziland, Zambia and Uganda.
31 Cf. *The Times*, 10 April 1970.
32 I. Delupis, *The East African Community and Common Market* (London: Longmans, 1970), p. 129 and Detter, *Law Making by International Organizations*, p. 269. For detailed provisions in the EEC see also the Transport Regulations, Regulation No. 11, *JO*, 16 August 1960, no. 53, p. 112; modes of transport sometimes rest with the member states, not with the Community.
33 Delupis, *The East African Community and Common Market*, pp. 129 et seq. for an analysis of African association agreements with the EEC.
34 Cf. Graf, 'Niederlassungsrecht und Assozierte', *Europarecht* (1970), pp. 366 et seq. On the Yaoundé convention, see Delupis, *The East African Community and Common Market*, pp. 131 et seq.
35 See articles 44, 47-48. Cf. the 'declaration of intent' in the agreement with Turkey, article 12 and in the agreement with Malta, article 2.
36 Statement by Mr Heath at the meeting of Commonwealth prime ministers in September 1962.
37 See Delupis, *The East African Community and Common Market* pp. 140 et seq.
38 Cf. Ewerling, *Das Niederlassungsrecht im Gemeinsamen Markt*, (Berlin/Frankfurt, 1964), p. 16.
39 On investment guarantee agreements, see further, Delupis, *Finance and Protection of Investments in Developing Countries*, pp. 34 et seq.

40 Some sectors may be excluded, Delupis, *Finance and Protection of Investments in Developing Countries*, p. 38.
41 *I.C.J. Reports 1960,* p. 6.
42 *Baarle-Duc* and *Baarle-Nassau* under article 14 of the boundary convention of 1842 between Belgium and Holland; *Büsingen* under articles 1 and 2 of the treaty of 1895 between Switzerland and Germany and under chapters 3-7 of the exchange of notes between Baden and Switzerland; *Llivia* under the treaty of the Pyrénées of 1659 between France and Spain and under a treaty of 1866 between the same states; *Campione* under the treaty of 1861 and under the treaty of 1923 between Italy and Switzerland.
43 Cf. Monaco, *Manuale di diritto internazionale pubblico* (Turin, 1971), p. 473.
44 *Dokumente zur Berlin Frage 1944-1966* (Munich, 1967), p. 58 and Bulletin Nr. 127 (3 September 1971), p. 1382.
45 See, treaty between Great Britain, USSR, United States and France, 3 September 1971, Bulletin Nr. 127, p. 1357; this is then a treaty concluded in favour of a third party as West Germany did not sign, cf. I. Detter, *Essays on the Law of Treaties* (London: Sweet & Maxwell, 1967), p. 115; but there is another treaty signed by the Federal Republic of Germany and DDR, which also guarantees transit to Berlin, Bulletin, Nr. 183 (11 December 1971), p. 1953.
46 J. B. Moore, *A Digest of International Law* (Washington: Government Printing Office, 1906), vol. 4, p. 557 and infra, p. 115.
47 [1891] A.C. 272.
48 (1892) 142 U.S.651. Cf. *Fong Yue Ting v US,* (1893) 149 U.S.698.
49 But cf. supra p. 62 and infra, pp. 86-7.
50 Statement by Zambian High Commissioner in London, *The Times,* 28 February 1973.
51 *The Times,* 22 May 1973.
52 Supra, p. 33 and note 21.

Chapter 5

Passage Through Air

5:1 HISTORICAL BACKGROUND

5:1:1 Is the Air Free?

Writers on international law at the beginning of this century often declared that the 'air is free' and that no state is entitled to monopolize the air over its territory.[1] As the importance of air navigation grew such statements were soon modified: states were said to enjoy a power to protect their 'security'.[2] The United Kingdom was one of the first countries to claim 'complete and absolute sovereignty' over its airspace and when it received too little support at the Paris conference in 1911 the United Kingdom enacted its own Aerial Navigation Act 1911 by which it confirmed its power of sovereignty above its territory and territorial waters and its right to establish, at its discretion, police, fiscal and other regulations regarding air navigation; no passage would be allowed through airspace without authorization.

In 1913 Germany and France concluded an agreement on rights of transit which were circumscribed by a number of safeguards.[3]

5:1:2 The Paris Convention

Although it had been advocated that the air was free to all states at the beginning of the century the pendulum soon swung the other way. The Paris convention of 1919 on civil aviation provided that states have complete and absolute sovereignty over their airspace. However, the convention—which was signed by 38 states—stipulated that civilian aircraft are, in times of peace, entitled to *innocent passage* through foreign airspace.[4] This right, however, was only granted to nonscheduled flights. Transit passage might have to be carried out within certain specified zones and certain areas could be closed to foreign aircraft. The right to land was subjected to express authorization usually in the form of a detailed bilateral treaty.[5] A permanent body, Commission internationale de la navigation aérienne (CINA) was established.

Other conventions on civil aviation were concluded within the Pan American framework,[6] and their provisions were usually based on the text of the Paris convention of 1919, with certain modifications.

5:2 ICAO REGULATIONS

The Paris convention and CINA were replaced in 1944 by the Chicago convention which established the International Civil Aviation Organization.[7] In June 1973, ICAO had 126 members. Article 5 of the Chicago convention provides that

> Each contracting state agrees that all aircraft of the other contracting states, being aircraft *not engaged in scheduled international air services* shall have the right, subject to the observance of the terms of this convention, to make flights into or in transit non-stop across its territory and to make stops for non-traffic purposes without the necessity of obtaining prior permission, and subject to the right of the state flown over to require landing. Each contracting state nevertheless reserves the right, for reasons of safety of flight, to require aircraft desiring to proceed over regions which are inaccessible or without adequate air navigation facilities to follow prescribed routes, or to obtain special permission for such flights.
>
> Such aircraft, if engaged in the carriage of passengers, cargo, or mail for remuneration or hire on other than scheduled international air services, shall also, subject to the provisions of article 7, have the privilege of taking on or discharging passen-

gers, cargo, or mail, subject to the right of any state where such embarkation or discharge takes place to impose such regulations, conditions or limitations as it may consider desirable.

In practice a number of ICAO's members require previous authorization for nonscheduled international air services under article 5 paragraph 2. According to a study by the Secretariat of ICAO such authorization should, however, not be necessary. The Secretariat was asked to review its opinion by the Air Navigation Commission of ICAO which considered the requirement of previous authorization reasonable.[8] In practice states continued to require such authorization for nonscheduled flights.[9] But, technically, for transit without landing, under article 5 paragraph 1, no authorization is necessary.

The ICAO convention only covers the transit rights of nonscheduled operations of civil aircraft. Military aircraft and 'state' aircraft are not covered. An attempt to embody the so-called Hague rules of 1923 on military aircraft in a separate convention failed.[10]

On the other hand, the minimum provision on transit for civil aircraft embodied in the ICAO convention itself is supplemented by two other conventions on transit—the International Air Services Transit Agreement (the so-called Two Freedoms Agreement) of 1944 and the International Air Transport Agreement (the so-called Five Freedoms Agreement of 1944). Under these supplementing agreements *scheduled air services* were granted certain rights of transit. The 'five freedoms' included the right to (1) fly across foreign territory (of a contracting state) without landing; (2) land for non-traffic purposes; (3) disembark in a foreign country from a flight originating in the home state of the aircraft; (4) pick up traffic in a foreign country to return to the home state of the aircraft; and (5) carry traffic between two foreign (contracting) countries. The 'Two Freedoms Agreement' included the first two of these 'freedoms'. Less than half the original members of ICAO signed the transport agreement allowing for five 'freedoms'; but the majority adhered to the transit agreement which thus actively supplements the ICAO convention itself for transit rights of scheduled flights among the majority of members. The ICAO convention is also, among some members, supplemented by the Paris convention of 1956 on Transit Rights for Scheduled Transport Flights, and the Convention on Commercial Rights of Non-scheduled Air Services also concluded in

Paris 1956. The Convention on Commercial Rights concerns, *inter alia*, rights of transit for planes for humanitarian or rescue purposes.

There are also numerous bilateral arrangements particularly regulating specific rights of scheduled air services.[11]

5:3 LIMITS OF THE AIRSPACE

If then, under various treaties, there exists a far-reaching right of transit without landing for both scheduled and nonscheduled services, it becomes important to establish to what airspace a modern state can actually claim sovereignty. For in this airspace a free right of transit or 'innocent passage' may exist for aircraft provided a state has adhered to special treaties.

The airspace of a state extends to its boundaries and includes the air above the territorial sea, even if underlying waters form part of international straits.[12] But the airspace does not include the air above fishing zones or other water zones, unless the superjacent air over such zones is claimed as special 'air identification' areas. Such 'air defence identification zones' are currently claimed by the United States and by Canada, and have been in use for over 20 years; also the Philippines apply this system.[13] Any aircraft which enters such a zone is required to report to the flight control centres of the littoral state. The zones extend in some cases to 200 nautical miles, and are, in the United States, supplemented by the rule that report shall be made no later than one hour from the coast, which with the speed of Concorde would involve a duty to report in the mid-Atlantic. It has been contended that the zones have already been accepted as international customary law, and that they would be justifiable as part of the right of self-defence; others have denied the legality of such zones under international law.[14] It is probably true that such claims must not be 'unreasonable';[15] but it is difficult to argue that zones that have been in use for a considerable number of years have not been recognized as forming part of regional customary law.

The vertical delimitation of the airspace also presents some problems. What is the upper limit of the airspace?

Neither the Paris convention of 1919 nor the ICAO convention stipulates any upper limit for the airspace that a state may claim as a part of its territory; but the phrasing of the first of these conventions that a state has 'complete and exclusive sovereignty' over the airspace above its territory seems to suggest that there was an *usque ad coelum* principle—that there was no upper limit to the airspace of a state. However, soon after the first Sputnik had been launched in 1957 it became evident that such claims would be absurd.[16] It was then suggested that a state's airspace extends as far as an aircraft can ascend;[17] but this fails to draw a precise line: the X-15, for example, possessed characteristics of both aircraft and spacecraft and could attain a height of 47 miles.[18]

Another theory claimed that airspace is equal to 'atmospheric space'. A state would then be able to claim sovereignty up to 10,000 miles where there are still traces of oxygen.[19] But, this theory is also unconfirmed by state practice. On the contrary, states have not protested when artificial satellites have been put in orbit and have not claimed that such spacecraft have violated their territorial airspace. Most states assumed, even before the United Nations resolution on the matter, that outer space is free for all.

It has been suggested that a state may claim territorial rights as far as it considers necessary for its national security.[20] Another proposal is that airspace should comprise what a state is able to control.[21]

The so-called Karman theory implies that a state is allowed territorial sovereignty over the airspace as far as the line where an object travelling at 25,000 feet per second loses its aerodynamic lift and the centrifugal force takes over; this would be at an altitude of some 53 miles.[22] A similar theory suggests that the line should be drawn at the lowest altitude at which an artificial satellite may be put in orbit around the earth, which is between 70 and 100 miles.[23]

United Nations resolution 1721 (XVI) declared that outer space is free for all but did not contribute to the attempts to determine the upper line for a state's territorial airspace; nor did the Treaty on Principles Governing the Activities of States in the Exploration and Use of Outer Space, including the Moon and other Celestial Bodies (1967), the Agreement on the Rescue of Astronauts, the Return of Astronauts, and the Return of Objects Launched into Outer Space (1968), the Convention on International Liability for Damage Caused by Space Objects (1972) and the draft Treaty on the Moon (1971).

The upper limit of national airspace is thus still undetermined.

However, it appears that the line is likely to be drawn somewhere above 20 and somewhere below 100 miles—that is, national sovereignty can probably be claimed up to where an artificial satellite can be put in orbit. Naturally, it would be more desirable to introduce fuller regulation of space activities, enforced by some inspection system, rather than insisting on demarcation lines; for the problem is only another facet of the disarmament problem.[24] Still, even though the security of a state can only be safeguarded by regulating activities rather than by excessive projection of sovereignty,[25] it is also clear that a customary norm has now emerged according to which a state may put a satellite in orbit without violating the territorial airspace of other states.[26]

It may be desirable to keep sovereignty claims fairly low for a number of reasons: most states do not possess the resources or the technical ability to exercise any effective control at great heights; exploration of outer space may be hampered by excessive claims; and a high sovereignty ceiling is also likely to penalize smaller states and make it difficult for them to launch and retrieve satellites without violating the sovereignty of neighbouring states—this would place them in an unequal position in regard to access to the resources of outer space.[27]

5:4 A GENERAL RIGHT OF TRANSIT?

The ICAO convention and the air transit agreement both have almost universal adherence: they reflect the opinion of the overwhelming majority of nations which have decided to grant each other a general right of transit through their airspace. It is of great importance to note that member states of ICAO have delegated powers to the organization to regulate the way in which the right of transit is to be operated in practice. The Council of ICAO, which is a restricted organ where not all member states are represented, can adopt 'annexes', which may embody further obligations for the member states, without their consent.[28] The burden is on the member states to avoid such obligations by a procedure of 'contracting-out', a procedure by which members can be allowed to depart from annexes. But under the contracting-out formula states avoid being bound only if they notify the organization within a certain time and declare that they find it 'impracticable' to comply with new rules adopted by the Council.[29]

The importance of the Chicago convention used to be greatly undermined by the fact that the USSR and a number of other states in eastern Europe were not parties to it. Instead the USSR and other states chose to conclude bilateral treaties to allow and obtain permission for air transit and/or landing rights. The USSR had, in 1965, concluded 31 such agreements.[30]

However, in November 1970 the USSR joined ICAO and by 1973 the organization had 126 member states including all eastern European countries except Albania.[31] The few states that are not members of the organization are mainly those which have little interest in civil aviation matters, perhaps because, like Andorra, Monaco and Liechtenstein, they have no large airport of their own.

Czechoslovakia, Poland and Bulgaria, together with 78 other states, have also signed the more far-reaching transit agreement which covers scheduled flights. But certain transit traffic for non-scheduled air services is guaranteed under the ICAO convention itself, and this rule has now achieved almost universal acceptance.

Even if there exists an almost universal right of transit for non-military aircraft, such a right is still based on treaty law and probably not on any general rule of international law.[32] On the other hand, to submit that such a right of innocent passage may gradually develop even in the airspace is not far fetched: in the days when states claimed unlimited sovereignty to their airspace they still allowed for a 'right of innocent passage' for nonmilitary aircraft.[33] However, if and when such a right develops again under international law it will be reduced by certain general principles. For example, a passage that involves sonic bangs can constitute a nuisance unless the effects are so trivial that the flight is protected by the maxim *de minimis non curat lex*.[34] In other words, if there were considerable nuisance, the passage would no longer be 'innocent'.

It has been claimed that a general right of 'innocent passage' in the absence of treaties already exists.[35] For example, Israel claimed before the International Court of Justice that Bulgaria, which had shot down an El Al plane on 27 July 1955 killing 58 people, did not enjoy such an exclusive right of sovereignty that it could prevent the 'innocent' passage of a civilian aircraft in distress which had lost its way and intruded on Bulgarian airspace.[36] There was, however, never any judgment by the Court in this case as Bulgaria agreed to make an *ex gratia* payment of 'compensation'. On the other hand, Israel has not argued that any such right of 'innocent passage' would subsist for a Libyan plane which, on 21 February 1973, was shot down over Israeli occupied Sinai killing 104 people.[37]

It may seem reasonable to assume that a general right of transit through a state's airspace has yet to develop. Furthermore, it is questionable whether a right of transit through airspace can ever develop through local custom. However, as previously mentioned, many states are bound by treaty to grant transit rights for civilian aircraft already. Yet, in analogy with ships in distress,[38] a state probably cannot refuse transit or even emergency landing, to an aircraft in distress, even in the absence of treaties.

It is obvious that the rules for transit through air are different from those for transit over land or water: the general security of a state is in peril when foreign aircraft, even civil aircraft, enter its airspace. It is far easier for a state to control and stop a motor vehicle on its roads than to reroute an aircraft or to force it to land if the state considers its security threatened. Above all, the risks of aerial photography of military installations and of espionage from the air make it reasonable to assume that the state must authorize transit by air in each case, unless general authorization has been given under special treaties. The right of air transit is therefore more restricted and, unlike passage overland or through territorial waters, there is almost a presumption that flights are a threat to a state's security; the right to transit is usually limited to specific corridors, previously approved by the territorial states. However, even if such a right of air transit is normally limited to civil aircraft travelling through delimited corridors, there does exist nowadays an almost universal right of transit through air under international treaty law.

Even if air services provide the quickest means of transport today they are not the only means of communication in the community of nations: landlocked states and enclaves, which, as has been suggested, must have some means of access to the sea and to international trade routes, can exercise their minimum rights of transit without claiming a right to flights through the airspace of foreign states. However, if there are no alternative transit routes, as in the case of certain commodities from Zambia when Rhodesia closed its borders in January 1973, it may well be justifiable to claim that an airlift must be allowed: Zambia even claimed that the costs for defraying such an alternative must be borne by the 'international community', an indication that the world as a whole has an obligation to safeguard the economic survival of landlocked states.[39]

NOTES

1. See Fauchille, 'Le domaine aérien et le régime juridique des aérostats', *Revue générale de droit international public* (1901), pp. 414 et seq. Cf. Hazeltine, *The Law of the Air* (London, 1911), pp. 12 et seq.
2. For example, articles drafted by Fauchille at the 1910 meeting of the Institute of International Law, where he stated 'la circulation aérienne internationale est libre, sauf le droit pour les états sous-jacents de prendre certaines mesures à examiner en vue de leur propre sécurité et de celle des personnes et des biens de leur habitants.' For a discussion, see Slotemaker, *Freedom of Passage for International Air Services* (Leiden, 1932), p. 11.
3. See, further, D. H. N. Johnson, *Rights in Air Space* (Manchester: Manchester University Press/New York, Oceana Publications, 1965), p. 24.
4. See, further Slotemaker, *Freedom of Passage for International Air Services*, pp. 14 et seq.
5. Chapter 4 article 15 of the Paris convention.
6. For example, the Ibero-American Convention of 1926, signed by seven states, the Pan American Convention of Havana, 1928, signed by 16 states.
7. On ICAO and its regulations, see I. Detter, *Law Making by International Organizations* (Stockholm: Norstedts, 1965), pp. 247 et seq.
8. For a discussion, see D. Goedhuis, 'Questions of public international air law', *Académie de droit international, Recueil des Cours*, vol. 81 (1952), ii, pp. 263 et seq.
9. Goedhuis, in *RCADI*, vol. 81, pp. 272 et seq.
10. See J. M. Spaight, *Air Power and War Rights*, 3rd edition (London: Longmans Green, 1947), p. 41.

11 The Bermuda Agreement between the United States and Britain of 1946 has been a 'model' agreement, see Bin Cheng, *The Law of International Air Transport* (London: Stevens, 1964), pp. 411 et seq.
12 Cf. supra, pp. 31-33 for width of territorial waters, pp. 41-3 for passage through straits, and pp. 32-7 for water zones.
13 See further, B. Johnson, *Suveränitet i havet och luftrummet* (Stockholm: Norstedt, 1972), pp. 270 et seq.
14 For example, Head, 'ADIZ, international law, and contiguous airspace', *Alberta Law Review* (1964), p. 186.
15 Johnson, *Suveränitet i havet och luftrummet*, p. 276.
16 McMahon, 'Legal aspects of outer space', in *The British Year Book of International Law, 1962* (London: Oxford University Press, 1964), p. 342.
17 Cooper, 'Flight space and satellites', *International and Comparative Law Quarterly* (1958), p. 82; Johnson, *Rights in Air Space*, p. 60; Rinck, 'Recht im Weltraum', *Zeitschrift für Luftrecht und Weltraumrechtsfragen* (1960), p. 191; Wright, 'Legal aspects of the U-2 incident', *American Journal of International Law* (1960), pp. 836 et seq.; cf. Lissitzyn, 'Some legal implications of the U-2 flight', *American Journal of International Law* (1962), pp. 106 et seq.
18 Cf. McMahon in *British Year Book of International Law, 1962*, p. 341. Cf. M. S. McDougal, H. D. Lasswell and I. A. Vlasic, *Law and Public Order in Space* (New Haven/London: Yale University Press, 1963), p. 335.
19 Cf. McMahon in *British Year Book of International Law, 1962*, p. 341. Cf. Meyer, 'Die Bedeutung der Festsetzung einer Grenze zwischen Luftraum und Weltraumgebiet', *Zeitschrift für Luftrecht und Weltraumrechtsfragen* (1962), pp. 106 et seq. Cf. N. M. Matte, *Aerospace Law* (London: Sweet & Maxwell, 1969), p. 21.
20 Galina, *Soviet Yearbook of International Law* (1958).
21 Zadorozhnyi, in *Sovetskaia Rossia*, 17 October 1957. Cf. Kelsen, *General Theory of Law and State* (Cambridge, 1945), p. 217.
22 This theory was developed by Haley in cooperation with the scientist Theodore von Karman; see Haley, Space Age Presents Immediate Legal Problems, International Institute for Space Law, The Hague 1958, pp. 8 et seq. Cf. Sontag, *Der Weltraum*

in der Raumordnung des Völkerrecht (Kiel, 1966) and McMahon in *British Year Book of International Law, 1962,* p. 344. See also Johnson, *Rights in Air Space,* p. 60; Bin Cheng in *International and Comparative Law Quarterly* (1957) and Cooper, 'High altitude flights and national sovereignty', *International and Comparative Law Quarterly* (1957).

23 McMahon in *British Year Book of International Law, 1962,* p. 343. Cf. the theory of a 'functional' rather than a 'territorial' limit, Ley and Taubenfeld, *The Law Relating to Activities of Man in Space* (1970), p. 47; J. E. S. Fawcett, *International Law and the Uses of Outer Space* (Manchester: Manchester University Press, 1968), p. 27 and C. Chaumont, *Le Droit de l'espace* (Paris, 1960), pp. 49 et seq.

24 McMahon in *British Year Book of International Law, 1962,* p. 344.

25 McMahon in *British Year Book of International Law, 1962,* p. 345.

26 But note Cheng, 'From air law to space law', *Current Legal Problems,* vol. 13 (1960), p. 237, who argues that such a right has not developed; states still give their 'tacit consent'. Cf. G. Gàl, *Space Law* (New York: Oceana, 1969), p. 103.

27 McMahon in *British Year Book of International Law,* 1962, p. 345.

28 See further, Detter, *Law Making by International Organizations,* pp. 248 et seq.

29 Detter, *Law Making by International Organizations,* p. 249.

30 See further, Rehm, 'Einige völkerrechtliche Betrachtungen zum Sowjetischen Souveränitätsanspruch im Luftraum', *Zeitschrift für Luftrecht und Weltraumrechtsfragen* (1959), pp. 174 et seq. Cf. Kislov-Krylov, 'State sovereignty in airspace', *International Affairs* (Moscow), 1956.

31 This point escapes Johnson, *Suveränitet i havet och luftrummet,* p. 259, who alleges that the USSR and other eastern European states were not members in 1971.

32 Cf. Bin Cheng, *The Law of International Air Transport,* p. 9.

33 A. D. McNair (Baron McNair), *The Law of the Air,* 3rd edition by M. R. E. Kerr and A. H. M. Evans (London: Stevens, 1964), p. 5.

34 McNair, *The Law of the Air,* p. 70.

35 C. N. Shawcross and K. M. Beaumont, *Air Law,* 3rd edition by P. B. Keenan, A. Lester and P. Martin (London: Butterworths, 1966) vol. 1, p. 190.
36 *I.C.J. Pleadings, Aerial Incident of 27 July 1955* (1957).
37 *The Times,* 22 February 1973. Note that Israel adhered to the Air Transit Agreement on 16 June 1954.
38 Supra, p. 48.
39 Cf. statement by the Zambian High Commissioner in London, *The Times,* 28 February 1973. Cf. supra, p. 74.

Chapter 6

Other Restrictions of Sovereignty Relating to Territory

6:1 QUESTIONS OF POLLUTION

The international community is increasingly concerned with the damage caused to the human environment by pollution. Some conventions already regulate certain aspects of the problem but their provisions are hardly adequate. Conventions that deal with these matters are, for example, the Convention for the Prevention of Pollution of the Sea by Oil (1954 amended 1962, 1969 and 1971), the Plant Protection Convention (1951), the Convention on Intervention on the High Seas in Case of Oil Pollution Damage (1969), the Convention on Civil Liability for Oil Pollution Damage (1969), the Treaty Banning Nuclear Tests in the Atmosphere, in Outer Space and Under Water (1963), the Treaty on the Prohibition of Emplacement of Nuclear Weapons on the Seabed and Ocean Floor (1971), the Treaty on Non-proliferation of Nuclear Weapons (1968), the Convention on Prevention of Marine Pollution (1973) and certain regional arrangements such as the African Convention on Conservation of Natural Resources (1968), the Latin American Convention on Prohibition of Nuclear Weapons (1967) and the Scandinavian Convention on Cooperation to Prevent Oil Pollution of the Sea (1971).

Even apart from such conventions a state is not entitled, under international law, to use its own territory in such a way as to cause damage to neigbouring states. This book is not concerned with pollution or other damage caused *outside* a state's territory; but I shall try to establish what rules on pollution under general international law actually restrict a state's exercise of sovereignty *in its own territory*.

If, for example, a state has in its territory an international river it cannot be allowed to pollute its waters by waste from oil or gas installations which will affect other states further along the river. The Rau arbitration between Sind and Punjab is illustrative although it only relates to the relationship between provinces, not between states. Here it was held that

> no new project, however beneficent in other ways should be allowed to impair existing inundation canals without payment of compensation.[1]

The same rule applies if a state has granted a concession to another state or to a foreign company to erect oil or gas installations: even if the state gives its consent it cannot empower someone else to pollute an international river so as to cause damage to neighbouring states.

Oil, gas or other petroleum products and coal slurry may escape or seep from pipelines or refineries and pollute the waters of a drainage basin. A state is internationally prohibited from causing such pollution through its own activity or by tolerating the activities of any concessionary on its territory. The chemical industry has created new pollution problems in connexion with new products. For example, household detergents, agricultural insecticides carried into streams and radioactive wastes may cause pollution of neighbouring states.[2]

In the *Trail Smelter* arbitration[3] it was held that a state should be responsible for damage resulting in a neighbouring state by fumes emitted from a smelter in its territory. In this case a smelter was operating in British Columbia and fumes were deposited over a large area of Washington in the United States. The tribunal emphasized that

Under the principles of international law, as well as under the laws of the United States, no state has the right to use or permit the use of its territory in such a manner as to cause injury by fumes in or to the territory of another or the property of persons therein.[4]

This leading case can, *mutatis mutandis,* give a guide to rules on pollution of international rivers or other damage caused to neighbouring states as well as to rules on damage caused to territory of a state over which it has no right to dispose—for example, an international waterway. These rules can also be deduced from the *Corfu Channel* case[5] where the International Court of Justice held that international law obliges every state 'not to allow knowingly its territory to be used for acts contrary to rights of other states'.

Thus, the maxim *sic utere tuo ut alienum non laedes*—one must so use his own as not to do injury to another—also applies to cases where a state does not cause damage itself but allows someone else to cause injury. The state must guarantee that no damage is caused to other states by allowing, for example, an oil concession in its territory. And if damage does occur in spite of all precautions the territorial state is liable to pay compensation to the states which suffer the damage.

Oil pollution of waters adjacent to a state is becoming an increasing problem. The *Torrey Canyon* disaster off the south coast of England in 1967 with a leakage of over 100,000 tons of crude oil indicated what damage may be caused by modern giant oil tankers. Some states have preferred to introduce preventive measures rather than relying on hazardous rules of responsibility and reparation. Thus Canada extended an oil protection zone by the Arctic Waters Pollution Prevention Act of 1970: within a distance of 100 miles offshore Canada held itself competent to lay down regulations and standards of construction and navigation, and to intervene or even seize ships violating the Act (cf. supra p. 34). When nuclear tests are likely to cause radioactive pollution affecting a state's territory even more vigorous action has been taken: in such cases rules on state responsibility and reparation provide little comfort if damage has already occurred by radioactive fallout. Australia and New Zealand thus approached the World Court for an injunction to stop French nuclear tests in the Pacific as such tests would, even if carried out outside their hegemony, have detrimental effects on areas under their sovereignty. The injunction was granted on 22 June 1973 although France boycotted the Court's proceedings and, a month later, exploded two nuclear devices. France contended that the Court had no jurisdiction in this affair which involved national defence. M. André Gros, the French judge on the International Court of Justice declared that the provisional measures based on article 41 of the Statute of the ICJ constituted an action *ultra vires* and Judge Isaac Forster, from Senegal, held that any state enjoys the right to 'undertake in full sovereignty on its own territory any action appropriate for ensuring its immediate or future national security and national defence ... Of course, in the exercise of this right, each state remains responsible for any consequent injury to third parties.'

However, as I have already emphasized, nuclear damage may be of such dimensions that reparation cannot be adequate or even possible. Preventive recourse must then be available. Territorial sovereignty cannot imply a right to take action within a territory when such action is likely to cause damage to neighbouring states.

Concerning the French contention that the International Court of Justice is incompetent in a matter concerning national security it may be pointed out that nuclear tests do, by definition, bear on national security. If the ICJ were deprived of all competence to hear a case involving such tests it would mean that states would have no remedy against pollution by radioactive fallout caused by such tests, either by seeking injunctions from the ICJ or by subsequently seeking reparation. However, whatever the connection may be between the *cause* of possible pollution and national security and defence it is inevitable that the *effects* of nuclear tests must be dealt with in analogy with classical cases like the *Trail Smelter* arbitration (see supra, p. 92). And, in view of the possibly catastrophic effects of nuclear bombs it is desirable that preventive action can be taken by injunction pending the hearing of the merits of the case.

To allow a state to prevent activity of another in the latter's own territory obviously depends on *how* likely it is that damage will be caused. The findings of substance in such a case therefore involve technical considerations of risk which modern science is capable of calculating. Another interesting problem arises if nuclear tests were not likely to cause damage to neighbouring states but merely to the high seas and the atmosphere and such damage were likely to interfere with international navigation. Which states would then be entitled to seek an injunction from the World Court?

The rule that the sovereignty of a state is restricted in so far as it may not use its territory as it pleases if it causes harm to other states could also be held to imply that a state must not pollute, or allow pollution of, its own groundwater which, in case considerable damage is caused, may have disastrous effects on neighbouring states.

Thus, a state may not pollute its own waters if that impairs the navigational rights of other states; it may not pollute its groundwater which may cause damage to neighbouring states; it may not pollute the waters of international waterways which may cause damage to other states downstream. This last form of damage may be caused by modern processes of irrigation for arid and semi-arid land which often has the effect of increasing the salinity of downstream waters. Similarly, industrial processes of valuable and useful products may inevitably result in deleterious wastes polluting the waters. Thus pollution may often be a by-product of beneficial uses of water. But a *substantial* injury must have occurred before a state is liable to pay compensation.[6]

6:2 EQUITABLE USE OF WATER

Every state is entitled, under international law, to use water in its territory for its own needs; but this right is limited, in the case of the waters of an international drainage basin, to what can be considered as reasonable and equitable use.

In many cases there may be a treaty which regulates the equitable use of, for example, international rivers. India and Pakistan have arrived at an understanding on the use of the waters of the Indus and concluded a treaty to this effect in 1960.[7] The Nile has also been subject to treaty regulation, first between the United Kingdom and Egypt in 1929 when the Nile Waters Agreement was concluded[8] and later, when the Sudan had become independent, between Sudan and Egypt in 1959.[9]

In the absence of treaties a state must still make reasonable use of international rivers and other water resources and not deprive a downstream state of its rightful enjoyment of the river for navigation, irrigation and other purposes.

An example of what might happen if states consider themselves free to use an international river as they please is an incident relating to the Nile.

After the independence of Egypt in 1922 Egyptians were gradually excluded from the Sudan which, technically, remained the condominium of the 'Anglo-Egyptian Sudan'. Irritation culminated in the assassination in Cairo of Sir Lee Stack, the Governor-General of the Sudan, in 1924. Viscount Allenby who at the time was British High Commissioner in Egypt then declared that, unless Egyptians evacuated the Sudan, his sappers would divert a great proportion of the Nile water so that it would never reach Egypt at all. This was virtually a threat of genocide for without water the population of the Nile Valley would perish in a few weeks.[10]

Now, some fifty years later, it appears that had a state, for whatever purpose, diverted an international river on which downstream peoples depend, it would have committed a crime under international law. The international legal system has now developed to safeguard, even in the absence of treaties, the equal right of states to natural resources, like water, common to them.

Support for this rule can be found in the *Trail Smelter* arbitration (see p. 92): no state may, deliberately or by negligence, cause damage to another state. Furthermore, the *Lake Lanoux* case[11] confirms the view that a state must not change the water conditions of an international drainage basin in a way that causes serious injury to downstream states. On the other hand, a territorial state is entitled to use the water, for example, for hydraulic purposes without asking the other riparian states for permission.[12] But such use must be 'equitable and beneficial'.

The Helsinki Rules[13] suggest, in article 5, what shall be considered as relevant factors in establishing what is, in an individual case, 'reasonable and equitable'. Article 5(2) provides that relevant factors to be considered include, but are not limited to,

> (a) the geography of the basin, including in particular the extent of the drainage area in the territory of each basin state;
> (b) the hydrology of the basin, including in particular the contribution of water by each basin state;
> (c) the climate affecting the basin;

(d) the past utilization of the waters of the basin, including in particular existing utilization;
(e) the economic and social needs of each basin state;
(f) the population dependent on the waters of the basin in each basin state;
(g) the comparative cost of alternative means of satisfying the economic and social needs of each basin state;
(h) the availability of other resources;
(i) the avoidance of unnecessary waste in the utilization of waters of the basin;
(j) the practicability of compensation to one or more of the co-basin states as a means of adjusting conflicts among uses; and
(k) the degree to which the needs of a basin state may be satisfied, without causing substantial injury to a co-basin state.

Naturally, many of these factors remain to be assessed and qualified in an individual dispute. It is certainly desirable for riparian states to regulate by treaty their use of an international drainage basin. If they refrain from doing so, a riparian state still remains protected, to some extent, by general international law, and if other states cause considerable damage to it, for example, by disproportionate use of an international river, then they are liable to pay compensation.

In recent international disputes concerning international rivers states have also recognized that all riparians have 'some right' to the waters. In the dispute between Bolivia and Chile, for example, concerning the use of the Lauca river, Chile recognized that downstream Bolivia had certain rights to the river.[14] Similarly, in the Jordan Basin dispute between Israel and the Arab states both sides adhered to the principle that they were all entitled to a 'reasonable share' of the basin waters.[15]

NOTES

1 (1930) *AD* 1931-2, no. 124.
2 Cf. International Law Association Report on Pollution of Boundary Waters, 1951, pp. 65-6.
3 *Reports of International Arbitral Awards,* vol. 3, p. 1905; *American Journal of International Law* (1941) p. 684.

4   *Reports of International Arbitral Awards,* vol. 3, p. 1965; *Missouri v Illinois,* 200 US 496 (1906); *New Jersey v City of New York,* 283 US 476 (1931).
5   *I.C.J. Reports 1949,* p. 22. Cf. also declaration by the Secretary-General of the United Nations that 'there has been general recognition of the rule that a state must not permit the use of its territory for purposes injurious to the interest of other states in a manner contrary to international law', Survey of International Law, 34 UN Doc. A/CN.4/1 Rev. 1 (1949).
6   Cf. International Law Association, Helsinki Rules, article X, Yearbook of ILA 1966, p. 500.
7   *American Journal of International Law* (1961), suppl., p. 797.
8   *LNTS,* vol. 93, p. 46. See, infra, on the problem of state succession, p. 182.
9   Khartoum *Morning News,* 13 November 1959.
10 Farran, 'The Nile Waters Agreements', *Yearbook of the AAA,* 1961, p. 77.
11 *Revue générale de droit international public* (1958), p. 79.
12 *Revue générale de droit international public* (1958), p. 79. On the distinction between 'sovereignty', 'ownership' and 'joint ownership' of such natural resources, see I. Delupis, *Finance and Protection of Invesments in Developing Countries* (Gower Press, 1973), pp. 59-64.
13 ILA, Yearbook, 1966, p. 488. The Helsinki Rules reject the so-called 'Harmon Doctrine' according to which a state would have an unqualified right to dispose of waters of an international river, ibid., p. 486.
14 OEA/Ser.B/VI.
15 SC, Off. rec., Jan-March 1962, p. 87, (S/5084).

PART THREE

RESTRICTIONS OF SOVEREIGNTY OVER INDIVIDUALS AND PROPERTY

Chapter 7

General Rules on Immunity for State Activities

Part two of this book discussed rules concerning restrictions of sovereignty with respect to the territory as such. A state may be bound under general international law to allow certain minimum rights of transit, provided that passage is 'innocent' and that it does not threaten the security of the state. The only other kind of restriction of sovereignty over the territory as such in the absence of treaties appears to be that a state must not use its territory in such a way as to cause damage to other members of the world community.

Part three will discuss cases in which a state's sovereignty is restricted, in the absence of treaties or special agreements, with respect to *individuals* in its territory or with respect to *property* in that territory. Individuals and entities representing foreign states, and property belonging to foreign states, may enjoy immunity under general international law. Individuals are furthermore exempt from certain sovereign functions, such as jurisdiction, if they are employed by the diplomatic mission of another state; consuls may also enjoy such immunity.

Traditional international law claimed that only *aliens* in a country enjoy certain minimum rights under international law. It will be shown that even nationals have such rights, by virtue of general rules on human rights. Thus, there is a limit to the state's sovereignty both as far as aliens and its own nationals are concerned.

7:1 STATE AGENCY TRADING AND PRIVATE ACTS OF HEADS OF STATE

Because all states are equal a foreign sovereign state[1] is held to enjoy immunity in another state on the basis of reciprocity. What foreign entities may claim such immunity? Must they be *organically* part of the foreign government?

The British Court of Appeal held in *Krajina v Tass Agency*[2] that there was no British competence to adjudicate as Tass is intimately linked to the Soviet state—in spite of the fact that Tass, under Soviet law, is a separate legal subject. However, it is submitted that such an extension of immunity goes further than international law requires. Although some states have recognized certain 'agencies' as forming part of a foreign government, those states have still exercised jurisdiction arguing that a particular transaction by that agency was carried out *de jure gestionis* and not as a 'sovereign function'. This was the situation in *USSR Trade Delegation v Borga* before an Italian court in 1952.[3] The trade delegation had been recognized as part of the Soviet government by an express provision in a treaty concluded between Italy and the USSR in 1924, and in at least one case the trade delegation had been held to enjoy immunity.[4] However, the court held in the *Borga* case that by virtue of the theory of acts *de jure gestionis* the court was competent to hear the case and the trade delegation could not claim immunity.

The distinction between acts *de jure imperii* and acts *de jure gestionis* is an artificial one which is usually drawn between acts which, according to their nature, can only be carried out by a state and those which do not differ from acts performed by private persons and corporations. The distinction has been much criticized by writers[5] but it is currently applied by courts in many cases (see p. 108).

Although there is no continuous practice there is a tendency in Great Britain to uphold immunity for all acts.[6] However, the trend in other states appears to be that the trading activities of a state ought to be exempted from immunity. In Italy court practice to this effect was developed early.[7] Soon Belgium followed[8] as did other states such as Switzerland,[9] France,[10] Austria[11] and, hesitantly, Sweden.[12] In a few cases American courts have also declined immunity for certain trading activities.[13] The idea behind refusing immunity to state organs in foreign countries was that a state was held to lose or forfeit its immunity by entering into private law contracts.

The trend to restrict immunity in cases of state trading may well be necessary to avoid arriving at completely different results for Eastern and Western states: if absolute immunity were granted then all trading activities of the socialist states would be exempt from jurisdiction in other countries as all their trade is administered by state agencies.

The distinction between a state's 'official and sovereign' acts and its 'private acts' is also, to some extent, reflected in the tendency to allow jurisdiction for private affairs of foreign heads of state. Such instances are invariably limited to non-British courts as Great Britain, in this respect also, is more generous in granting immunity than international law demands.[14]

An Italian court has held that the private affairs of a foreign head of state can be brought before a court and no immunity is granted;[15] similar views have been expressed by French courts.[16] In numerous French cases courts have held that they have full jurisdiction for all the private affairs of a foreign head of state after he has ceased to be in office: in *King Farouk v Christian Dior*[17] it was held that an ex-king does not enjoy immunity for private debts. If some medals had been ordered by a head of state they may be 'official' in which case a court should grant immunity; if they were ordered from the jewellers as 'private decorations' the former head of state, or his successors, enjoyed no immunity for debts. This is the rule developed by *Emperor Maximilian's Heirs v Lemaître*, before a French Court.[18] Foreign heads of state may not be subjected to income tax for private income[19] but death duties may be imposed in other states.[20]

7:2 JURISDICTION OVER FOREIGN SHIPS

It appears to be an established rule that warships enjoy immunity.[21] However, they are subject to local regulations relating to navigation, anchorage and public health.[22] If immunity is waived local law will apply.[23] There is even considerable ground for assuming that criminal acts committed ashore are not covered by immunity.[24]

Other foreign ships have traditionally been treated differently depending on whether they are 'public' ships or ordinary merchant ships. The very fact that a foreign sovereign owned a ship has precluded courts from jurisdiction. The leading case has been *The Parlement Belge* (1879)[25] in which a British court granted immunity to a Belgian post boat owned by the Belgian king as there was a question of 'public property destined for public use'. Similarly, in the American case *Berizzi Bros. v SS Pesaro*[26] it was held that a commercial ship was immune as it was state owned.

Applying the theory of acts *de jure gestionis* (see pp. 102-3) the trend may now be reversing. It does not appear feasible to let foreign state-owned vessels enjoy immunity if they engage in ordinary international trade: this would lead to a privileged position for all the state trading countries under international law. But international law is a universal system and should not favour any particular economic structure but must grant the same rights and obligations to all states, whatever economic policy they pursue; and this assertion is only limited in so far as there are special treaties.

By conventional regulations states have agreed to submit their public ships which carry goods and passengers to the same regime as their merchant ships. One early convention is the Brussels agreement of 1926. The same rules are applied by the Montevideo Treaty on International Sea Trade concluded in 1940, and by the Geneva Conventions on the Territorial Sea and the Contiguous Zone and on the High Seas of 1958. The general adherence to the last two conventions may indicate that there is a changing trend in general international law. The Convention on the High Seas, which, in some respects, may be 'declaratory' of existing customary rules, provides for the same rules for merchant ships and public ships if the latter do not exercise proper state functions but indulge in trade and carry goods and passengers. But eight Communist countries had reservations about this provision, article 9 of the convention; similarly, there were reservations about article 21 of the Convention on the Territorial Sea and the Contiguous Zone, which dealt with the same matter. It must be emphasized that it is only reasonable that public ships should enjoy immunity under international law if they exercise proper state functions: for this is the very *raison d'être* of that immunity. Rules on immunity have been devised to safeguard the undisturbed exercise of such official functions. If a state engages in trading and uses one of its public ships to this end, there is no reason under international law why such a ship should be exempt from the jurisdiction of the states it purports to visit. Not only would such extended immunity lead to discrimination between state-trading and private-trading nations; it would also mean that immunity is granted although the very reason for such immunity—to let a foreign state exercise its official functions without interference—is absent.

On the other hand, nothing in international law prevents a state from granting immunity to state trading vessels. But it is then a matter of generosity, of international courtesy, and not a question of a binding rule under international law. The United Kingdom has, as with diplomatic immunity (see p. 117), been more generous in granting immunity than other states. Immunity has been extended to all foreign public ships, whether or not they have been trading vessels.[27]

A state enjoys full jurisdiction over ordinary merchant vessels, in port or in passage. However, most states prefer not to exercise criminal jurisdiction unless effects of a crime extend to the coastal state.[28] States do not normally claim civil jurisdiction unless specifically requested to do so.[29]

7:3 JURISDICTION OVER VISITING FORCES AND FOREIGN MILITARY BASES

No foreign military forces may pass through a state's water, land or air without *special* authorization (see pp. 40, 43, 45, 47, 74 and 86). A state may impose any conditions or restrictions in connection with such authorization and any lengthy stay is invariably regulated by *treaty* (see pp. 195-219 on military bases). But what immunity do foreign forces enjoy in the absence of treaties? In other words, what immunity is *implicitly* granted by an authorization of a visit by foreign forces? It has been claimed that *The Schooner Exchange* case indicates that warships have extensive immunity.[30] But, as has been shown above (p. 103), this is certainly not so in the majority of states. Furthermore, the Supreme Court of the United States—the court that gave the ruling in *The Schooner Exchange* case—held, in the *Girard* case (1957),[31] that a sovereign nation has exclusive jurisdiction to punish offenses against its laws committed within its borders unless it expressly or impliedly consents to surrender its jurisdiction.

Far from enjoying any 'automatic' immunity, it is up to foreign forces to show that the territorial state has given its consent. There is a presumption in favour of jurisdictional competence of the territorial state until evidence of consent is produced. The consent to a surrender of jurisdiction implied by an authorization for a visit by foreign troops may be assumed to cover: (*a*) acts committed on board a warship or aircraft or in barracks, provided their is no effect on the receiving state (the local and interest criteria); (*b*) acts relating to discipline and internal administration (the functional criterion); acts against the interest of the sending state alone (the interest criterion). It does not seem to be relevant to assess whether or not an act was committed 'on duty' as only the sending state can ascertain this and any exception from jurisdiction may lead to abuse.[32] However, problems of concurrent jurisdiction have rarely occurred when questions of competence have been covered by treaty. Such treaties may *extend jurisdiction of the receiving state*.[33] This is a natural development as the stationing of armed forces in foreign territories has become a regular measure of foreign policy. Powers of jurisdiction have usually been reserved for the territorial state by bilateral and multilateral agreement. The Brussels defence treaty and the Western European Union, for example, provided that members of foreign forces who commit offences in a receiving state can be prosecuted in the courts of that state. Some agreements, such as the NATO and Warsaw Pact agreements,[34] give predominance to the 'interest criterion'. The NATO agreement provides that the sending as well as the receiving states exercise complementary jurisdiction. The agreement provides, in article 7, that

> (*a*) the military authorities of the sending state shall have the right to exercise exclusive jurisdiction over persons subject to the military law of that state with respect to offences, including offences relating to its security, punishable by the law of the sending state, but not by the law of the receiving state.
> (*b*) The authorities of the receiving state shall have the right to exercise exclusive jurisdiction over members of a force or

civilian component and their dependants with respect to offences, including offences relating to the security of that state, punishable by its laws but not by the law of the sending state.

To avoid conflict another article provides that, if both states are competent, the sending state shall exercise jurisdiction for offences against its property or against its security; it is equally a matter for the sending state to exercise jurisdiction for offences arising out of any act of omission done in the performance of official duty. But in the case of any other offence the receiving state shall have the 'primary right' to exercise jurisdiction.

Other agreements may *extend jurisdiction of the sending state*. For example, the United States has concluded numerous agreements supplementing the NATO agreement to ensure immunity for all acts.[36]

Thus, it is necessary to distinguish between, on the one hand, *criminal jurisdiction,* which is normally retained by the territorial state unless otherwise regulated by treaty, and, on the other hand, *disciplinary jurisdiction* which, by implication, must be granted to the visiting forces when they obtain permission to be stationed in a state. *Civil jurisdiction* is also retained by the territorial state, but such a state may bind itself not to exercise this jurisdiction by concluding a treaty to this effect.[37]

7:4 IMMUNITY OF FOREIGN STATE PROPERTY?

In spite of the abovementioned trends of state practice some writers still claim that it is a 'well established rule of international customary law' that the property of sovereign states situated abroad is 'immune' from the jurisdiction of the territorial sovereign.[38]

However, this is only true in so far as the United Kingdom, by tradition, refuses to deal with claims relating to foreign state property. Indeed, as soon as a dispute in any way concerns foreign state property English courts declare they are not competent.

Immunity has thus been extended in Britain in cases merely bearing on foreign state-owned property: the very fact that a foreign sovereign has ownership, or even factual possession of property involved in a dispute, has precluded courts from dealing with a claim.[39] Still, the Privy Council held in *Juan Ysmael & Co. Incorporated v Government of the Republic of Indonesia* that the foreign sovereign may have to produce evidence to satisfy the court that its claim is not merely illusory but well substantiated.[40]

Practice in the majority of other states is far more restrictive. Foreign states must naturally not be disturbed in the exercise of sovereign functions; therefore, property intimately linked with such activity is immune from jurisdiction. On the other hand, most states distinguish between such property (for example, warships, aircraft and weapons) and property connected with commercial activity. In the latter case, numerous states even allow attachment and seizure in execution. This is the position in Italy,[41] France,[42] Switzerland,[43] Belgium,[44] and Greece.[45]

All these cases have, however, one thing in common: they all concerned the much refuted distinction between acts *de jure imperii* and acts *de jure gestionis* (see p. 102). But whatever troubles the distinction has caused scholars, courts have not hesitated to draw a line between acts of a commercial nature which do not differ from those carried out in ordinary international trade and acts performed by a foreign state in its capacity of a sovereign. Naturally, there are bound to be many borderline cases, like that before the Egyptian Mixed Court,[46] in which the Spanish state argued that it was immune as it had bought as a 'sovereign' to alleviate a famine in Spain. The Court held that the Spanish state had acted in no way different from an ordinary businessman; the motives for its action could not alter the commercial character of the transaction. Nor have courts hesitated to distinguish between property connected with commercial activity and property connected with sovereign functions: if government bonds are deposited as security for the purchase of army boots it does not appear unreasonable to refuse immunity if there is default in payment.[47]

It must be recognized that, in the absence of special treaties, the practice of most states is not, in commercial disputes, to allow for any immunity of foreign state property. If Britain and, perhaps, the United States allow for more extensive immunity against jurisdiction and other measures they do so by international courtesy and generosity. When identifying what is a general rule of international customary law it is necessary to accept only the lowest common denominator of immunity cases: and it is then clear that a state loses its immunity for state property in a foreign state if that property is connected with commercial activities.

Ironically, it is precisely in the countries which pay tribute to the extensive line of immunity that foreign state property, in the form of liquid assets, has been withheld pending rectification of international claims. Britain refused, for example, to release Egyptian assets in the United Kingdom before the settlement of compensation for nationalization of the Suez Canal Company.[48] Similarly, the United States withheld Indonesian gold reserves after nationalization of American property in Indonesia.[49]

This is interesting in so far as this is not a question of a dispute before judicial organs of a state; here, it is a matter of measures imposed by the executive itself. Although these measures are taken as 'reprisals' they are still, from a point of law, surprisingly similar to the kind of sequestration applied by many civil law countries as a measure independent of a pending suit.

These acts of interference with foreign state property are not caused by acts *de jure gestionis*, but are retaliation for acts *de jure imperii*. For what can be more *de jure imperii* than the exercise of the eminent domain of a state for the purpose of nationalization?

NOTES

1 *Krajina v Tass Agency* [1949] 2 All E.R. 274. Cf *Dexter & Carpenter v Kungl. Järnvägsstyrelsen*, 1930 43 F 2d 705 on Swedish Railways which enjoyed immunity from seizure or attachment although not organically tied to the government. But Swedish railways had waived its immunity in the suit by appearing, initially, as plaintiffs. Cf. Swedish Supreme Court, NJA 1934 206 and NJA 1949 C 398. On the question of degree of incorporation as an organ of a state, see also *Baccus S. R. L. v Servicio Nacional del Trigo*, [1957] 1 Q. B. 438, [1956] 3 All E. R. 715.

2 [1949] 2 All E. R. 274. On the relevance of recognition, see *Carl Zeiss Stiftung v Rayner & Keeler Ltd (No. 2)*, [1967] 1 A. C. 853, [1966] 2 All E. R. 536: acts of 'governing bodies' in East Germany would be recognized not as those of a sovereign

East German state but as 'acts done by a subordinate body which the USSR set up to act on its behalf'.
3. *USSR Trade Del. v Borga*, (1952), Foro Padano 1952, I, 696.
4. *Tani v USSR Trade Del.*, c cass, Foro it, 48 I 855.
5. For a critical discussion, see I. Brownlie, *Principles of Public International Law*, second edition (Oxford: Clarendon Press, 1973), pp. 323 et seq.
6. See, *Compania Naviera Vascongado v SS Cristina*, [1938] A.C. 485; cf. *The Arantzazu Mendi*, [1939] A.C. 256.
7. Cass. Naples (when independent) 1886 I 1 288; Rome Giur. it. 1893 I 1 1213; *Rumania v Trutta*, Riv. 18 1926 252.
8. *SA des chemins de fer liègeois-luxembourgeois v Netherlands*, PB 1903 I 294, cass.
9. BGE 44 I 49; BGE 56 I 237.
10. *Soc. Le Gostrog et l'URSS v Ass. France-Export*, C 54 1927 406.
11. *Dralle v Czechoslovakia*, GRUR 52 1950 531.
12. Svea Ct of Appeal, SvJt 1939 1; but cf. NJA 1942 65, NJA 1946 719 and SvJt 1950 202.
13. For example, *Pan American Tankers Corporation v Republic of Viet-Nam* (1969) 296 F. Supp. 561; *Amkor Corporation v Bank of Korea* (1969) 298 F. Supp. 143. Cf. *U.S. v Deutsches Kalisyndikat Gesellschaft* (1929) 31 F (2d) 199.
14. *Duke of Brunswick v King of Hanover* (1848), 2 H.L. Cas. 1.
15. *Prince Danilo of Montenegro*, Milan, Monitore dei Tribunali 46 (1905) 776.
16. Trib. civ. Seine C1 44 (1917) 146.
17. 1957 C 716.
18. C. app. Paris (1872) S 1871-5 II 95.
19. *Queen Mary of Rumania*, G. H. Hackworth, *Digest of International Law* (Washington: Government Printing Office, 1940-4), vol. 2, p. 404.
20. *Prince of Monaco in the United States*, Hackworth, *Digest of International Law*, vol. 2, p. 404.
21. *The Schooner Exchange v M'Faddon*, 1 Cranch 116.
22. See article 23 of the Geneva Convention on the Territorial Sea. Cf. supra, pp. 39-40, 47.
23. *Chung Chi Cheung v The King* [1939] A.C. 160.
24. The Machel case C. cass. (Crim) S 1868 1 351 (France); ILR 1952 C 47 (Japan); cf. C. cass. (Egypt), A.D. 1919-42, Supp.

C. 86, 87, 1943-5, C. 33, 34, 38. Cf. article 20, Stockholm rules 1928 of the Institute of International Law. Gidel claims this is 'une régle sur laquelle tout le monde est d'accord', see *Le Droit international public de la mer,* vol. 2 (Paris, 1932), p. 295.

25   (1880), 5 P.D. 197.
26   (1926), 271 US 562.
27   *The Porto Alexandre,* [1920] P. 30. See, S. Sucharitkul, *State Immunities and Trading Activities in International Law* (London: Stevens, 1959); T. K. Thommen, *The Legal Status of Government Merchant Ships in International Law* (The Hague: Nijhoff, 1962). See, also, Baldoni, *RCADI* (1938) iii p. 185; Böger, Die Immunität der Staatsschiffe, 1921; McNair, BYIL, 1921-1922; Quadri, Le navi private del diritto internazionale, 1939; Maiwald, Die Entwicklung zur staatlichen Handelsschiffahrt im Spiegel des internationalen Rechts, 1946.
28   Under article 19 of the Convention on the Territorial Sea, jurisdiction may be exercised: (*a*) if the consequences of a crime extend beyond the vessel, (*b*) if the peace of the country or the good order of the territorial sea is disturbed, (*c*) if assistance is requested by the ship's captain or the flag state's consul, (*d*) if necessary to suppress illicit traffic in drugs. Cf. the classic cases on access to ports, *The Sally* and *The Newton, Bulletin des lois,* 1806, no. 126 p. 602 discussed supra, p. 47. See also notes 81 and 82 to Chapter 3 and pp. 40-1.
29   Cf. article 20 of the Convention on the Territorial Sea. There must be no executory measures except for obligations assumed for navigation through territorial waters. Innocent passage must also not be disturbed. See supra, pp. 39-40. Civil jurisdiction may be exercised if the peace of the littoral state is disturbed, cf. C. J. Colombos, *The International Law of the Sea,* sixth edition (London: Longmans, 1967), pp. 318, 320.
30   For example, J. L. Brierly, *The Law of Nations,* 6th edition, edited by Sir Humphrey Waldock (Oxford: Clarendon Press, 1963), p. 267; L. Oppenheim, *International Law,* vol. 1, 8th edition, edited by H. Lauterpacht (London: Longmans Green, 1953), p. 846. Cf. Bathurst, 'Jurisdiction over friendly foreign armed forces: the American law', in *The British Year Book of International Law 1946* (London: Oxford University Press), p. 338; King, 'Jurisdiction over friendly armed forces', *Ameri-*

can *Journal of International Law* (1942), p. 529; Flory, 'Les bases militaires à l'étranger', *Annuaire français de droit international* (1955), p. 5.

31 Girard case, 354 U.S. 524 (1957); *Schooner Exchange v M'Faddon*, 1 Cranch 116. Supra, pp. 47 and 105.

32 *Japan v Smith* and *Stinner* ILR 1952, No. 47. For the need of an 'interest' criterion, see the *Gilbert* case *AD* 1946 No. 37. Cf. Barton, 'Foreign armed forces: immunity from supervisory jurisdiction', in *The British Year Book of International Law 1949* (London: Oxford University Press, 1950), p. 412; cf. Barton, 'Foreign armed forces: immunity from criminal jurisdiction,' in *The British Year Book of International Law 1950* (London: Oxford University Press, 1951), p. 186; cf. Barton, 'Foreign armed forces: qualified jurisdictional immunity', in *The British Year Book of International Law 1954* (London: Oxford University Press, 1954), p. 341.

33 Agreements concluded under the Visiting Forces Commonwealth Act 1933; Allied Forces Act 1940; Maritime Forces Act 1941.

34 For example, agreements between USSR and Poland, 1957, *UNTS*, vol. 155; between USSR and Czechoslovakia, 1968, *International Legal Materials*, vol. 7, p. 1331.

35 Agreements concluded under Visiting Forces Act 1952 and Anglo-American Agreement of 27 July 1942.

36 For example, agreement between the United States and the Netherlands, 1954, *TIAS*, no. 3174.

37 For example, the Anglo-Egyptian treaty of 1936, *LNTS*, vol. 173, p. 433.

38 G. Schwarzenberger, *Foreign Investments and International Law* (London: Stevens, 1969), p. 3.

39 *The Porto Alexandre*, [1920] P. 30. Cf. case law in the USA, M. M. Whiteman, *Digest of International Law* (Washington: Government Printing Office, 1963-5), vol. 6, pp. 709-26.

40 [1955] A.C. 72. *Compania Naviera Vascongado v SS Cristina*, [1938] A.C. 485; *The Arantzazu Mendi*, [1939] A.C. 256; see, for a discussion, Brierly, *The Law of Nations*, p. 253.

41 *Hamspon v Bey of Tunis*, Foro it. 1887 I 474; *Rumania v Trutta*, Riv. 18 1926 252. Cf. law of 18 August 1925.

42 (Paris) Cl. 54 (1927) 406 and (Paris) C.cass 56 (1929) 1042. S

1947 I 137. See note by Niboyet in *Revue générale de droit international public* (1936), p. 541.
43 BGE 44 I 49, 56 I 237. Cf. *AD* 1941-1942, No. 60.
44 *Socobelge v Greece*, Cl. 79 (1952) 244.
45 *AD* 1927-1928, No. 109.
46 *AD* 1943-1945. No. 27, *Egyptian Delta Rice Mills Co. v Comisari General de Madrid*. Cf. comments by Hjerner on the Swedish Case NJA 1965 145 in 'Nytt Misstänkt fall av immunitet' in *Festskrift till Nial* (Stockholm, 1966), pp. 296 et seq.
47 *Rumania v Trutta*, Riv. 18 1926 252.
48 I. Delupis, *Finance and Protection of Investments in Developing Countries* (Gower Press, 1973) pp. 103 et seq.
49 Delupis, *Finance and Protection of Investments in Developing Countries,* pp. 73 et seq.

Chapter 8

Immunity of Diplomats and Consuls

8:1 IMMUNITY OF DIPLOMATS

8:1:1 Historical Background

The sovereignty of a state is restricted with regard to diplomats accredited to its government; such diplomats are immune from civil and penal jurisdiction, at least for most acts. Furthermore, they are exempt from other authoritative measures of the territorial state.

The law of diplomats is the oldest part of international law. As soon as there were any states a need appeared to send messengers to another sovereign; on the basis of reciprocity the immunity of such emissaries soon developed. From the thirteenth century onwards several permanent missions were established—the Duke Sforza of Milan was for example accredited to the Medicis in Florence.[1] When nation-states emerged during the sixteenth and seventeenth centuries such permanent missions became the rule. Then the immunity previously only enjoyed by the envoy, the 'ambassador', soon extended to his suite, his household and to the very building where he resided. The rule of 'extraterritoriality' developed: the diplomat, and the embassy itself, were considered to form part of his own country 'for all purposes'.

The personal immunity of a diplomat may not originally have consisted in more than a guarantee that he should be able to travel home freely to his own sovereign. It was considered to be quite in order, for example, to shake his clothes to make sure he did not abuse his privileges by being armed.[2] However, the rules of immunity soon became far more comprehensive and it became an offence to lay hands on a diplomat. A violation of the rights of a diplomat was a 'violation of the law of nations', yes, a crime 'against the whole world'.[3]

The privileges of diplomats appear to have been at their height when the functions of diplomats were indispensable for the communications between nations. It was diplomats who negotiated treaties, who even concluded them, who declared war and negotiated for peace. Nowadays the importance of diplomatic functions has been reduced in so far as a number of matters are taken care of by direct negotiations between foreign secretaries, between prime ministers and even between heads of state or are considered within international organizations. At the same time the privileges of diplomats have diminished correspondingly and it is no longer implied that diplomats are 'extraterritorial'. On the other hand, immunities are nowadays enjoyed not only by ordinary diplomats sent by states to other states, but also by some international civil servants employed by international organizations and by diplomats accredited to such organizations.[4]

The immunity now enjoyed by state diplomats is largely codified by the Vienna convention of 1961. This convention is perhaps exceptionally important since it entails not only contractual obligations for those who sign it but also appears to lay down authoritatively what is actually *lex lata* for states who do not adhere to it.[5]

8:1:2 Specific Rights and Privileges

A diplomat has a right to work undisturbed. He has a right to respectful treatment as the representative of his state. His embassy archives and official correspondence are 'inviolable'. He cannot be subjected to the judicial courts and other authorities of the host state in connection with *official* or *private* acts, unless immunity is expressly waived.[6] He and members of his immediate family[7] are immune from arrest, criminal proceedings and execution, and exempt from taxes, dues and public service. He is also immune from civil proceedings unless they are of the type specified in article 31 of the Vienna Convention on Diplomatic Relations 1961 which embodies rules of general international law and specifies that immunity is not given for (1) a real action relating to private immovable property unless the diplomat holds it on behalf of his sending state for the purposes of the mission or (2) an action relating to succession to real property provided it concerns the diplomat as a private person or (3) an action related to professional and commercial activities of the diplomat outside his official functions as a diplomat.

Some states had, even before signing the Vienna convention, restricted diplomatic immunity so that certain private activities were not covered. In Italy, for example, the *Rinaldi* case[8] shows that a court could go as far as ordering the sequestration for private debts of a car belonging to a diplomat. In another Italian case damages were awarded against a first secretary who had injured a person when driving a car,[9] as a diplomat could not avoid such consequences if he was a danger to public order and life. In some cases Italian courts went perhaps further in restricting diplomatic immunity than international law allowed: for example, in *Perruchetti v Puig y Casauranc*[10] a court refused immunity for a dispute concerning the purchase of an embassy building.

Other states, above all Great Britain, have been far more generous in granting diplomatic immunity. However, the statement by Lord Campbell in the *Magdalena Steam Navigation Company v Martin*[11] that a diplomat is considered 'for all judicial purposes still to be in his own country', is no longer valid. In *R. v Kent*[12] in 1941 it was made clear that extraterritoriality is no more than a fiction and any crime committed in a foreign embassy in Great Britain is, unless protected by diplomatic immunity, to be prosecuted under English law in English courts. Furthermore, under the Diplomatic Immunities Restriction Act of 1955 immunity for private acts of diplomats may be 'withdrawn' if the sending state does not grant such immunity to British envoys.

France adhered previously to the ideas of absolute immunity for diplomats and fairly late cases went on this line.[13] Later, however, immunity for diplomats was much reduced and was held not to cover, for example, debts entered into by a wife of a diplomat before her marriage.[14] A disputed lease of a flat which was neither connected with the official function of a diplomat nor used as his private dwelling was also brought before a French court and immunity was refused.[15]

The three important exceptions laid down by the Vienna convention will affect jurisdiction in, for example, England in so far as it will restrict immunity previously granted by courts. In other countries, like France and Italy, the Vienna convention will probably extend immunity in cases where such privileges have previously been denied, such as the aforementioned contractual disputes.

The conclusion that may be drawn is that diplomatic immunity is neither absolute nor must it be so relaxed and watered down that a diplomat, and his household, cannot be left undisturbed so that he can discharge his official functions. It is suggested that the Vienna convention carries considerable weight as a codification of general international law and that it has decided on certain previously uncertain nuances. It is therefore of the greatest relevance to a state which has not adhered to it as it appears to lay down rules which are binding as universal customary rules of international law.

Diplomats represent their governments and this has sometimes been taken to mean that they could also be held responsible for the actions of their state. But, of course, no litigation can be instigated for such purposes. Thus, when an Australian businessman, Mr Ross Milner Cameron, took out a private summons in June 1973 alleging 'assault by nuclear fallout' due to French nuclear tests in the South Pacific in 1972 the French Ambassador to Australia, M. Gabriel van Laetham, did not answer the summons and claimed diplomatic immunity (cf. supra pp. 93-4).

There is a growing tendency to dispense with the provisions on immunity as laid down by customary law or by the convention in cases where there is reason to believe that a diplomat has abused his privileges, or when there is danger to the general public. For example, when an Algerian diplomat arrived at Schiphol Airport in Amsterdam with two suitcases containing unaddressed letter bombs, explosives, handgrenades, arms and ammunition, the Dutch authorities did not hesitate to arrest him. When he was subsequently released, the Dutch police declared that this was not because he enjoyed diplomatic immunity but because they 'could not prove that he knew what was in the suitcase'.[16]

In another case, suspected criminals were arrested in the home of an Israeli diplomat in Norway; the diplomat was subsequently declared *persona non grata*. Here the Norwegian Supreme Court directed a lower court to consider whether the arrests had 'violated' the Geneva convention or whether the diplomat had 'abused his rights'.[17]

However, if on the one hand states tend to dispense privileged treatment if a diplomat abuses his position, on the other hand, diplomats have themselves recently been the target for numerous acts of terrorism and to afford greater protection to envoys and other internationally protected persons a number of supplementary conventions have recently been concluded. Within the framework of the Pan American Union one convention was, for example, concluded during 1971 'to prevent and punish the acts of terrorism taking the form of crimes against persons and related extortion that are of international significance'. The Convention for the Suppression of Unlawful Acts against the Safety of Civil Aviation of 1971 may also be relevant in this context as well as the Convention for the Suppression of Unlawful Seizure of Aircraft of 1970. A Convention on Special Missions, and an optional protocol concerning the compulsory settlement of disputes relating thereto, was concluded in 1969. This convention was designed to afford protection to *ad hoc* diplomats—such as itinerant envoys (see p. 73), diplomatic conferences and special missions sent to a state for a limited purpose— to supplement the Vienna convention which only covers permanent diplomatic missions. Finally, an important convention is currently being drafted by the International Law Commission on the 'prevention and punishment of crimes against diplomats and other internationally protected persons'. Under this draft convention, states would pledge themselves to introduce criminal legislation to punish crimes against diplomats and to cooperate with other contracting parties for the purpose of extraditing persons guilty of such crimes. Not only diplomats are covered by the convention but also consuls (see pp. 119-21), heads of state, heads of government, *ad hoc* envoys and certain officials of international organizations (see pp. 121-2).

8:2 IMMUNITY OF CONSULS

The position under the Convention on Consuls signed in Vienna in 1963 is different from that under the Vienna Convention on Diplomatic Relations. If the latter one was said to codify existing international law with respect to diplomats this cannot be said of the

Convention on Consuls. The Convention on Consuls is far more progressive than at least present customary international law demands and, therefore, a number of governments have not yet been able to accept it. The convention assimilates a consul to a diplomat and grants almost as far-reaching immunity to consuls, contrary to the previous practice of states. Therefore, if a new nation has not adhered to this particular convention old customary legal rules will still apply.

The origin of consuls is different from that of diplomats: in the early Middle Ages consuls were appointed, by election, among merchants abroad in the first instance to solve disputes among the merchants. This was their primary function in the days of personal laws—that is, when each person who travelled abroad was still subject to his national law or his religious law and therefore could only be tried by his compatriots or his coreligionists.[18] When the new ideas of territorial laws developed at the time of the creation of nation-states, above all in Europe, the functions of consuls changed. For a while territorial sovereigns refused to restrict their jurisdiction by allowing consuls to adjudicate among their compatriots. But towards the end of the eighteenth century the importance of consuls in international relations had a revival: they were no longer exercising jurisdiction but instead were in charge of the naval and commercial interests of their home state in other countries. A consul thus has technical, not political functions. He is not 'accredited' to the government as a diplomat. Unless he is a consul-general, in which case he is formally accepted by an exequatur, he is not even accepted—merely tolerated. He does not 'transact business between two crowns' but merely safeguards commercial interests.[19]

In some cases a consul may enjoy the immunity of a diplomat if he appears on the list of diplomats which an ambassador hands to his host country.[20] But otherwise a consul enjoys only three privileges under general international law: he is immune from penal and civil jurisdiction for official acts; he has the right to make direct contact with local authorities in his area; his consular archives and correspondence must not be violated.

It may not always be easy to distinguish between official and private acts of a consul; such acts may be interconnected, as shown in *Bigelow v Princess Zizianoff*.[21] In this case an American consul in Paris refused to issue a passport to a former citizen of Russia. He then telephoned the French newspapers in Paris to inform them that she was a spy employed by a foreign power. The French court held that it had jurisdiction for the second act but not for the first; the issuing of passports was part of the official duties of a consul for which he could not be tried.

Numerous treaties have been concluded to increase the immunities of consuls, such as the aforementioned Vienna convention of 1963, the Havana treaty of 1928 and the European Convention on Consular Functions of 1967.[22] However, unless a state has agreed to such extension of immunity of consuls they enjoy only some minimum privileges under general international law.

8:3 IMMUNITY OF STATE DELEGATES AND INTERNATIONAL CIVIL SERVANTS

Diplomats enjoy immunity under general international law not only when they are accredited to another state but also, it is submitted, when they are representing their country in an international organization. Such organizations have recently been considered to possess the right of legation—that is, the right to send and to accept envoys, although only the passive right to receive envoys is usually exercised.[23] Privileges of state representatives are sometimes specified by conventions on privileges of organizations or by special headquarters agreements.[24] But the International Law Commission found it important to codify immunities and privileges of state representatives separately in a general convention. A draft convention was drawn up in 1971 on the 'representation of states in their relations with international organizations'. This convention covers, *inter alia*, facilities, privileges and immunities of permanent missions, and an annex deals with permanent observer missions and delegations to organs or to conferences.

Another group of persons enjoy far-reaching important immunity under treaty law: they are the international civil servants employed by the organizations themselves and who are ensured, by special conventions, that their work will be undisturbed by interference from the territorial state in which the organization has its offices. However, such immunity, derived from the immunity of the organization itself, covers only official acts and is thus less extensive than the immunity of diplomats. Most international organizations have entered into conventions on privileges and immunities and there are usually a number of headquarters agreements by which the immunity of the organization and its employees is guaranteed.[25]

It may be important to emphasize that immunity of civil servants of organizations is based on treaty law and that international law does not, in the absence of treaty provisions, grant such employees any special protection. Certain recent general conventions have increased privileges and protection granted under specific treaties. There is, for example, the Draft Convention on Prevention and Punishment of Crimes against Diplomats and Other Internationally Protected Persons of 1971, which in parts also covers officials of international organizations (see p. 119).

NOTES

1 See, Hill, *A History of Diplomacy in the International Development of Europe* (New York, 1905), vol. 2, p. 154.
2 Krauske, *Die Entwicklung der ständige Diplomatie* (Leipzig, 1885), pp. 12 et seq.
3 *Respublica v De Longchamps,* 1 Dall. 111.
4 See, I. Detter, *Law Making by International Organizations* (Stockholm: Norstedts, 1965), pp. 90 et seq. and pp. 123 et seq. and infra, pp. 121-2.
5 On treaties binding third parties, see, I. Detter, *Essays on the Law of Treaties* (London: Sweet & Maxwell, 1967), pp. 117 et seq.
6 Cf. article 32 of the Vienna convention. Waiver of immunity for all acts must be express and must be made by the sending state's government, *Balmaceda* case, Cl. 33 (1906) 751; *Re Republic of Bolivia Exploration Syndicate Ltd,* [1914] 1 Ch. 139. But cf. *Dickinson v Del Solar,* [1930] 1 K.B. 376. Immunity for official acts is 'permanent' whereas immunity for private acts ceases with employment. Cf. article 39 of the convention and supra, p. 103 on heads of state.
7 Members of technical and administrative staff, if not nationals of the host state, enjoy immunity only for official acts. Staff in the domestic service of a diplomatic mission presumably have no

immunity as in their case there is no *raison d'être* for such privileges. However, the Vienna convention goes further in this respect than general international law and accords immunity from criminal jurisdiction even for private acts to technical and administrative staff, and immunity for 'acts performed in the course of their duties' to service staff—see article 37. This is not consistent with the trend of state practice, see pp. 101-9.

8 Riv. 9 1915 215, c.cass. Rome; cf. *Comina v Kite*, Riv. 16 1924 174, c.cass. Rome.
9 *Balloni v Chilean Ambassador*, Riv. 27 1935 375.
10 Riv. 20 1928 521.
11 (1859), 2 E. & E. 94.
12 *R. v A.B.* (*R. v Kent*), [1941] 1 K.B. 454. Cf. promissory notes and insurance policies which are governed by the laws of the host state, *Dickinson v Del Solar*, [1930] 1 K.B. 376, and *General Accident Fire & Life Ass. Comp.*, A.D. *1938-40*, case 163, before High Court of Eire.
13 *De Fallois*, S 1938 I 117.
14 C. app. Paris, C 82 1955 390.
15 *Freeborn v Fou Pei Kouo*, S 1949 II 153.
16 *The Times*, 26 October 1972.
17 Decision of the Supreme Court of Norway, 23 August 1973. For earlier cases see *Revue générale de droit international public* (1928), p. 184. Cf. *Rose v R. AD 1946*, case 76; *R. v Lunan, AD 1947*, case 72; *The Queen v Turnbull* (1971), 17 FLR 438.
18 Cf. Detter, 'The problem of unequal treaties', *International and Comparative Law Quarterly* (1966), pp. 1077 et seq.
19 *Barbuit's* case (1737), Ca. *t.* Talb. 281.
20 *Engelke v Musmann*, [1928] A. C. 433 (House of Lords); *Parkinson v Potter* (1885), 16 Q. B. D. 152.
21 *Revue générale de droit international public* (1929), p. 77.
22 Cf. the draft convention on prevention and protection of diplomats and other internationally protected persons of 1971; see supra p. 119. See also a number of bilateral agreements—for example, between the USA and the USSR, *TIAS* 6570 (1964), between the USA and Japan, *TIAS* 5602 (1963) and between the USA and South Korea, *TIAS* 5469 (1963).
23 Detter, *Law Making by International Organizations*, pp. 118 et seq.

24 See Detter, *Law Making by International Organizations*, pp. 123 et seq.
25 Detter, *Law Making by International Organizations*, pp. 123 et seq. The classic work on the legal position of international civil servants remains S. Basdevant, *Les Fonctionnaires internationaux* (Paris: Sirey, 1931).

Chapter 9

Treatment of Individuals

9:1 TREATMENT OF ALIENS

9:1:1 Aliens and Human Rights

The traditional view of international law has been that the sovereignty of states over aliens—other than state agents, diplomats and consuls—in its territory is limited in so far as aliens are entitled to 'decent treatment' or a 'minimum standard'.[1] Before a state violates such rights there must, it is claimed, be an obvious 'outrage'.[2] Another, equally traditional approach, which perhaps has not received as much support in case law as the former line, is that aliens should be entitled to the same treatment as nationals as far as civil rights are concerned: but it has not been claimed that they should enjoy political rights such as the right to vote.[3]

It is submitted that neither of these lines is suitable for identification of an alien's rights under international law. A 'minimum standard' for aliens only is too vague to furnish any useful guidance. And the rules on national treatment would not offer sufficient guarantees under international law if, for example, a state enacted legislation, for own nationals and aliens alike, on compulsory sterilization.[4] It has also been noted that international law does not prohibit discrimination between nationals and aliens with respect to exchange control.[5]

Therefore, rather than adopting a 'minimum standard for aliens' or advocating national treatment, it appears more realistic to apply the safeguards of human rights to protect aliens and nationals alike in a state's territory. International law affords protection, even in the absence of treaties, of the most *fundamental* human rights (see p. 129). The fear that such *fundamental* human rights would differ according to the particular socioeconomic system of a country[6] does not seem warranted provided the term 'fundamental' is interpreted strictly. For example, one can hardly count the right to acquire real property or the right to transfer currency as fundamental. A state which imposes exchange restrictions or which prohibits aliens from buying real estate can hardly be said to violate the fundamental human rights protected by international law; nor would it violate such rights by nationalizing property of aliens.[7]

Of the human rights enumerated in the Universal Declaration of Human Rights and in the European Convention on Human Rights none appear to be tied to any particular form of economic system apart from provisions in the European Convention whereby nationals and aliens alike are granted the right of compensation in the case of nationalization, a right to which only aliens are commonly entitled under international law.[8]

By relating treatment of aliens to the rules on human rights it is submitted that the position of aliens is not, in fact, different from that of nationals. With regard to both aliens and nationals there are binding rules of international law which restrict the exercise of sovereignty of the territorial state.

Only in two respects may aliens be entitled to better remedies in cases of violation of these rights. The first is that an alien's home state may intervene diplomatically on his behalf and may also take an offending state to court in some instances to obtain redress.[9] Traditionally such intervention is permissible provided that all local remedies have been exhausted and the alien has attempted to have justice done in the local courts.[10] But the obligation to seek justice in the courts in a state only exists if there are any 'effective' local remedies to exhaust.[11]

The second way in which an alien has better remedies is that if a state should proceed to nationalization then an alien may be entitled to better treatment under international law. An alien has, under general international law, a right to be compensated,[12] whereas a national does not have such a right. In many countries nationals may enjoy this right of compensation, perhaps even guaranteed under their constitution,[13] but it is not, in the case of nationals, a right guaranteed by international law. For if it were, international law would virtually prohibit a state from introducing a new economic system for redistribution of wealth.[14]

9:1:2 The Calvo Clause

It is questionable whether an alien may deprive himself of the right of diplomatic intervention by including a so-called 'Calvo clause' in a contract with a foreign government.

The doctrine of the Calvo clause originated last century in Argentina where the international lawyer Carlos Calvo suggested that a sovereign state has the right to be free from interference of any sort and that therefore an alien cannot have a better right to redress than the state's own nationals.[15] Some states have included a clause to this effect in treaties, particularly those concluded between Latin American countries. In accordance with such treaties, an alien is to be governed completely by the laws of the foreign state and if he suffers from denial of justice, delay of justice or other gross injustices he can take the matter no further; he has no further right of appeal than a national of that state.

There are different considerations when a Calvo clause is included in a constitution and prescribes that an alien has to waive his right of diplomatic protection if he is to enjoy a national's right to natural resources.[16] A state cannot by including provisions in its own constitution affect the rules of public international law and it is questionable whether an alien would be validly deprived of the diplomatic protection of his home state by such provisions. Constitutions that have provisions of this type often include a 'safeguard' that property acquired by an alien who subsequently invokes intervention by his home state, is *forfeited*; naturally, a clause like this is very cogent. On the other hand, it is precisely in the case of expropriation or nationalization that the alien turns to his home state for diplomatic protection and if the property has been taken from him the safeguard can no longer work as a deterrent.

If a Calvo clause is included in a contract between an alien and a government then the problem is different. It is doubtful whether an alien is validly precluded by such a clause in a contract from asking his home state for protection. It is also doubtful whether the home state is barred from intervening on its own initiative. In one case it was held that a Calvo clause of a contract entailed the incompetence of an international tribunal for all aspects of the contract.[17] But other cases have shown that a claimant would not be barred from appearing before an international commission.[18] There is a tendency to presume that redress by diplomatic intervention of the home state is left open even if a Calvo clause has been incorporated in a contract between an alien and a government.[19]

9:1:3 Nationality of Claims

It is becoming increasingly important to establish when a home state may intervene on behalf of its nationals whose business enterprises are in another state—for example, in the case of nationalization.[20] It is relatively easy, in international law, to establish the nationality of a natural person[21] but it is rather more difficult to establish the nationality of an artificial legal person or corporation. It may be held that the country under whose laws a company was incorporated is the company's home country and may intervene on the company's behalf during a dispute.[22] Another rule, influenced by French theory, is that the home state is the one in which the *siège social* is located.[23] Other theories that have been advanced suggest that the country in which the management resides or from where the actual control of a company is exercised is the true home state of the company.[24]

It appears that each of these tests has some importance but for different purposes. If one wants to establish which law shall govern a business contract under private international law or conflict of laws, one of these facts may be weighed against another to establish where the company 'belongs' and where the contract has its 'weight'. If, on the other hand, one wants to ascertain whether a company has 'enemy character' during war then special importance may be attached to the fact that it is controlled from a particular country.[25]

However, practice shows that a company which by any of the abovementioned tests is linked to a particular state is regarded as a national of that state on whose behalf the state can intervene. Furthermore, a state may sometimes intervene if its nationals are among the shareholders of a company. This is of particular importance in developing countries where foreigners often invest nowadays by forming a new company under local laws. Then, even if head office, management and full control are established in the developing state itself, a foreign state may still be entitled to intervene on the ground that it has an 'interest' in the matter because a number of shareholders of the company are its own nationals.[26] But such intervention on behalf of shareholders must, after the ruling of the International Court in the *Barcelona Traction* case,[27] be considered as exceptional. The court held that as a *general rule,* the national state of shareholders of a company cannot intervene to protect such shareholders against loss caused by an international wrong suffered by the company. The findings of the Court in this respect were based on the argument that under most municipal systems company law does not allow shareholders to claim damages from outsiders who have violated rights of the company in which they hold stock.

9:2 TREATMENT OF A STATE'S OWN NATIONALS

9:2:1 Nationals and Human Rights

In spite of abundant evidence that the treatment of a state's own nationals is no longer the concern of that state alone some international lawyers continue to emphasize that international law does not grant nationals of a state any right except by express treaties.[28] This can hardly be correct any more: the right to treat both aliens and national subjects is limited by an individual's general human rights. This does not mean that the whole set of human rights have broken through the national walls of a state. But some such rights are undoubtedly enjoyed by nationals of modern states—for example, the right not to be subjected to genocide or slavery, the right not to be tortured, the right to appear in courts and other fundamental rights. It cannot be correct as some claim that if a state has not signed conventions on these matters and provided for the conversion of such rules into internal legislation then nationals are, under international law, deprived of all such rights. Is it reasonable to presume that a state, in 1974, can validly enact legislation on slavery or genocide and claim that since it is not party to the conventions on these matters it is free to do as it pleases in its 'reserved domain'? There may be limits at present to the powers of the United Nations to intervene in these questions; and other states may also be precluded from taking action to rectify the situation. In other words, human rights are not often directly enforceable. But a state may, sooner or later, have to face international jurisdiction in one form or another for delicts it has committed. After the precedents of the Nürnberg trials no state can validly claim that acts violating human rights are not punishable under general international law and are of no concern to the world community. Human rights are at present protected under general international law which, in the absence of treaties, probably covers the fundamental rights of individuals referred to above. Other rights may be enjoyed by *groups*: for example, certain aspects of the rule of self-determination itself (see pp. 13-18); and other rights may be emerging, for example, the various nuances of the rule of nondiscrimination. The crystallization of such rights into general international law is greatly promoted by the increasing contractual network on human rights.

Some of the provisions of the Charter of the United Nations and in the constitutions of the specialized agencies concern human rights. However, these instruments merely proclaim that human rights should be 'respected' and do not define the rights; nor do these instruments ensure their enforcement. It is, perhaps, even questionable whether these instruments impose any legal obligations on the member states. On the other hand, there are some other important international agreements on human rights. The most important conventions concluded so far on human rights are the two International Covenants (1966—see pp. 11-13, 15), the Convention on the Prevention and Punishment of the Crime of Genocide (1948), the Agreements for the Suppression of the White Slave Traffic (1904 and 1910)—both amended by a protocol of 1949—the International Conventions for the Suppression of Traffic in Women and Children (1921), and for the Abolition of Slavery and the Slave Trade (1926 and 1956); the Convention Relating to the Status of Refugees (1951) with protocol of 1966; the Conventions Relating to the Status of Stateless Persons (1954), the Reduction of Statelessness (1961), and Political Rights of Women (1953) and the Conventions on the Elimination of all Forms of Religious Intolerance (1967) and all Forms of Racial Discrimination (1966).

Other instruments important to the protection of human rights have been drafted in the form of conventions by the International

Labour Organization (ILO), for example conventions concerning Forced or Compulsory Labour (1930), Abolition of Forced Labour (1957), Freedom of Association and Protection of the Right to Organize (1948), Application of the Principles of the Right to Organize and to Bargain Collectively (1949), Equal Remuneration (1951), Discrimination (Employment and Occupation) (1958), Equality of Treatment (Social Security) (1962), Social Policy (Basic Aims and Standards) (1962); and Employment Policy (1964).[29] Under the auspices of UNESCO another convention on discrimination—in education—was concluded in 1960-2.

As far as Europe is concerned there is also the important European Convention of 1950 under which individuals are granted a right of petition and the European Social Charter of 1961.[30] An 'American Convention on Human Rights' was concluded in 1969 under the auspices of the Pan American Union.

By numerous other treaties states have bound themselves to safeguard rights of minorities. The treaties of Versailles, Neuilly, Trianon, Lausanne and St Germain all contained such provisions and under these peace treaties, and by special minorities treaties of 1919 and 1924, Poland, Czechoslovakia, Yugoslavia, Romania, Greece, Austria, Bulgaria, Hungary and Turkey pledged themselves to afford equal treatment to racial, religious and linguistic minorities. Other states are bound by their unilateral undertakings to this effect proclaimed in connection with their entry into the League of Nations. Albania and Iraq, as well as the three Baltic states, Lithuania, Estonia and Latvia, all made such declarations.[31] Provisions of the Charter of the United Nations concern the interest of certain minority groups, but they merely state, as for example in article 55 (c), that the organization shall 'promote' respect for human rights without distinction as to race, sex, language or religion. Provisions on minorities also appear in the 1947 peace treaties (on the South Tirol question, cf. pp. 152-3) and in the Austrian State Treaty (1955).

Certain 'declarations', especially by the United Nations, have been of great importance for the development of human rights. For example, the Universal Declaration of Human Rights of 1948, the Declarations on the Granting of Independence to Colonial Countries and Peoples—resolution 1514(XV) of 1960—on the Elimination of Discrimination against Women of 1967, and on the Rights of the Child of 1959. Other UN declarations of principles are also of importance such as the principles of international law recognized by the charter and judgment of the Nürnberg Tribunal of 1946 covering human rights in war; the draft declaration on rights and duties of states of 1949 and the draft code of offences against the peace and security of mankind of 1951 and 1953.

Other regional declarations are also worth noticing, such as the Latin American Declaration of the Rights and Duties of Man of 1948; the Declaration of Punta del Este of 1961; the Declaration of the First and Second Conferences of Independent African States of 1958 and 1960; the Declaration of the Lagos Conference on the Rule of Law of 1961 and the Declaration of the OAU of 1964.

Among these Declarations the Universal Declaration of Human Rights of 1948 has proved to be of outstanding importance. Although it is not technically binding as a treaty, writers and commentators refer to it as an instrument of 'considerable authority'.[32] A number of regional organizations have been much influenced by the Universal Declaration, both in their own charters and in their subsequent declarations on human rights. For example, the Charter of the Organization of American States 'adheres' expressly to the Universal Declaration and the so-called Law of Lagos pledges adherence to it.[33]

The Universal Declaration has also had a great impact on the constitutions adopted by developing countries: for example, Algeria, Dahomey, Gabon, Guinea, Ivory Coast, Malagasy Republic, Mali, Mauritania, Niger, Rwanda, Senegal, Somalia, Upper Volta and Zaïre all expressly 'adhere' to the Declaration in their constitutions. Other constitutions, such as those of Ethiopia and Libya are based on the Declaration without any express adherence. And Kenya, Nigeria, Sierra Leone and Uganda have taken over even more far-reaching provisions from the more comprehensive European Convention.

The fact that such an overwhelming majority of developing nations subscribe in their constitutions to human rights as laid down in the Universal Declaration or in the European Convention shows that they, perhaps more than the older states, are aware of their importance in the modern international society. It confirms the view advanced above that there is no difference in the treatment that aliens and nationals may demand. Also nationals enjoy such human rights which were formerly the 'minimum standard' enjoyed only by aliens. Numerous cases may be quoted to support that at least two basic human rights, the right to life and the right to personal liberty, have been protected by international courts without relying on treaties or other contractual undertakings.[34] The basic human rights enjoyed by both aliens and nationals (see p. 129) in the territory of a state are not based on how nations treat foreigners, but on how they treat all within their jurisdiction.[35]

9:2:2 *Jus cogens?*

I submit that a number of rules contained in the Universal Declaration of Human Rights are peremptory norms from which derogation, either by legislation or by treaty, is not permitted.[36] Furthermore, a number of rules laid down in the conventions on genocide and slavery also have this character and bind third states by virtue of forming part of the general principles of law.[37] This conclusion is made abundantly clear as far as the genocide convention is concerned by the *Genocide* case[38] before the International Court of Justice. But the Universal Declaration, which does not itself constitute a binding document, lays down rules which, irrespective of whether they are embodied in a binding document or not, are binding as customary international law. No state can rightly believe after the Nürnberg trials that international law, in the absence of treaties, contains no rules which forbid atrocities and genocide.

The International Law Commission's draft for a convention on the law of treaties suggested that treaties violating *jus cogens* would be void, *ab initio*. A conference in Vienna adopted this part of the draft and the Convention on Treaties now provides, in article 62, that treaties in conflict with *jus cogens* are void from their inception; the convention furthermore recognizes, in article 64, the dynamic character of international law prescribes that: 'If any new peremptory norm of general international law emerges, any existing treaty which is in conflict with that norm becomes void and terminates.' This implies a recognition that international law is no static legal system but may change to satisfy new demands of a changing community. But neither the ILC nor the convention indicates what exactly is to be understood by such 'peremptory norms': how are they identified? It is questionable what norms could reasonably form part of such *jus cogens* from which derogation by treaty is not allowed;[39] but the minimum rules concerned must at least comprise fundamental human rights (see pp. 129-30). States are bound to respect these whether they have signed conventions to that effect or not; and they are obliged to respect them under general international law from which they have no right to rid themselves by signing agreements violating human rights. For such rights belong to the individuals, and not to the state itself, and the state is not entitled to waive the rights of its citizens by concluding any treaty infringing upon those rights.

9:3 DEROGATION FROM SOVEREIGNTY BY EXTRATERRITORIAL ASYLUM

Provided there is no extradition treaty or other contractual undertaking applicable to a specific case a state is always free to grant territorial asylum to aliens should it wish to do so. The power to grant territorial asylum is incidental to the sovereignty of a state. But in some exceptional cases a state's territorial sovereignty may be limited by a right of refuge granted by a foreign embassy, consulate or public ship in its territory—that is, by so-called extraterritorial asylum. Refuge may be granted to either a national or to an alien of the territorial state and such asylum is a derogation from the sovereignty of the territorial state.

It was earlier suggested in international law that the sovereignty of a state was restricted, on the basis of reciprocity, by the rights enjoyed by foreign legations in its territory to grant asylum. The right to give refuge in embassy and consulate buildings, as well as in public vessels, stemmed from the concept of extraterritoriality of the diplomatic and consular buildings as well as of the extraterritoriality of foreign public ships which were thought of as parts of their home country.[40] It has been shown (see p. 105 and p. 117) how the principle of extraterritoriality has been abandoned as a fiction both in the case of buildings of foreign missions and in the case of public ships.

It is questionable whether a right to grant extraterritorial asylum still exists in international law[41] outside the framework of specific treaties; such treaties have been concluded by a number of South American countries.

It may perhaps be suggested that there exists a right of extraterritorial asylum under general international law in certain cases—for example, when a person seeks refuge from mob violence.⁴² But this is merely a question of temporary asylum and the embassy or public ship must hand the person back once the violence has subsided. There may also be another case where more permanent asylum could validly be accorded under international law, namely where there is abundant evidence that the authorities of a state will violate fundamental human rights on genocide or torture. It may then be a matter of power politics if the person is handed back but international law cannot demand that this is done.

The case of extraterritorial asylum—whether temporary or permanent—is quite exceptional: the territorial sovereignty of a state must not be undermined by foreign missions or ships sheltering criminals who should rightly be convicted and punished by the territorial state.

NOTES

1. J. L. Brierly, *The Law of Nations*, 6th edition edited by Sir Humphrey Waldock (Oxford: Clarendon Press, 1963), p. 276.
2. *Neer's* claim (1926), Mexican Claims Commission, *Reports of International Arbitral Awards*, vol. 4, p. 73.
3. For example, *Canevaro* case (1912), Permanent Court of Arbitration, J. B. Scott (ed.), *The Hague Court Reports*, vol. 1 (New York: Oxford University Press, 1916), p. 285.
4. I. Brownlie, *Principles of Public International Law*, second edition (Oxford: Clarendon Press, 1973), p. 511.
5. Brownlie, *Principles of Public International Law*, p. 511.
6. Brownlie, *Principles of Public International Law*, p. 513.
7. Cf. I. Delupis, *Finance and Protection of Investments in Developing Countries* (Gower Press, 1973), p. 67.
8. Delupis, *Finance and Protection* . . . , p. 88.
9. *Panevezys-Saldutiskis Railway*, Judgment, *1939*, P.C.I.J., Series A/B, No. 76, p. 4.
10. *Ambatielos* claim (1956), *Reports of International Arbitral Awards*, vol. 12, p. 83.
11. *Robert E. Brown* claim (1923), *Reports of International Arbitral Awards*, vol. 6, p. 120.
12. See Delupis, *Finance and Protection* . . . , p. 88.
13. Delupis, *Finance and Protection* . . . , p. 88.

14 Delupis, *Finance and Protection* . . . , pp. 88 *and* 113.
15 Calvo, *Droit international public théorique et pratique* (Paris, 1868).
16 For example article 17 of the Mexican constitution of 1917 declared that 'Only Mexicans by birth or naturalization and Mexican Corporations have the right to acquire ownership of lands, waters and their appurtenances or to obtain concessions for exploring mines, waters or mineral fuel in the Republic of Mexico provided they agree before the Secretariat of Foreign Relations to consider themselves as nationals in such property and accordingly not invoke the protection of their government in matters relating thereto; under penalty in case of non-compliance, of forfeiture to the nation of property so acquired.'
17 *North American Dredging Co.* (1923), *Reports of International Arbitral Awards*, vol. 4, p. 26.
18 G. H. Hackworth, *Digest of International Law* (Washington: Government Printing Office, 1940-4), vol. 5, p. 639.
19 *Orinoco Steamship Co.* (1910), J. B. Scott (ed.), *The Hague Court Reports*, vol. 1, p. 230.
20 See Sinclair, 'Nationality of claims', in *The British Year Book of International Law 1950* (London: Oxford University Press, 1951); Parry, 'Some considerations upon the protection of individuals in international law', *Académie de droit international. Recueil des cours* (1956), iii; Bagge, 'Intervention on the ground of damage caused to nationals', in *The British Year Book of International Law 1958* (London: Oxford University Press, 1959).
21 But the claimant must have had 'continuous' nationality—see *Panevezys-Saldutiskis Railway, Judgment, 1939, P.C.I.J., Series A/B, No. 76*, p. 4—unless otherwise agreed between the parties to an arbitration, as held in the *Landreau* claim (1921), *Reports of International Arbitral Awards*, vol. 1, p. 347.
22 *Appeal from a Judgment of the Hungaro/Czechoslovak Mixed Arbitral Tribunal (The Peter Pázmány University), Judgment, 1933, P.C.I.J., Series A/B, No. 61*, p. 208. Cf. *Ruden's* case (1870), J. B. Moore, *A Digest of International Law*, vol. 1 (Washington: Government Printing Office, 1906), p. 1653.
23 *Canevaro* case (1912), Permanent Court of Arbitration, J. B. Scott (ed.), *The Hague Court Reports*, vol. 1, p. 285. In the

Flack claim (1929), *Reports of International Arbitral Awards*, vol. 5, p. 61, nationality was held to depend both on the country of incorporation, *siège social* and domicile.
24 *Daimler Co. Ltd v Continental Tyre & Rubber Co. (Great Britain) Ltd*, [1916] 2 A.C. 307.
25 For example the *Daimler* case quoted in the previous note.
26 *Delagoa Bay Railway Company* case (1899), *Reports of International Arbitral Awards*, vol. 2, p. 230. Cf. also *Ruden's* case (1870), Moore, *A Digest of International Law*, vol. 1, p. 1653.
27 *I.C.J. Reports 1970*, p.3. Protection could only be enjoyed if the corporation had ceased to exist in law (ibid, p.41).
28 For example, Kelsen, Principles of International Law, London, 1952, p. 143; Lauterpacht (ed. Tucker), Principles of International Law, New York, p. 236.
29 See C. W. Jenks, *Human Rights and International Labour Standards* (London: Stevens/New York: Praeger, 1960) and C. W. Jenks 'ILO standards and procedures', in *International Protection of Human Rights: Proceedings of the Seventh Nobel Symposium, Oslo, September 25-27, 1967* edited by A. Eide and A. Schou (New York/ Chichester: Interscience, 1968), pp. 230 et seq.
30 Even individuals have the right of petition before the European Commission of Human Rights. See for example, Partsch, *Die Rechte und Freiheiten der Europäischen Menschenrechtskonvention* (Berlin 1966); Ermacora, *Handbuch der Grundfreiheiten under der Menschenrechte* (Vienna, 1963); Morrison, *The Developing European Law of Human Rights* (Leyden, 1967). On the work of the European Commission, see, in particular, Monconduit, *La Commission européenne des droits de l'homme* (Leyden, 1965); Lodigiani, *La Commissione nella Convenzione europea dei diritti dell'uomo* (Milan, 1970). Cf. Pinto, 'Régionalisme et universalisme dans la protection des droits de l'homme', in *International Protection of Human Rights*, pp. 183 et seq. For a useful collection of most human rights documents, see United Nations, *A Compilation of International Instruments of the United Nations on Human Rights*, UN Doc. A/Conf.32. Cf. I. Brownlie, *Basic Documents on Human Rights* (London: Oxford University Press; 1971).
31 All such provisions were 'guaranteed' by the League of Nations.

For other treaties on minorities, see the treaties of Dorpat (1920), Riga (1920), Brünn (1920) and Upper Silesia (1922).
32 Brierly, *The Law of Nations*, p. 294.
33 See further, Pinto, in *International Protection of Human Rights*, pp. 183 et seq.
34 See Cheng, 'The contribution of international courts and tribunals to the protection of human rights', in *International Protection of Human Rights*, p. 169.
35 Cheng, in *International Protection of Human Rights*, p. 170.
36 On *jus cogens*, see, for example, Verdross, *American Journal of Inernational Law* (1966), p. 56; Jacovides, *Treaties Conflicting with Peremptory Norms of International Law and the London-Zürich Agreements* (Nicosia, 1966); cf. Schwarzenberger, *Texas Law Review* (1965), pp. 455 et seq.; in private law, cf. Eek, *Recueil des Cours de l'académie de droit international* (1973, I).
37 On treaties apparently binding third states, see I. Detter, *Essays on the Law of Treaties* (London: Sweet & Maxwell, 1967), pp. 117 et seq.
38 *I.C.J. Reports 1951*, p. 23 Cf. *Barcelona Traction, I.C.J. Reports 1970*, p. 3 at p. 32.
39 See, for example, Jacovides, *Treaties Conflicting with Peremptory Norms. . . .* Cf. infra p. 198.
40 See, further, International Law Association, *Report*, 1964.
41 Cf. Hackworth, *Digest of International Law*, vol. 2, p. 622 and A. D. McNair (Baron McNair), *International Law Opinions* (London: Cambridge University Press, 1956), pp. 74-6.
42 *Asylum, Judgment, I.C.J. Reports 1950*, p. 266 at p. 294. On the Spanish civil war, see Toynbee, Survey, 1937 II, 388.

PART FOUR

COERCION AND CONSENT

Chapter 10

Coercion of a State to Conclude Treaties

10:1 DEVELOPING COUNTRIES' NEED FOR SAFEGUARDS

It has been shown that territorial sovereignty is limited by a number of rules under *general international law*. A state can, of course, restrict its territorial competence *further* by concluding *treaties* limiting its power in its own country—for example, by allowing grazing,[1] construction of railways (see pp. 60-3) or oil pipelines (see pp. 63-5). Treaties may also concern delegation of more specifically sovereign functions—for example, the treaties establishing the European Communities limit the legislative power of the member states, which agree to let their citizens be bound by regulations of the Communities and grant these regulations the force of law in their territories (see p. 21). By the capitulation treaties China delegated an important part of its sovereignty in so far as it allowed foreign consuls to exercise jurisdiction in its territories (see p. 21). Agreements on military bases indicate how sovereign functions can be delegated by treaty or express consent (see pp. 196-219) as do agreements concerning refuge or exile governments[2] or international control commissions.[3]

It is of paramount importance to developing nations that such restrictions of territorial sovereignty by treaty or contract are granted of their own free will: in other words the question of consent to treaties has special importance for developing nations. Many developing nations are bound by agreements on military bases and by agreements for exploitation of natural resources. However, because they are newly independent, they find it difficult to make their voices heard in international negotiations. Therefore, any new rule for voidability of 'imposed' treaties is of crucial importance to developing nations. For it is such nations which are in need of special safeguards in order to ensure that they are not exposed to undue pressure, especially when they conclude treaties which limit their territorial sovereignty further than general international law demands.

If a treaty is 'imposed' upon a newly independent state, or indeed on any state, then it is, according to the Vienna Convention on the Law of Treaties, void. It is necessary to examine the kind of force applied: is any pressure sufficient for the treaty to be called void? Or, to put the question differently, are not all treaties concluded under some kind of force? According to the Vienna convention, which is based on a draft prepared by the International Law Commission, some treaties concluded under duress shall be invalid. It appears to be important therefore to qualify what kind of force shall cause such invalidity. It may be possible to suggest rules after analysing incidents in which states have claimed to be legally entitled to repudiate agreements concluded under force: although the convention on treaties has not yet entered into force there is reason to believe that some of the principles on coercion and consent embodied in the convention are already *lex lata* of the international community.

When a treaty is forced upon a state there is obviously a lack of consent on the part of that state: it is not its will to enter into an agreement on those terms. But the weaker party can never, in international law, enjoy the same protection as an 'inferior' or 'dependent' party to a contract under municipal law, for example in a hire-purchase transaction; but *de lege ferenda* it is to be hoped that international law will one day provide safeguards for the free consent of a state, for

> A dictated treaty obviously violates the first principle of any civilized law of contracts, which is the freedom of consent on both sides.[4]

Thus, as I shall attempt to show, there is reason to believe that certain types of coercion, but not every form of pressure, invalidate an agreement under international law as it stands. The freedom of consent of states in the conclusion of 'imposed' treaties is only safeguarded to a certain extent. However, I shall show that some new rules relating to state succession and state continuity have emerged and the requirement of free consent to restrictions of territorial sovereignty can be protected in other ways and not only by insisting that there must be absence of every form of coercion in the treaty-making process.

10:2 COERCION AND ITS HISTORICAL BACKGROUND

10:2:1 Before 1919

The traditional doctrine, before the League of Nations, was that the validity of treaties was not affected even if they had been concluded under duress against the state, but a treaty was void if the person signing it had been subjected to force.[5] Thus, even in the case of treaties concluded by military coercion a state was presumed to have given its 'consent': the State Department of the United States pronounced, in relation to the signatures of the treaty of Versailles, that

> even though a vanquished nation is in effect *compelled* to sign a treaty, I think in contemplation of law its signature is regarded as voluntary.[5]

Although the Versailles treaty was often subject to litigation before the Permanent Court of International Justice no party to the treaty ever put forward a plea of coercion to claim that the treaty was void or voidable.[6] Courts have consistently upheld the validity of peace treaties.[7]

10:2:2 1919-1945

(a) Opinion of Writers
After the signing of the Covenant of the League of Nations (1919) and the Pact of Paris (1928) a 'strong body of opinion' began to claim that treaties procured by the illegal threat or use of force

should no longer be recognized as legally valid.[8] Soviet writers claimed that coercion invalidates a treaty.[9] But Lauterpacht asserted in 1927 that there were

> few questions in international law in which there is such a measure of common agreement as this, that duress, so far as states are concerned, does not invalidate a contract.[10]

Other writers went as far as to support a contention that *de lege ferenda* coercion ought to invalidate an international agreement.[11]

(b) Attitude of States
It has been suggested that the idea of invalidating treaties concluded by force is supported by the so-called Stimson doctrine. After Japan had occupied most of Manchuria in 1931-2, Henry Lewis Stimson, Secretary of State of the United States, sent identical notes to the Chinese and Japanese governments in which he stated that the United States

> cannot admit the legality of any situation *de facto* nor does it intend to recognize any treaty or agreement entered into between those governments which impaired the open-door policy or treaty rights of the United States, particularly those arising from the Nine-Power Treaty of 1922 by which Japan had undertaken to respect the sovereignty and territory of China.[12]

Furthermore, the United States

> does not intend to recognize any situation, treaty or agreement which may be brought about by means contrary to the covenants and obligations of the Pact of Paris of 27 August 1928, to which both China and Japan, as well as the United States, are parties.[13]

Shortly after the Stimson declaration the Assembly of the League of Nations adopted unanimously a declaration that

> it is incumbent upon the members of the League of Nations not to recognize any situation, treaty or agreement which may be

brought about by means contrary to the Covenant of the League of Nations or to the Pact of Paris.[14]

In the Stimson doctrine and in this declaration of the League of Nations there is an attempt to define the attitudes of states other than the contracting parties: they are not to *recognize* treaties procured by force. There is also the idea that *force* must be illegal to merit such nonrecognition. It is interesting to note that attitudes of noncontracting states are made relevant: in other fields of treaty law the position of third states is never brought in as a corollary of the validity of a treaty.

Another example of nonrecognition of imposed treaties is in a clause in the Turkish-Soviet agreement of 16 March 1921. By this agreement both parties bound themselves *not to recognize* peace treaties or other international agreements which were imposed by force on the other party.[15] But the Stimson doctrine and the declaration of the League of Nations are different from this general clause in the Turkish-Soviet treaty: the latter does not specify that the 'force' must be *illegal*. In the Stimson and League of Nations declarations, on the other hand, there is the important qualification that the treaties must be brought about by means contrary to the Covenant of the League of Nations or the Pact of Paris.

10:2:3 After 1945

The law on treaties procured by force was reinforced and consolidated in three significant stages:

1 The endorsement of the criminality of aggressive war in the charters of the Allied military tribunals for the trial of Axis war criminals.
2 The clear-cut prohibition of the threat or use of force in article 2(4) of the Charter of the United Nations.
3 The practice of the United Nations.[16]

But, in spite of the tentative development in state practice of a new principle of nonrecognition of illegally imposed treaties described above, most writers continue to assert, even after the birth of the United Nations, that coercion does not invalidate a treaty. In 1961

Lord McNair declared that Great Britain has never dissented from the traditional doctrine that the validity of a treaty is not affected even if it has been imposed by force.[17] In his drafts on the law of treaties submitted to the International Law Commission, Sir Gerald Fitzmaurice suggested that coercion of a state should not invalidate a treaty under the new codified law of treaties.[18]

But in subsequent drafts submitted to the International Law Commission by Sir Humphrey Waldock there is an article on the invalidity of treaties concluded under duress. Thus, in the final draft the International Law Commission suggested that

> A treaty is void if its conclusion has been procured by the threat or use of force in violation of the principles of the Charter of the United Nations.

The substance of this article was adopted by the conference on the law of treaties in Vienna 1968-9; the conference added, however, that the applied force must violate not only the principles of the Charter of the UN but, more generally, principles of international law of the Charter. Thus, the adopted article reads:

> A treaty is void if its conclusion has been procured by the threat or use of force in violation of the *principles of international law embodied in the Charter* of the United Nations.[19]

The present Convention on the Law of Treaties (which has not yet entered into force) thus lays down that a treaty procured by force is void whether or not third parties 'recognize' it (as previously suggested by the Stimson and League of Nations declarations—see pp. 144-5). Furthermore, it is void, and not voidable, and hence there is no need for a statement by, for example, the International Court of Justice to *declare* it invalid (as previously suggested in the ILC).[20]

One important qualification retained by the Convention on Treaties from the previous Stimson and League of Nations declarations is that the force applied must be *illegal*: it must violate the principles of international law as laid down in the Charter of the United Nations.

It is important to emphasize the requirement of illegality for, unless it is clear that only unlawful pressure will invalidate agreement, both states and doctrine will be reluctant to agree with the apparently far-reaching article on coercion of states. It has been claimed that

> the United Nations has advanced beyond the League system and generally prohibited the 'threat or use of force'.[21]

But surely it is a misconception that all use of force is illegal?[22] On the contrary, international society is being developed to provide for force in a number of ways, for example by organizing sanctions. Article 2(4) prohibits the threat or use of force—probably only armed force[23]—in *some* cases but it does not outlaw force used by the organization, or by its member states, in the form of sanctions. Therefore, when examining the validity of treaties procured by force it is important not only to examine what force is envisaged by article 2(4) of the Charter of the United Nations but to establish what force is incompatible with international law as a whole. The issue may be narrowed down in the following way:

> ... if we look forward to a time when, we may hope, the law will have been provided with a workable system of sanctions against aggression; surely then we shall not say that if, under pressure of sanctions, an aggressor state has been forced to accept certain onerous obligations, those obligations ought not to be upheld by the law.[24]

and therefore,

> ... the change to which we ought to look forward is not the elimination of the use of coercion from the transaction, but the establishment of international machinery to ensure that when coercion is used it shall be in a proper case and by due process of law, and not, as at present it may be, arbitrarily. The problem of treaties imposed by force is therefore in its essence not a problem of treaty law, but a particular aspect of that much wider problem which pervades the whole system, that of subordinating the use of force to law.[25]

10:3 TYPES OF ILLEGAL FORCE

10:3:1 What Force?

In 1964 the UN arranged a special conference on friendly relations and cooperation among states. One of the tasks of the conference was to attempt a definition of illegal force. The Eastern bloc wanted to include economic and political force and other forms of pressure or coercion falling short of armed force for, as they argued, such non-military forms of pressure are often far more potent in their effects than actual armed force. Other states at the conference insisted that it is both desirable and inevitable in an interdependent world that states attempt to influence the actions and policies of other states and it would be impossible to outlaw all such forms of pressure.[26]

In the International Law Commission there was also discussion on whether the article in the convention on treaties on validity of treaties imposed by illegal force should cover 'other forms of coercion which obviously (have) serious effects in international life'.[27] In the Sixth Committee of the United Nations, there were also demands that any provisions on coercion must cover not only armed force but also economic and political pressure.[28]

When the draft article on coercion of states was discussed at the conference on treaties in Vienna considerable time was devoted to a proposal by Afghanistan[29] supported by 18 Afro-Asian and Latin American states. The proposal was that in the article on coercion, after the words 'threat or use of force', there should be inserted the words 'including economic and political pressure'.

This proposal would have imposed an interpretation on the international legal principles embodied in the Charter. The United Kingdom claimed at the conference that article 2(4) of the Charter certainly only envisaged physical force and the threat of physical force: concepts like economic and political force are too vague to be included as a ground for invalidity of treaties without endangering the paramount principle of *pacta sunt servanda*.[30] Eventually it was agreed at the conference that rather than amending the article on coercion in this respect the conference would make a declaration 'condemning' treaties imposed by all types of force.[31] The declaration was annexed to the convention and read:

The United Nations Conference on the Law of Treaties,
Upholding the principle that every treaty in force is binding upon the parties to it and must be performed by them in good faith,
Reaffirming the principle of the sovereign equality of states,
Convinced that states must have complete freedom in performing any act relating to the conclusion of a treaty,
Deploring the fact that in the past states have sometimes been forced to conclude treaties under pressure exerted in various forms by other states,
Desiring to ensure that in the future no such pressure will be exercised in any form by any state in connection with the conclusion of a treaty,
1. *Solemnly condemns* the threat or use of pressure in any form, whether military, political or economical, by any state in order to coerce another state to perform any act relating to the conclusion of a treaty in violation of the principles of the sovereign equality of states and freedom of consent,
2. *Decides* that the present declaration shall form part of the Final Act of the Conference on the Law of Treaties.

But, obviously, because it does not form part of the article that declares void all treaties concluded under illegal pressure, it must be assumed that the declaration does not possess the same legal force as the convention itself. Article 52 on coercion of states still leaves open whether 'force' and 'threat of force' shall include political and economic pressure: the article was purposely left in broad terms because a specification of 'armed force' might have excluded other force *e contrario*. As things now stand it appears that it has been left to practice to define the exact meaning of illegal force under article 52 of the convention and indeed under article 2(4) of the Charter but that, at any rate, armed force must be included.

By July 1973, 18 states had ratified or acceded to the Vienna convention. Among these states is the United Kingdom, and it may be assumed that numerous other states will follow suit. The convention requires, under article 84, no less than 35 ratifications or accessions before it enters into force, but, as the convention will be of great importance to states with regard to the law of treaties, it is interesting to remark already at this stage that the coercion article of the convention will only cover instances of armed force, in accordance with the intention of the parties.

Syria acceded to the convention with the reservation, among others, that

> The expression 'the threat or use of force' used in [Article 52] extends also to the employment of economic, political, military and psychological coercion and to all types of coercion constraining a state to conclude a treaty against its wishes or its interests.[32]

The United Kingdom, on the other hand, made a reservation against this 'interpretation' by Syria and emphasized that it did not accept the view of Syria that article 52 would have such an extensive application. Such an interpretation, said the government of the United Kingdom, does not correctly reflect the conclusions reached at the conference of Vienna on the subject of coercion; the conference had 'dealt with this matter by adopting a declaration on this subject which forms part of the final act'.[33]

The declaration by the United Kingdom may not constitute a reservation properly so called in so far as it does not alter the legal effect of the agreement.[34] It must be established that the intention of the parties was that the coercion article will only extend to armed force and will not affect the validity of agreements concluded under political or economic pressure.

Syria is, of course, free to *extend* the application of the Vienna convention by a reservation. But it is not capable of doing this for other states but itself and if only Syria's own rights and duties can be affected it becomes dubious whether its reservation does take any effect in law. For a treaty must, at least, be bilateral and another party to a treaty with Syria can never be affected by Syria's 'interpretation'.

It may be interesting to note that Syria, in spite of its far-reaching interpretative reservation, excludes, by another reservation, the application, for its part, of the annex which deals with obligatory conciliation. To this reservation the United Kingdom took a stronger view and appended a special declaration, also in the form of a reservation, by which the United Kingdom *objected* and *excluded* the application of the convention between the United Kingdom and Syria.[35]

10:3:2 Military Force

Apart from peace treaties, which are obviously concluded under military force,[36] numerous agreements on trade and other matters have in the past been concluded by states occupied or threatened by armed forces. Thus in 1853 Commodore Matthew Perry of the United States Navy

> arrived at the Japanese coast off Yokohama and backed by an imposing squadron he proposed to open trade relations. His offer was rejected and he said he would be back the following year for an answer. He did so with an even more imposing squadron . . .

when his 'offer' was accepted by Japan.[37] No one would, in those days, have questioned the validity of the agreement. In 1915 an agreement between the United States and Haiti was concluded under military force: the United States occupied the island to 'ensure' ratification of the treaty.[38] The treaty gave the United States a right of intervention and Haiti was pledged to preserve its sovereignty intact and not to lease or cede territory, nor to give other states a right of jurisdiction.

(a) *The Munich agreement*
Another agreement that was procured under the threat of aggression is the Munich agreement of 1938. On 29 September 1938 France, Britain, Germany and Italy signed this agreement which ceded Sudetenland from Czechoslovakia to Germany. On 30 September Dr Krofta, foreign minister of Czechoslovakia announced, in the presence of the foreign ministers of France, Great Britain and Italy that

> in the name of the President of the Republic and in the name of the Czechoslovak government we accept the decisions taken at Munich without us and against us.[39]

By this 'acceptance' Czechoslovakia must be considered to have become a party to the agreement itself. Furthermore, the government of Czechoslovakia had addressed separate notes to the signatory powers including Germany stating that it had fulfilled all its obligations for carrying out the guarantee promised under the agreement.[40]

At least in one case a state has disputed the validity of a peace treaty dealing with boundaries after the Second World War. Austria has repeatedly asserted that it was not a free agent in the Paris agreement of 1946 as it was at the time occupied by the four Allied Powers.[41]

(b) Question of Retroactivity

According to the ILC's draft it seems that the coercion article in the Vienna convention (article 52) applies *at least* to treaties concluded after the end of the Second World War. Although the ILC refrained from indicating the date from which treaties concluded under duress would be void it had considered it sufficient to mention 'the Charter of the United Nations' which, in itself, would give some idea of the relevant time period. The Vienna conference went even further than the International Law Commission: by including in the coercion article the words 'principles of international law as embodied in the Charter of the United Nations' the conference sought to indicate that the prohibition against the use of illegal force was *lex lata* even before the establishment of the United Nations.[42]

Consequently, even treaties concluded just before the war appear to be covered by the coercion article.

(c) Problems of Peace Treaties: the South Tirol Question

What then about peace treaties? Are all peace treaties concluded after the Second World War void? And will it, in the future, be impossible to conclude a valid peace treaty which is not struck by the coercion article of the Vienna convention? The thinking of the International Law Commission, and of the Vienna conference, has apparently been that since aggressive war is forbidden by contemporary international law, at least for all states bound by the Charter or other treaties, an aggressor has forfeited his right to invoke the coercion article as a ground for a claim that a subsequent peace treaty is void *ab initio*.

But, if the Vienna convention is to have retroactive operation, at least as far back as 1945, how are the South Tirol provisions concerning Austria in the 1947 peace treaty with Italy affected? Austria's position was not really that of an aggressor and so it cannot be deprived of the right to invoke coercion as a reason for nullity. But as the Vienna convention does not allow severance of the imposed and not imposed provisions of a treaty the whole treaty runs the risk of being considered void.

As for peace treaties concluded in the future, not only may it be difficult to assess who is an aggressor, but if a state is brought into a war by annexation then it may also, in many instances, be difficult to ascertain who, in an actual conflict, took the first aggressive step. It may seem that there is a risk of reverting to the principle *vae victis*[43] if certain states, but not all, are allowed to invoke the coercion article.

Still, as will be seen, identification of an aggressor causes comparatively few problems compared to the difficulties raised by disputed boundary treaties.

(d) *The Question of Subsequent Approval: the Munich Agreement Again*

Article 52 of the Vienna convention prescribes that treaties procured by force are 'void'—not merely 'voidable'. By choosing the term void the International Law Commission intended to leave it open to the forced party to conclude a new treaty; for the imposed treaty could not be brought to life by subsequent approval for the very reason that a violation of the principles of the Charter could not be 'approved'.

But how then does this affect an existing agreement? The ILC explained in its commentary that

> Even if it were conceivable that after being liberated from the influence of a threat or use of force a state might wish to allow a treaty procured from it by such means, the Commission considered it essential that the treaty should be regarded in law as void *ab initio*. This would enable the state concerned to take its decision in regard to the maintenance of the treaty in a position of full equality with other states. If, therefore, the treaty were maintained in force it would in effect be by the conclusion of a new treaty and not by the recognition of the validity of a treaty procured by means contrary to the most fundamental principles of the Charter of the United Nations.

Still, it is technically difficult to preclude states from approving an imposed treaty; and as a 'treaty' can be entered into without any specific form apart from the requirement that it must be embodied in a written document, the difference between a 'new treaty' and subsequent 'approval' is not great. What is required appears to be not a mere unilateral declaration of approval, but some written fresh 'understanding' between the parties.

The difficulties to be faced with respect to the prohibition of subsequent approval may be illustrated by the events following the Munich agreement.[44]

After Germany had violated the Munich agreement by annexing Bohemia and Moravia and by creating a German protectorate in Slovakia, as well as by other breaches, the United Kingdom declared in a note to the German government that it

> cannot but regard the events of the last few days as a complete repudiation of the Munich agreement and a denial of the spirit in which the negotiators of that agreement bound themselves to cooperate for a peaceful settlement.[45]

Later Mr Eden, British Foreign Secretary, stated in the House of Commons,[46] as well as in a note to the Foreign Minister of Czechoslovakia[47] that his government regarded itself free from any engagement. Furthermore, he said

> At the final settlement of the Czech frontiers to be reached at the end of the war they will not be influenced by any changes effected in and since 1938.[48]

The same day, on 5 August 1942, Jan Masaryk, Czech Minister for Foreign Affairs, fully endorsed the denunciation by the British government based on the German violation of the treaty.[49]

The same year France denounced the treaty, and Italy followed suit in 1943.

After the war West Germany under Adenauer insisted that the Munich agreement had been a valid treaty and that the Sudeten Germans had a right to their homeland. But West Germany never demanded Sudetenland as a rightful part of Germany as it did the Polish territory east of the Oder until 1970. Under Brandt, West

Germany has recently agreed that the Munich agreement is now without force. However, the government has declined to claim that it was void *ab initio*. If the line is taken that the Munich agreement is void from the start two million Sudeten Germans would stop being German citizens. They would lose their rights to German compensation grants, and, in theory, be open to Czech prosecution as traitors for serving the Germans.

Britain has also taken the view that the Munich agreement lost force but that it was once valid; it may be that, to British thought, it is conceptually weird for diplomacy to claim that any treaty is void from the moment of signature.[50]

Czechoslovakia, on the other hand, has all along claimed that the Munich agreement was void from the start.

Article 52 of the Vienna convention covers, in accordance with its wording, instances of coercion which violate the principles of international law as embodied in the Charter of the United Nations. It appears reasonable that its operation would retroactively affect agreements at least as recent as the Munich treaty. But should the International Law Commission, and the Vienna conference, have made an exception for treaties dealing with boundaries: is it of benefit to the international community to consider such treaties void from the beginning if millions of individuals derive their citizenship from them?

According to article 62 of the Vienna convention parties are empowered to denounce a treaty in the case of fundamental change of circumstances *unless the treaty in dispute establishes a boundary*. I question whether the same exception, in the interest of the stability of relations within the international community, should not have been incorporated in the coercion article.

In one case, which has been given little attention, a municipal court held that the Munich agreement was valid from the start and that it was capable of creating rights of nationality. In *Nederlands Beheers Institut v Nimwegen*[51] a Dutch court held that the Czech accession in 1938 to the Munich agreement was void under international law as the agreement had been forced upon Czechoslovakia under the threat of aggression. Therefore, a deceased person whose estate was in dispute had not acquired German nationality. The Court of Appeal, on the other hand, reversed the decision. In part, the Court of Appeal founded its judgment on the ground that a

Czech decree of 1945 implicitly recognized and confirmed the Munich agreement so that it was clear that the treaty, initially, had been valid. Consequently, the decedent had actually become a German national.

However, as the principle of consent is the most essential basis in all treaty and contract law, it may be preferable to tolerate complications about nationality of individuals rather than to exempt boundary treaties from coerced treaties. In other words, in my opinion treaties can still be vitiated if they have been imposed, even if they concern boundaries which are important for the stability of international relations.

(e) The Question of Intertemporality
As I have shown difficulties will not be avoided even if the application of the coercion article of the Vienna convention is restricted to future agreement. But even if the coercion article did not, contrary to its wording, affect the validity of existing agreements, there is still the question of how existing agreements are to be reconciled with the new legal rule. This has been called the problem of intertemporality, frequently encountered by students of the conflict of laws. As Huber expressed the rule in the *Island of Palmas* case.[52]

> The same principle which subjects the act creative of a right to the law in force at the time the right arises, demands that the existence of the right, in other words its continued manifestation, shall follow the conditions required by the evolution of law.

10: 3: 3 Economic Force and Political Pressure

Most treaties are concluded under some sort of economic or political force. Such 'force' may result from the fact that one of the contracting parties is a larger or more powerful state which, by its very size and strength, exercises pressure on weaker parties to an agreement. In some cases political pressure may be clearly pronounced, as in the recent events following the Moscow treaty, between the Soviet Union and West Germany, which is still unratified by West Germany. Mr Gromyko, on 12 April 1972, announced that there will be no friendly and good-neighbourly relations if the necessary understanding of the Soviet Union's interest, the minimum of which are reflected in the Moscow treaty, is not displayed in the Federal Republic.[53]

But such pressure does not, to be effective, have to be pronounced by the larger power; on the other hand, if it is claimed that such pressure is 'illegal' that is virtually to claim that states can no longer conclude treaties. For treaty relationship will always, by necessity, be established between states of different size and different power.[54]

The problem has special relevance for developing countries. An *obiter dictum* by the representative of India in the United Nations suggests that a marked political dependence, as between the emerging new nations and their previous metropolitan countries, would deprive treaties of their legal force. Thus,

> In determining the validity of territorial claims no reliance [can] be placed on treaties concluded between expanding colonial powers such as France and Spain and declining indigenous kingdoms like Morocco.[55]

But if this far-reaching view is accepted, it would be virtually impossible for a new nation to conclude any agreement with its previous mother country; and at least in some instances it must be assumed that such agreements may be in the interests of the emerging state and not contrary to its wishes.

One group of treaties that a state contracts at the time of independence may, however, be signed under considerable pressure: the new state signs these agreements as a price for its independence, although the treaties may be 'dictated by necessity'.[56]

It has been shown (p. 148) that the Vienna convention is not intended to cover treaties concluded under political or economic force. Still, it will be seen (pp. 196-219) that in certain cases the contents of such treaties may be such that they may be repudiated on other grounds under international law.

It may be important to emphasize, in this context, that political pressure *per se*, as well as economic force, may be illegal.[57]

10:3:4 Illegal Economic or Political Force?

It has been alleged in the Sixth Committee that retaining a state within the currency area of a former metropolitan country constitutes a form of economic pressure.[58] The fact that the United States suspended economic aid to Laos to force the right-wing group of the Laos government to enter into a coalition has been quoted as another example of 'economic force'.[59] In the Indonesia crisis the United States suspended Marshall aid to secure the rapid settlement of the dispute,[60] and in a fishing dispute with Ecuador, the United States declared it would 'reconsider' all economic aid (see p. 36). Although the effectiveness of such force may be questioned,[61] it could hardly be contended that such pressure is, in itself, 'illegal' under international law. For the states in question could not claim any internationally established *rights* to aid and agreements on aid usually allow for suspension.

Similarly, when France suspended wine imports from Algeria in 1970 to press Algeria to conclude a treaty that was then under negotiation[62] it was hardly a question of 'illegal' pressure. It is unlikely that a state commits any offence by refraining from importing commodities.

Another case in which economic pressure cannot be illegal is when a state is exposed to organized economic *sanctions* because of some irregular acts committed by that state.[63]

It could be argued that if the economic measures are seen in a greater context they could, in some instances, be viewed as unjustified 'reprisals'.

After Fidel Castro came to power in Cuba, the United States reduced the Cuban sugar quota. This reduction caused, in its turn, the Cuban government to nationalize the property of American citizens in Cuba.[64] The act of the United States was in itself legal, as it has not bound itself by any treaty to keep the sugar quota at any particular level. The action of Cuba was also legal in so far as any state is entitled to nationalize property provided it pays adequate compensation and that nationalization is done in the public interest. However, it has been argued on the one hand that the action of the United States constituted an 'act of aggression' and, on the other, that Cuba violated international law by discriminating against aliens when it nationalized property; furthermore, the compensation was said to be 'illusory'. But what, in fact, the parties have argued about then are the *motives* behind intrinsically legal acts: thus, if a state nationalizes *in retaliation* for what it considers a violation of its interests, the *motives* for such nationalization would, it has been argued, be 'illegal'. This has recently been held with respect to the Libyan nationalizations.[65] But do we not then face an embarrassing twofold problem: how can we ever establish what act constitutes a reprisal and what act is the initial 'offensive' one? If a state suspends, for example, commodity imports from another state as a means of disapproval of a political decision of that other state, it acts legally although its motives are to 'retaliate'. If then the other state proceeds to nationalize property it acts legally (provided there is a 'public purpose', provided there is no discrimination and provided there is adequate compensation) although its motives are to 'retaliate'. The first state may then take some other action, which in itself is legal but which causes difficulties to the other party, and the game can go on and on, until we perhaps lose track of who 'retaliated' first.

Another problem is connected with the expression of the motives. In the recent debate on Libyan nationalization it has been claimed that Libya's emphatic assertion that her measures were retaliatory constituted a particularly compromising indication of guilt. But how can we then ever achieve complete knowledge of the motives[66] of a foreign state? In other words, will not a state which is wise enough to keep the motives to herself be unduly privileged?

NOTES

1 See, for example, the new convention on grazing between Sweden and Norway concluded on 9 February 1972. Cf. the the previous convention of 1919, which was denounced by Norway in 1961. On the Somali-Ethiopian arrangement, see infra, p. 188 n101.
2 Cf. *Re Amand*, [1941] 2 K.B. 239; *Lorentzen v Lydden & Co. Ltd*, [1942] 2 K.B. 202.
3 For example, the 1954 Geneva Agreement on Indo-China.
4 J. L. Brierly, *The Law of Nations*, 6th edition edited by Sir Humphrey Waldock (Oxford: Clarendon Press, 1963), p. 318.

5 G. H. Hackworth, *Digest of International Law* (Washington: Government Printing Office, 1940-4), vol. 5, p. 158. Cf. Detter, 'The problem of unequal treaties', *International and Comparative Law Quarterly* (1966), p. 1085.

6 A. D. McNair (Baron McNair), *The Law of Treaties* (Oxford: Clarendon Press, 1961), p. 209.

7 *Free Zones of Upper Savoy and the District of Gex, Judgment, 1932, P.C.I.J., Series A/B, No. 46*, p. 96 on the Paris treaty of 1815; *S. S. 'Wimbledon', Judgments, 1923, P.C.I.J., Series A, No. 1* on the Versailles treaty (1919); *Customs Regime between Germany and Austria, Advisory Opinion, 1931, P.C.I.J., Series A/B, No. 41*, p. 37 on the treaty of Saint-Germain-en-Laye (1919); *Treaty of Neuilly, Article 179, Annex, Paragraph 4 (Interpretation), Judgment No. 3, 1924, P.C.I.J., Series A, No. 3* on the treaty of Neuilly-sur-Seine (1919); *Interpretation of Article 3, Paragraph 2, of the Treaty of Lausanne, Advisory Opinion, 1925, P.C.I.J., Series B, No. 12* (the Mosul case) on the treaty of peace with Turkey, 1923; *Interpretation of Peace Treaties with Bulgaria, Hungary and Romania, First Phase, Advisory Opinion, I.C.J. Reports 1950*, p. 65 at p. 89.

8 Commentary to the draft convention on the law of treaties by Sir Humphrey Waldock in *Yearbook of the International Law Commission 1966*, vol. 2 (New York: United Nations, 1967), pp. 246 et seq.

9 Korovin, *Sovremennoe meshdunarodnoe publichnoe pravo* (Moscow/Leningrad, 1926), p. 93.

10 H. Lauterpacht, *Private Law Sources and Analogies of International Law* (London: Longmans Green, 1927), p. 161.

11 Brierly, 'Some considerations on the obsolescence of treaties', *Transactions of the Grotius Society* (1926), pp. 11, 19.

12 Hackworth, *Digest of International Law*, vol. 1, p. 334.

13 Hackworth, *Digest of International Law*, vol. 1 p. 334.

14 League of Nations, *Official Journal*, spec. suppl. no. 101 (1932), p. 87. See further, Langer, Seizure of Territory: The Stimson Doctrine and Related Principles (1947).

15 RSFSR 1917.

16 Cf. Sir Humphrey Waldock, in *Yearbook of the International Law Commission 1966*, vol. 2, pp. 246 et seq.

17 McNair, *The Law of Treaties*, p. 208.

18 For example, Sir Gerald Fitzmaurice, 'Third report on the law of treaties', in *Yearbook of the International Law Commission 1958* (New York: United Nations, 1958), pp. 20, 26. Note that Lauterpacht had previously suggested in his report—*Yearbook of the International Law Commission 1953*, vol. 2 (New York: United Nations, 1959), p. 47—that 'Treaties imposed by or as the result of the use of force against a state in violation of principles of the Charter of the United Nations are invalid if so declared by the International Court of Justice at the request of any state.'
19 Italics added for the alteration made at the Vienna conference.
20 See note 18.
21 Blix, *Sovereignty, Aggression and Neutrality* (Dag Hammarskiöld Foundation, Stockholm, 1970), p. 124.
22 I. Brownlie, *International Law and the Use of Force by States* (Oxford: Clarendon Press, 1963) on instances where the use of force is permissible—for example, pp. 317 et seq.
23 Brownlie, *International Law and the Use of Force by States*, p. 362.
24 Brierly, *The Law of Nations*, pp. 318-19.
25 Brierly, *The Law of Nations*, p. 319.
26 See *American Journal of International Law* (1966), p. 9. Further, Pugh, Definition of Aggression.
27 For example, *Yearbook of the International Law Commission 1963*, vol. 1 (New York: United Nations, 1963), p. 52.
28 UN Doc. A/CN.4/175, 254-267 and Adds. 1-4 (1965).
29 UN Doc. A/Conf. 39/20.
30 Canada, Australia, the Netherlands and Uruguay made similar statements. On the standpoint before the Vienna convention, see McNair, *Law of Treaties*, pp. 210-11.
31 UN Doc. A/Conf. 39/20 (17 May 1969),
32 UN Doc. ST/Leg.Ser.D/4.
33 UN Doc. ST/Leg.Ser.D/4.
34 On this point, see I. Detter, *Essays on the Law of Treaties* (London: Sweet & Maxwell, 1967), pp. 51 et seq.; cf. Waldock's report on the law of treaties in *Yearbook of the International Law Commission 1962*, vol. 2 (New York: United Nations, 1962), p. 62.
35 UN Doc. ST/Leg.Ser.D/4.

36 See infra, pp. 195 et seq. and Detter in *ICLQ* (1966), pp. 1073 et seq.
37 McGraw-Hill (ed.), *World History* (New York, 1964), p. 325.
38 Harvard Research, *American Journal of International Law* (1935), p. 1157.
39 Taborsky, 'Munich: the Vienna arbitration and international law', *Czechoslovak Yearbook of International Law, 1942*, p. 25.
40 See, for example, France, Min. aff. étr., Documents diplomatiques, 1938-1939, Doc.45.
41 GAOR 15th Sess., Spec. Pol. Cttee, 176th mtg. and Fenet, *La Question du Tyrol* (Paris, 1968).
42 UN Doc. A/Conf. 39/C.1/L.289.
43 Cf. Detter, in *ICLQ* (1966), p. 1085.
44 See, for the conclusion of this agreement, supra, pp. 151-2.
45 Documents Concerning German–Polish Relations and the Outbreak of Hostilities between Great Britain and Germany on September 3, 1939 (London: HMSO, 1939), Cmd. 6106, document 10.
46 *Parliamentary Debates (Hansard), House of Commons*, 5th series, vol. 382 (1942), cols. 1004-5.
47 *British and Foreign State Papers 1940–42*, vol. 144, (London: HMSO, 1953), p. 986.
48 Ibid., loc. cit.
49 Ibid., loc. cit.
50 *The Observer*, 7 November 1971.
51 (1951), ILR 249 No. 63.
52 (1928), *Reports of International Arbitral Awards*, vol. 2, p. 825.
53 *The Times*, 13 April 1972.
54 McNair, 'Equality in International Law', *Michigan Law Review* (1927), p. 136.
55 *GAOR*, 15th sess., Spec. Pol. Cttee, 1116th mtg.
56 Statement by Archbishop Makarios signing the Cyprus Agreement. Cf. SC/S/PV 1098 (1964), p. 16; see, further infra, pp. 211-14.
57 Brownlie, *International Law and the Use of Force by States*, pp. 369 et seq.
58 Detter, in *ICLQ* (1966), p. 1083.
59 Williams, *Unequal Treaties* (Dag Hammarskiöld Foundation, cycl., Uppsala, 1966).

60 A. M. Taylor, *Indonesian Independence and the United Nations* (London: Stevens, 1960), p. 396.
61 Taylor, *Indonesian Independence and the United Nations*, pp. 396 et seq.
62 *Documentations sur les relations entre l'Algérie et les sociétés pétrolières françaises* (Alger, 1971), p. 38.
63 On economic sanctions see Doxey, *Economic Sanctions and International Enforcement* (London, 1971). Cf. supra, p. 21.
64 Cf. the *Sabbatino* case, 376 US 398, 84.S.Ct.923,11L.Ed.2nd 804 (1964), See further, I. Delupis, *Finance and Protection of Investments in Developing Countries* (Gower Press, 1973), pp. 70, 89-90.
65 *The Times*, 17 January 1972, letter to the Editor by Professor Schwarzenberger. On the Libyan nationalization see further, Delupis, *Finance and Protection of Invesments in Developing Countries*, pp. 74 et seq.
66 On the problem of intention see further, Delupis, *Finance and Protection of Investments in Developing Countries*, pp. 76 et seq.

Chapter 11

Expression of a State's Consent

11:1 FORCE AGAINST WHOM?

11:1:1 The Panama Treaties and the Problem of Representation

It has been claimed that Panama was 'forced' to accept the Hay-Varilla treaty by which Panama ceded a strip of land for the Canal.¹ But in fact the force was not applied against Panama so much as against Colombia. The United States encouraged a revolutionary clique in Panama to declare themselves independent from Colombia, which possessed sovereignty over the Canal Zone, and assisted the revolution—carried through by seven persons—by United States warships.² This was the result of the unsuccessful pressure the United States had applied on Colombia which had refused to sign a treaty, the so-called Hay–Herran treaty of 1903. This treaty would have authorized the United States to obtain a strip of land across Panama. Colombia would have granted a lease for a hundred years but the United States would not have enjoyed any sovereign rights. The United States would have paid $10,000,000 cash in addition to $250,000 yearly for the privileges granted. The United States had ratified the treaty in February 1903 but months later Colombia still had not ratified. On 13 June 1903 the United States informed its Ambassador in Bogotá that the peaceful relations between Colombia and the United States would be endangered if Colombia did not speedily proceed to ratify the treaty. The Senate of Colombia viewed this intimidation as 'unlawful pressure' and rejected the treaty altogether; apart from the pressure unduly applied by a foreign power Colombia felt that the treaty would virtually amount to the establishment of an annex government in the Canal Zone and lessen the sovereignty of Colombia in this region. The United States then encouraged Panama to declare its independence which followed on 4 November 1903. Two days later the United States recognized the new state.

The Hay–Varilla treaty which is nowadays contested by Panama as being contrary to international law was concluded on 18 November 1903 between the new state and the United States. By this treaty Panama transferred to the United States all 'rights, power and authority' over a strip of land 'as if the United States were the sovereign of the territory'. The United States was given the right of intervention with armed forces to secure its rights to the Canal and a right to build military bases to this end (see pp. 182 and 200). The United States was also given certain fiscal rights, rights of jurisdiction and a monopoly over building roads and railways. The treaty also ensured the free immigration of American workers. Panama even bound itself to 'sell' further land, if needed by the United States, for naval and coaling stations.

It seems untenable to claim that this treaty was concluded by the use of armed force against Panama: on the contrary, Panama was *assisted* by armed force to achieve a secession from Colombia and it was against Colombia that the United States exercised its armed force and threat of armed force.

11:1:2 Consent of the People

The example of the Panama agreement procured by assistance in seceding from another state raises the question whether a state, after a change of government, can argue that the 'people' had been forced to accept a treaty although the previous government had given its consent. Some authorities claim that the people must give their consent to secession. Hyde maintained in 1922 that a treaty forced upon a state providing for the cession of a portion of the state's territory without the consent of the population is 'internationally illegal . . . or voidable'.[4] In Soviet doctrine the consent of the people is often made one of the most important preconditions for a valid treaty. Thus, the consent expressed by a state to an international agreement must be the real will of the people not merely the formal will of the state.[5] The Soviet Union would, claim its own writers, be particularly conscientious to conclude treaties which express the will of the entire people, as opposed to agreements concluded by the 'Western world'.[6] The fact that 'peoples' had been coerced was the reason why one of the first steps of the Soviet Union in the first few years of its existence was to release contracting parties of the former Russian empire from treaties to which the 'peoples' had not given their consent.[7]

However desirable it may be that the entire people of a state give their consent to an international agreement it is not possible to count such popular consent among the requirements for the validity of a treaty under modern international law. A state is always free to release other contracting parties from their obligations if it considers that the popular support of the treaty is lacking in the cocontracting states; but there can be no obligation under international law to do so. A state is unable to ascertain whether a treaty has the approval of the population of other states which sign the agreement; it must be enough for a state to rely on the consent as expressed by the competent organs of the other states, organs which normally represent the states in their international relations. Or as Sir Gerald Fitzmaurice expressed the thought in 1958:

> States have no choice but to accept as internationally authentic the acts of the legitimate executive authority of another state carried on in the international plane in an *apparently regular manner*.[8]

On the other hand, if it is necessary to accept the rule that a treaty is validly concluded once the authority legitimately entitled to represent the state has given its consent, this does not mean that the consent of the people is irrelevant. As has been described above (pp. 13-18) political rights of citizens to self-determination are emerging as human rights guaranteed by international law; but their assent to a treaty would have to be expressed by the organ authorized to represent them. The importance of the people's assent and approval of a treaty is growing in the present-day international community; in many cases states release contracting parties from agreements that lack popular consent (see p. 204); and it is of special importance to new nations which have recently attained independence. It is also significant that the Rhodesian draft settlement of 24 November 1971—although it is not technically a treaty between two states—provided that the settlement was to be 'subject to its being acceptable to Rhodesians as a whole in the opinion of the [Settlement] Commission'.

11:1:3 Relevance of Changes of Government

Thus a government cannot argue that since its 'people' had been forced by a previous government into a treaty binding the country it can now validly abrogate the agreement. To allow this would not only cause great uncertainty in international relations and undermine the important maxim *pacta sunt servanda* on which treaty law is based, it would also provide a valid reason for a state to rid itself of any undesirable international obligation by a mere change of government.

The Panama agreement discussed earlier (p. 164) was concluded not with the reluctant consent of the state but with the express and emphatic approval of the Varilla government which had been helped to power by the other party to the treaty, the United States. Subsequent governments of Panama have attempted to rid the state of this agreement, on various grounds: but the agreement was never concluded under armed force applied against Panama (see p. 165); nor is it possible to argue that the 'people' did not give their consent as the government was able to act validly on their behalf. The rule of self-determination as discussed above (pp. 14-18) does not, as far as its internal aspects are concerned, entail any right to affect the validity of a treaty to which the executive has given its consent on behalf of the state. Thus a subsequent government cannot attack an international agreement on this ground.

11:1:4 State Succession and Changes of Governments

The prevailing view appears to hold that a change of government does not affect the position of the state under international law.[9] The state is not identical with its constitution and

> Changes in the government or the internal policy of a state do not as a rule affect its position in international law. A monarchy may be transformed into a republic or a republic into a monarchy; absolute principles may be substituted for constitutional, or the reverse; but though the government changes, the nation remains, with rights and obligations unimpaired. . . . The principle of the continuity of states has important results. The state is bound by engagements entered into by governments that have ceased to exist.[10]

A change of government also covers any revolutionary change according to numerous writers[11] although some Soviet writers have taken another view (see p. 170).

Cases which have dealt with the problem of changes of government and state continuity appear to show that certain rights and obligations are unaffected by a change of government. The right to sue, for example, or the right to continue an already instigated legal action, is—perhaps one should not say transmitted—enjoyed by any subsequent government.

In *The Sapphire*[12] a court held that the legal action of Napoleon III could be continued by a subsequent French government. And the Permanent Court of Arbitration held in a case between France and Peru which concerned claims by the French firm Dreyfus & Cie that the state had been bound by a decision of a previous dictator and a subsequent government could not declare his acts as null.[13] Equally if a treaty has been concluded by an unrecognized government it still binds a subsequent government.[14]

Even in radical changes of government, as for example in Russia after the Revolution the identity of the state is preserved. The Court of Appeal of the United States said in *Lehigh Valley Railroad Co. v the State of Russia*[15] that 'we must juridically recognize that the state of Russia survives' and consequently the Soviet Union could make claims in respect of an explosion, caused through negligence, in the United States before the Revolution and could continue legal action instigated by an earlier government for damages in the United States.

The famous *Concordat* case[16] also indicates that the German *Bundesverfassungsgericht* found that there was identity even of the Third Reich and postwar Germany.

Only a few international lawyers equate change of government with state succession, and then only if there has been a *coup,* and thus a revolutionary change of government. Feilchenfeld assumes—without analysing the revolutionary change of the Russian state—that the Soviet Union is a new state and a successor state of Russia.[17] O'Connell claims that there would be 'virtual irrelevance of the distinction, save in form, between state succession and government succession'.[18]

Some Soviet writers also regard the USSR as a new state which is not bound by Tsarist treaties.[19] But this view appears to be exceptional in the Soviet Union itself: the line is generally taken that although there is a 'new state' this is only so from a sociological angle; from a legal point of view there is full continuity because the October Revolution did not create any new subject of international law.[20] And, what matters more than the opinion of writers, state practice confirms that treaties concluded by Tsarist Russia were not subject to any general abrogation by the Soviet Union.[21] The Soviet Union considers itself bound by prerevolutionary treaties which 'do not contradict the foreign policy' of the USSR.[22] As far as military pacts or defence alliances are concerned this view may not be too unreasonable: there is ground to believe that a state cannot bind itself eternally to a particular political course.[23]

As far as some other treaties were concerned the Soviet Union could quite validly at any given time annul them, as they only granted *rights,* and no obligations, to Russia. Such treaties can always be renounced without the consent of the other parties.[24] This was, for example, the case with the Capitulation Treaties with China which granted certain jurisdictional privileges to Russian consuls in China[25] but which were incompatible with the principles of the USSR and with the equality of states. All such treaties were denounced.[26]

Thus, a change of government does not *ipso facto* abrogate existing treaties. On the other hand, a change of government, particularly a revolutionary change, may cause a rupture of diplomatic relations and, in some cases, *suspend* treaties and international agreements. But rupture of international relations does not necessarily revoke the recognition of a state, nor of its government.[27] And the Vienna conference on the law of treaties emphasized this by including certain additions to the draft presented by the International Law

Commission. Articles 63 and 74 of the Vienna convention on treaties now provide that

> The severance of diplomatic or consular relations between the parties to the treaty does not affect the legal relations established between them by the treaty except in so far as the existence of diplomatic or consular relations is indispensable for the application of the treaty. (Article 63.)

and

> The severance or absence of diplomatic or consular relations between two or more states does not prevent the conclusion of treaties between those states. The conclusion of a treaty does not in itself affect the situation in regard to diplomatic or consular relations. (Article 74.[28])

The Federal Tribunal of Switzerland had as early as 1923 emphasized that courts must enforce treaties in a state even after revolutionary changes of government in another state that is party to that treaty. This was held in the famous case *Lepeshkin v Gossweiler & Co.*[29] The Tribunal of the Canton of Zürich had, on the advice of the Swiss Department of Justice and Police, held that The Hague convention of 17 July 1905 concerning civil procedure was suspended with respect to Russia. The Federal Court of Appeal found that as the convention had not been abrogated and since internal legislation enacted to give the treaty force in Switzerland had not been revoked by a contrary act of the legislature, courts had to respect the treaty in question. For, said the Court, it is a universally recognized and incontestable principle of international law that modifications in the form of government and in the interior organization of a state can have no effect upon its rights and obligations under international law: in particular a state cannot after a change of government abolish obligations resulting from treaties previously concluded by that state.

Still there was in other countries a marked uncertainty with regard to the legal force of treaties with Russia after 1917. Great Britain treated them as largely suspended and subsequently notified the Soviet Union in 1924 that the recognition of the Soviet government of Russia will, according to the accepted principles of international law, automatically bring into force all the treaties concluded between the two countries previous to the Russian Revolution except where they have been denounced or have otherwise juridically lapsed.[30]

The Soviet Union answered that they were prepared to arrive at an 'understanding' with the British government to replace those former treaties which had either been denounced or had lost their juridical force as a result of events during or after the war.[31]

On 28 October 1924, the President of the Council, Minister for Foreign Affairs of France, also notified the Soviet government that he recognized the government *de jure* and that he proposed to open negotiations of a general nature. Until the outcome of these negotiations, treaties and arrangements between France or French citizens and Russia would have no effect.[32]

Treaties can thus be 'suspended' and come into effect again upon recognition of the new government. But it is important to emphasize that recognition cannot in any way be important in the question of the existence of a state.[33]

It is only reasonable to assume that international law cannot allow a state to relieve itself of previous international obligations by a mere change of government although a change of government may cause a state's 'discontinued consent' to a special group of treaties (see pp. 197-9).

But a change of government may be internationally relevant in several ways: under the rules of conflict of laws, for example, foreign courts will have to take changes of government into account when they examine the acts of a new government. For it is *new governments* as well as *new states* that may be recognized under international law if there has been a *coup d'état*.[34] It has been suggested that the same, or at least similar, rules apply to recognition of a new government as to recognition of states.[35] Recognition of a new government is connected with the question of who is competent to represent the state.[36] Recognition of a new government is relevant for the establishment of new diplomatic relations[37] and it is also important in so far as courts may have to take recognition into consideration when they adjudicate a case relating to confiscation or similar matters.[38]

11:2 THE REQUIREMENT OF CONSENT AND THE PROBLEM OF STATE SUCCESSION

11:2:1 Need for Consent *in casu*

If a change of government does not affect the continuity of a state or the validity of its treaties, what happens if the continuity *is* broken and there is a new state? Is that new state bound by the treaties concluded by its predecessor?

This is a problem which all new nations have had to face. Most writers claim that numerous treaties are 'inherited' by new states, whether or not they give their consent.[39] But it does not seem tenable to claim that treaties are automatically transmitted to a newly independent state. What has happened to the important requirement of consent which international law traditionally counts among the preconditions of a valid treaty? Brierly states that

> In principle the mere cession of a piece of territory from one state to another does not affect the treaty rights or obligations or either. Nor are these rights and obligations affected when part of an existing state breaks off and becomes a new state. They remain with the old state and the new state starts its career without any.[40]

But most writers have held other opinions: traditional law allowed for universal succession in analogy with private law.[41] The doctrine soon distinguished between personal and dispositive treaties.[42] 'Personal' treaties are those which establish contractual rights and duties of states. 'Dispositive' treaties require territorial performance —that is, they are 'real' treaties which 'run with the land'. A number of writers claim that dispositive treaties are transmitted to a new and independent state under the 'law' of state succession.[43]

Nowadays some writers are prepared to go even further. They feel they can dispense with the abovementioned distinction and that an *even wider category* than dispositive treaties are, in fact, transmitted to newly independent states. However, they feel that dispositive treaties are

> the hard core of the ensemble of transmissible treaties, and this

makes it imperative, if not to find a touchstone of 'dispositive' character, at least pragmatically to examine the classes of treaties which, on analogy with those held to be transmissible in the past, could well be included in the list of dispositive treaties.[44]

I do not question that a variety of treaties are transmitted to or 'inherited' by newly independent nations although the analogies to the private law of succession do appear inaccurate. But what I should like to establish, and what others have declined to discuss, is *how* the treaties are handed from an ex-mother country to an independent state. Various techniques such as devolution agreements between a metropolitan power and a new nation have been examined in detail;[45] but no one has discussed the form in which the *consent* of the new state is given.

An analysis of available instances of treaties transmitted to independent states shows that new states have invariably declared themselves willing to be bound by the treaties. The technique as far as multilateral conventions are concerned is that new states are 'consulted' or 'asked' *whether they consider themselves bound* by the conventions. For example, Cameroon, the Congo Republic (Congo-Brazzaville), Cyprus, Dahomey, Malagasy Republic, Mali, Niger and Republic of the Congo (now Zaïre) declared themselves bound by the Berne convention of 1886 for the protection of literary and artistic works. They did so on a specific request by the Director of the Bureaux internationaux réunis pour la protection de la propriété intellectuelle who asked the independent states to 'confirm' whether they proposed to continue to apply the Berne convention.[46] The fact that the newly independent states declared themselves to be contracting parties *by means of state succession* then merely implies that they chose to let their declaration have *retroactive effect* as from the date of independence.

Other newly independent states such as the Ivory Coast, Gabon, Upper Volta and Senegal preferred to adhere by *accession* which entails no retroactivity;[47] other new states declared that they did not wish to be bound.[48] Some states had been members of the Berne Union even before independence as international organizations often admit territories which are not yet independent. Thus, Tunisia and Morocco (French Zone) had joined the Berne Union in 1887 and 1917 respectively. They then ranked as contracting parties with equal voting rights and when they became independent there was no change of their status in the Berne Union; and there was no question of state succession.[49]

Similarly, the Administrative Council of the Permanent Court of Arbitration began, in 1955, to adopt a general procedure of consultation to regularize the situation resulting from the appearance of new states. As a result of decisions taken by the Administrative Council during the following two years after *consultation with the new states* nine states became contracting parties to The Hague conventions of 1899 and 1907, namely Australia, Cambodia, Canada, Ceylon, Iceland, India, Laos, New Zealand and Pakistan. These states had expressed a desire to adhere by state succession; the Philippines, on the other hand, declared that it did not consider itself bound by the convention.[50] The states which wished to succeed to these treaties showed their consent not only by an initial declaration but also by taking part in the decisions of the Administrative Council where they had a voice; subsequently, they also expressed their consent by means of diplomatic notes or letters.

New states have also by their own will succeeded to the Red Cross conventions: a statement by Nigeria declares that it agrees to be bound as from the date of independence[51] and Tanganyika stated that it would 'continue to be bound'.[52] An 'instrument of ratification' submitted by Sierra Leone was treated as a declaration of continuity which was more consistent with its wording.[53] Other declarations of continuity were construed as such even if they were not always clearly formulated.[54] Some other states, like Kenya, Uganda and Zambia chose to use the accession formula by which they did not succeed to obligations entered into on their behalf by the United Kingdom but became 'new parties'. The only difference between the succession formula and the accession mechanism is that the first method entails, with the express consent of the new state, the retroactive operation of the conventions as from the date of independence.

The same mechanisms have been adopted for a number of other multilateral conventions and for conventions establishing international organizations:[55] in each case in which new states have been 'approached' by the depositary or by the secretary-general of an organization, they have been asked 'whether they consider themselves bound' by the treaties in question. In a few cases the burden of action may rest with the successor state: it will be considered bound as by acquiescence unless it produces a declaration to the contrary. This is, for example, the case with the International Tin Council.[56] If the new states consider themselves bound, by declaration or acquiescence, the treaties will be considered to have been in continuous force all through the independence phase. This is often of little importance to a new state in the case of general lawmaking treaties like the Red Cross conventions. There is very little difference between acceding to such conventions and declaring oneself 'still bound': but the latter formula is easier and simpler. It is, therefore, submitted that far from constituting automatic state succession to conventions the procedure indicates that a new way to adhere to treaties has emerged. Adherence by state succession is the simplest and shortest method[57] available to a new state and if it desires to be a party to a convention it may, for convenience, adhere by the summary procedure of succession. But its *consent* is most certainly required in one form or another and, even if the question of retroactivity presents no problem, there are reasons such as simplicity and convenience why a state may choose to adhere by this method.

It may perhaps appear unfair that a state can rid itself of public debts by losing its identity under international law.[58] But although most writers uphold the theory that the debt should be divided between successor states the few cases there are on this matter do not support this contention.[59] The consent of new states is usually obtained in the form of a new treaty apportioning the debt between the various successor states.[60]

11:2:2 Devolution Agreements

It has been suggested that a devolution agreement is one way by which a new state can validly take over all previous treaty commitments assumed by its metropolitan country on its behalf.[61] Such devolution agreements have predominantly been concluded by Great Britain with its ex-colonies and other territories under its administration.[62]

It is questionable whether such devolution agreements have any effect in international law.[63] The Secretary-General of the United

Expression of a State's Consent

Nations has, at any rate, not accepted them as sufficient evidence of the consent of new states to multilateral conventions: unless he has heard from new states of their own accord that they wish to 'remain bound' by a convention he sends them a letter asking for their consent to succession. If there is a devolution agreement he phrases the letter in the following way:

> It is the understanding of the Secretary-General based on the provisions of the aforementioned (devolution) agreement, that your government recognizes itself bound, as from (the date of independence), by all international instruments which had been made applicable to (the new state) by (its predecessor) and in respect of which the Secretary-General acts as depositary. The Secretary-General would appreciate if you would *confirm this understanding* so that in the exercise of his depositary functions he could *notify all interested states* accordingly.[64]

This letter indicates two interesting points: first, it appears necessary for a new state to confirm the devolution; thus, it must give its consent in the form of a declaration addressed to the Secretary-General. This may indicate that the devolution agreement is some sort of internal understanding between the new state and its ex-metropolitan country on which not too much reliance may be placed, perhaps because it was concluded as a necessary link in the independence process when the new state may not have been a free agent able to express its own consent.

Second, the letter raises the question whether in any case two states, by an understanding between them, can substitute a contracting party to a multilateral convention. It does not appear unreasonable to let the other contracting states have a say in this matter.[65] At least in some cases, when it is not a question of a straightforward lawmaking convention like the Red Cross agreement, where both metropolitan country and the new state become bound, states may be reluctant to find a contracting party *substituted* by another. If they are notified, as they invariably are by a depositary of a multilateral convention, they can make their comments or protests or, by acquiescence, give their tacit approval to a state succeeding to another contracting party. But this is very different from allowing two states to decide on their own that state succession is to take place to a multilateral convention.

The most important point may be that it is questionable whether a metropolitan country can, by a devolution agreement or in any other way, bind a newly independent state to take over treaty obligations. Devolution agreements are registered with the United Nations as proper treaties; but it is questionable whether they can take effect outside the parties.

A devolution agreement between the Netherlands and Indonesia was invoked by the Netherlands when it was asked whether Indonesia was a contracting party of the Berne convention of 1886 for the protection of literary and artistic works. The government of the Netherlands declared that:

> The former Netherland East Indies, later called Indonesia were part of the Berne Union (under article 26) . . . Her Majesty's government of Indonesia has not altered the situation, bearing in mind the charter of transfer of sovereignty dated 27 December 1949. Indeed, article 5 of the transitional agreement concluded on the occasion of the transfer was adopted precisely with a view to situations such as this.[66]

The Swiss government 'accepted', as depositary of the convention, the standpoint of the Netherlands and notified other parties that Indonesia was a member. Indonesia, however, chose to denounce the convention in 1959.[67] But far from indicating that this

> implicitly confirmed the Netherlands government's view that Indonesia had become a member state of the Union by state succession[68]

it shows that Switzerland was at fault when it sought the consent to succession from the metropolitan power and not from the newly independent state; it also shows that a new state retains its power to decide for itself in these matters and that Indonesia could not become a member until it gave its own consent. The fact that it chose to denounce the convention—which would not be necessary unless it was a member—cannot be held to imply any acceptance of the Dutch view: denunciation was merely intended to clarify matters and Indonesia cannot be held liable for defraying expenses of the Union for the period when it did not even notify its class of contribution.[69]

11:2:3 'Dispositive' Agreements

Are 'dispositive' or 'real' treaties which deal with territorial or localized rights inherited by a new state?

It has been suggested[70] that 'dispositive' treaties present the prototypes of agreements which are automatically transmitted to successor states and this is held even by some who doubt that other treaties are inherited.[71] What then do such treaties concern? An analysis of examples given by writers[72] shows that a large category contain provisions *in rem*, concern rights of transit and other localized rights which have been treated above as general principles of modern international law. But newly independent states do not *succeed* to treaties on such matters without their own consent: they merely *accede* to the whole system of international law. New states do not have to give their approval to rules of the legal system which applies in the world community; they are automatically bound by all legal norms from the moment they emerge as states. But they have no obligation to take over treaties that provide for any expanded rights of transit—for example, they never have to tolerate the transit of military personnel and arms unless they have given their express consent to such operations (see pp. 105, 195-219). A newly independent state presumably cannot deny another state a minimum right of transit for civilians and goods—for example, to reach the sea or to reach international trade routes from which the other state otherwise would be precluded. But such rules, as has been suggested above (see pp. 71-5), form part of the general principles of law which must exist if the international community is to prosper.

Typical treaties *in rem* which, it is said, are automatically transmitted to a newly independent state are treaties concerning boundaries. But, surely, new states merely succeed to the legal situation resulting from the implementation of such treaties and not to the treaties themselves.[73] In other words, if there has been a boundary treaty and this has been respected and implemented for a certain time, a legal regime has thereby been created which is firmly established through customary law. As will be seen, there is not one case before an international tribunal where the court has not attached far more importance to the use of the boundary regime—that is, to custom—rather than to the provisions of a treaty. The only cases in which a court has held that a successor state is bound by a *treaty provision* are ones in which the new state has accepted the treaty regime, either expressly, or by acquiescence or by custom (see the *Right of Passage* case, supra, p. 72).

Other types of treaties which are thought to be 'dispositive' and therefore to be transmitted to independent states are those which concern military 'servitudes'. One writer claims that

> To treat the question [of agreement on military bases] as exclusively one of assimilation with a treaty of political alliance would appear to beg for it, for treaties of alliance are inherently terminable and contingent, whereas the *conveyance of base rights is expressly interminable*.[74]

But is this really possible? Is a newly independent state to be bound eternally by treaties establishing military bases under colonial rule? Treaties concerning military bases are precisely those which are usually contested by new states, not only in connection with state succession but also when one and the same state is bound by such a treaty but wishes to denounce it after a change of government or after a change of foreign policy. And, indeed, as some have noticed,[75] military base treaties are the expression of a very personal foreign policy.

The question will be examined in its broader context and not solely from the viewpoint of state succession.

11:2:4 'Servitudes'

Authors who defend the theory of acquired rights in public international law[76] usually also claim that a newly independent state can be validly fettered by *servitudes*. The definitions of such servitudes vary; but most protagonists of the idea of 'international servitudes' claim that it is a matter of rights related to territory, or so-called 'real rights'.[77]

In spite of the difficulties caused by any such analogy between national and international law the theory has become quite popular and few[78] have taken a firm stand against it, and then without developing their reasons for rejecting it.

But it is obvious that the theory of servitudes, as understood in Roman law and in most modern national systems of law, has its only real application when there is a change of ownership: it is then that the mechanism of servitude is brought into its fullest operation. It is only then that the *real* character of a servitude has its practical application: it is valid *erga omnes* and not only in the previous relationship between the owner of the property and the benefiting party or parties. The ownership of the property is limited to every new owner, and the parties who benefit may also, in many cases, subrogate their rights.

How then can the theory of servitudes apply in international law? Perhaps if there is a question of state succession one could see the similarities to the servitude situation under international law and then reference may be made to the considerations above relating to 'dispositive' treaties (see p. 179). But many writers accept that a theory of servitudes applies without the test of state succession; to them any contractual restriction of the territorial rights of a sovereign state is called a 'servitude'.[79] But then we could, in such cases, do well without such a legally confusing term which to most lawyers retains a specific meaning but in international law is bound to cause nothing but confusion.

Is the use of the term servitude not justified even in the case of state succession? Then, after all, there is a change of 'ownership', there is a new sovereign and then the theory could surely be brought to the test. One writer does claim that the test cases prove that the theory of servitudes does merit application in international law, that 'real' rights exist and 'servitudes' survive state succession.[80] But let us look at some of the test cases again; and we shall see that they are hardly conclusive as they do not prove 'that there are servitudes' which survive a change of sovereignty in the absence of specific consent by the successor state.

(a) *Free Zones Case*[81]

The treaty of Turin of 1816 had, when laying down boundaries between Sardinia and Switzerland, restricted the customs rights of Switzerland in the St Gingolph area. A Sardinian manifesto of 1829 settled certain details of the customs regime enjoyed by Switzerland under the treaty. In 1860 France succeeded Sardinia in the zones adjoining Switzerland and after this date France continued to respect Switzerland's privileges under the previous treaty. In 1919, however, France suggested that the customs regime should be revised, and a declaration of intent was incorporated in article 435 of the treaty of Versailles; under this article France and Switzerland declared themselves willing to agree to an amendment of the status of the zones. In 1932 a case was before the Permanent Court on whether the status of the zones could, as alleged by France, be abolished without the consent of Switzerland.

The Court found that the treaty of Versailles, by article 435, had not, as France contended, abrogated the earlier treaty on the customs regime; nor had the Sardinian manifesto abolished this regime. On the contrary, France had, as successor to Sardinia, *acknowledged* the regime created by its predecessor. Consequently, France was bound to obtain Switzerland's consent before altering the status of the zones.

The case is obviously concerned with contractual relationships and not with any 'real' rights which, contrary to the *serviens* power would survive: the rights created are only 'real' in so far as they relate to property; but not in the sense that they would survive a change of sovereignty in the same way as a servitude survives changes of ownership under Roman law. In this case, France had acknowledged, applied and respected the customs regime for *59 years,* between 1860, when it succeeded Sardinia in sovereignty, until 1919, when the article on proposed revision was included in the Versailles treaty. It is only reasonable to assume that such prolonged application of the regime implied a new contractual undertaking *vis-à-vis* Switzerland to accept, as a party, the regimes established under the treaty of Turin.

(b) Nile Waters Agreement
This is quoted by many as another example of 'servitudes' that survive a change of sovereignty.[82] However, it is shown on pp. 95-6 that a completely new treaty regime was actually introduced after the Sudan succeeded Great Britain in sovereignty.

(c) Panama Canal Agreement
Territorial restrictions in Panama have also been called a 'servitude'.[83] The nature of the regime in the Canal Zone is discussed on pp. 164-8, 200 and 214 and therefore this section will deal only with aspects relevant to the theory of 'servitudes'. The concessions have never been put to the test as there has not been any state succession. That the rights in themselves would merit being called 'servitudes'

as they are granted in 'perpetuity' may seem questionable. One important point, however, is that the use of the Canal may have surpassed the mere level of territorial restriction and may have become valid *erga omnes* in so far as all ships of all nations now enjoy the right of passing through the Canal (see p. 43). But such rights, although they apply *erga omnes*, are not necessarily best described as 'servitudes': they are no different from other transit rights granted under international law (see pp. 41-3). Similar rights exist under numerous national legal systems and are not then usually described as servitudes; for example, a right of way that members of a community have over someone else's property is, in many countries, of such a general nature that it is not accurate to classify it as a servitude, which, by its usual definition, is a benefit to one or more specified parties.

(d) *Guantánamo Base Treaty with Cuba*
The Guantánamo Base treaty has not been put to the test of state succession as it is only the government, not the state, which has changed in Cuba (see pp. 201-3). A new government is not, as has been pointed out, generally allowed to repudiate international agreements although other grounds for repudiation may exist (see pp. 168-72).

(e) *Hüningen Treaty*
It has been argued that this is a case of a 'negative servitude'; there would be an obligation not to fortify territory and this obligation would be transmitted to successor states.[84] But it appears that there were a number of purely contractual reasons why fortifications should still not take place and it is far fetched to use this case as proof of the existence of 'negative servitudes' which survive change of sovereignty.[85]

(f) *Åland Islands*
By an annex to the peace treaty of 1856 at the end of the Crimean War, Russia was pledged not to fortify the Åland islands in the Baltic; but the islands were not 'neutralized' under the treaty.[86]

Later Russia sought to rid itself of the obligations assumed under this annex and during the First World War Russia obtained the consent of England and France to fortify the islands. None of the other contracting parties protested against this. Only Sweden objected but then it had not been a party to the 1856 convention.

When Finland achieved independence in 1917 a new treaty was concluded between it and Sweden and Germany under which the fortifications on the Åland islands were to be demolished.

In 1920 the Åland islands were granted limited autonomy by Finland following attempts by the island population to secede from Finland and seek association with Sweden. In spite of the limited autonomy enjoyed under the 1920 arrangement, there was still much dissent among the islanders, and the matter was soon taken to the Council of the League of Nations on Britain's instigation. Finland agreed to submit to the Council's decision although it was not a member of the League. A three-party commission then declared that the obligation not to fortify the islands under the 1856 convention was still binding upon Finland, as the convention had created 'objective law'. Another commission established by the League decided, also in 1920, that the islands should remain under Finland's sovereignty in spite of the wishes expressed by the islanders to associate themselves with Sweden: a right to secession in such circumstances would create 'anarchy' in the international community (see p. 16). The commission further decided that the islands should be neutralized by a new treaty to be concluded by the relevant parties and that this treaty should also prohibit all fortifications on the islands.

On 24 June 1921 the Council of the League of Nations took a decision based on the recommendations of the commission. However, the Council did not repeat the expression 'objective law' but merely stated that a new international understanding would be desirable to safeguard the neutralization and nonfortification of the Åland islands. And, said the Council, 'For this purpose the 1856 convention ought to be replaced by a more far-reaching agreement concluded under the guarantee of all interested parties, including Sweden.'[87]

To ensure that such an agreement was concluded the Council requested the Secretary-General to 'invite' interested governments to nominate representatives for the negotiations of a new convention.

Only four months later, on 20 October 1921, a new convention was signed by the British Empire, Sweden, Finland, Denmark, Estonia, Lithuania, Latvia, Poland, Germany, France and Italy; but the Soviet Union was not a signatory. By the first article of the convention—which entered into force in 1922—Finland 'confirmed', as far as it was concerned, the declaration given by Russia in 1856 not to fortify the Åland islands. Under article 6 the islands were declared neutral in wartime although Finland retained the power to mine the territorial waters, 'if necessary'. The other contracting parties would 'guarantee' that the system of neutralization and non-fortification was respected and to this end they pledged themselves under article 7 of the convention to 'contribute to any measures decided' in the matter. And, if Finland was attacked, the other contracting parties could come to her rescue under the terms of the convention.[88]

The neutrality of the islands was violated during the Finnish Winter War 1939–40 but the other contracting parties to the 1921 convention did not take any action. Finland then mined the territorial waters of the islands and also erected fortifications without any protests from the parties to the 1921 agreement. On 22 October 1940 Finland concluded an agreement with the Soviet Union under which the islands were completely demilitarized and subjected to a new obligation of not being fortified. This agreement may appear to be incompatible with the earlier 1921 convention in so far as it made impossible any 'rescue' operation from the parties to the 1921 agreement.[89]

Finland entered the war again in 1941 against the Soviet Union and remined the territorial waters of Ålands and built new fortifications, without any protests from the parties to the 1921 agreement. However, in 1944 the preliminary treaty between Finland and the USSR again entered into effect by virtue of a special agreement signed in Moscow, and the obligation not to fortify the islands again became effective.

The 1921 convention may no longer be in force; the guarantees under the 1921 convention proved ineffective and Finland had to defend the integrity of the zone on its own. The agreement thus became one for which there was no quid pro quo.[90] The very fact that fortifications were erected on the islands contrary to the letter and spirit of the 1921 convention, and that this was done with the acquiescence of the other parties,[91] may perhaps contribute to the assumption that the 1921 convention has lapsed.

The Åland islands have been discussed in some detail as many writers refer to this example as a prototype of a servitude.⁹² It is clear from the historical facts that there was never any question of Finland's accepting any obligation without its own will and no question of ever dispensing with its consent concerning the demilitarization and the neutralization of the islands. It is equally obvious that there would have been little or no point in asking Finland to agree to a new regime on the islands in 1921 if Finland had simply 'inherited' the obligations assumed by Russia in 1856, as it would have done had there been a servitude properly so called.

Some writers may have been deluded by the expression 'objective law' used by the League of Nations commission; but it is more important to establish what state practice considered relevant rather than attaching importance to a wording which had no foundation in political realities.

Finally, in support of my contention that there never was any true 'servitude' of the Åland islands it may be pointed out that the 1921 convention has now probably lapsed, and it is difficult to see how this would ever be possible had there existed a servitude *in rem*.

(g) *North Atlantic Fisheries Arbitration*
The award in the *North Atlantic Fisheries* arbitration⁹³ appears to support my contention that servitudes do not exist in international law.⁹⁴ To allow for such rights *in rem* the consent of a successor state must be dispensed with and no right can pass on from one state to another as 'running with the land' without consent expressed in some contractual form by the state which is going to endure the 'servitude' in question.

(h) *Right of Passage over Indian Territory*
Another case sometimes referred to as relevant to the problem of 'automatic succession' of treaties is the case concerning *Right of Passage over Indian Territory* (see supra, p. 72).⁹⁵ Here the Court was even more emphatic in so far as it found that India had succeeded to the legal situation created by bilateral custom. Even if that custom had initially been created between Great Britain and Portugal, India had succeeded to the legal situation unaffected by the change occurring when India became independent. But India, as an independent state, had given its initial consent to the transit traffic and, as remarked elsewhere (pp. 72-5) a minimum right of transit may exist under general international law.

11:2:5 Boundary Regimes

Some of the cases discussed in the previous section on servitudes have also concerned boundaries. As has been shown, successor states, which no doubt often respect previously established boundaries, invariably have given their consent in one form or another to any treaty provisions relating to boundaries concluded by a preceding state. In this context it must be emphasized also that cases where boundaries are in fact established by treaty by no means constitute the general rule: in most cases there are no treaties and then a successor state succeeds to a legal situation created and continued by custom. A newly independent state could then conceivably object to established boundaries only in the first few years of its life as custom, as far as boundaries are concerned, must be held to develop fairly quickly in the absence of objections or protests. In some cases even the initial right to object may be waived by express approval of borders existing at the time of independence. Such acceptance has, for example, been given by heads of state within the OAU.[96]

The case of the *Temple of Preah Vihear*[97] has been thought to demonstrate the existence of a distinct group of dispositive treaties which, as they concern boundaries, should remain unaffected by state succession.[98]

The International Court of Justice had to consider the boundary treaty between Siam and France of 1904. Neither Thailand nor Cambodia disputed that the treaty now applied to them but it was alleged that there had been an error in executing the treaty by the Franco–Siamese commission which had demarcated the boundary. The Court decided the case giving primary importance to a map resulting from the demarcation and to Cambodia's acceptance of the boundaries depicted on that map. It is therefore clear that the Court found *consent* to the boundary situation essential: and any analysis of the pleadings on the preliminary objections filed by Thailand only reinforces this view.

It has been argued[99] that considerations which led to exclusion of boundary treaties from the rule concerning fundamental change of circumstance in the Convention on Treaties 'apply with the same force to succession of states, even though the question may have presented itself in a different context'.[100] On p. 155 it was suggested that boundary treaties should—contrary to the International Law

Commission's thinking—have been excluded from the article on coercion in the Convention on Treaties. But to hold that such treaties should be automatically transmitted to a *new* state—that is, a new subject of international law—as the Commission has done in the draft convention on succession, is to discard the vital principles of self-determination: a new state must retain at least some initial right to object against a regime established by its predecessor. It is highly unlikely that such protests would concern actual boundaries which, as has been pointed out, are rapidly settled under customary law. But it is important to retain this right to object because a treaty concerning boundaries may also include other burdensome provisions relating to the boundary regime which would, at least according to the Commission's draft article 29(b), be automatically binding upon a successor state. To fetter a newly independent state in this way by claiming that onerous provisions 'relating to the regime of a boundary'—for example, grazing rights[101] should bind a new nation without its consent appears not only incompatible with the principles of independence but also politically unrealistic.

A preceding state's opinion in this respect[102] is surely relevant: how can it matter under international law whether Great Britain, which may have ruled a territory as a colony, considers that a certain regime still 'applies' to a newly independent nation? Only the bordering nations themselves can, by their custom and acquiescing behaviour indicate that the regime is still in force. Unless the initial consent of a new state is made a precondition for the subsistence of any regime relevant to its territory the principle of equality is not fully implemented. On the other hand as has been pointed out, a border regime, whether established by a treaty or not, soon crystallizes into customary law unless objected to at the time of independence.

NOTES

1 Nozari, *Unequal Treaties and International Law* (Stockholm, 1971), pp. 212 et seq.
2 For exchange of telegrams, Morrison-Comager, ii, p. 446.
3 W. M. Malloy, *Treaties, Conventions, International Acts, Protocols and Agreements between the United States and Other*

Powers, vol. 2 (1910), pp. 1349 et seq.
4 2 Hyde, 1922 p. 9. Cf. infra, p. 204.
5 Lukashuk, 'The Soviet Union and international treaties', *Soviet Yearbook of International Law, 1959,* pp. 44-5.
6 Lukashuk, in *Soviet Yearbook of International Law, 1959,* p. 18; Pashukanis, *Ocherki po mezdunarodnomu pravu* (Moscow, 1935), X, pp. 156-7; Cf. Shurshalov, *Osnovaniia deistvitel 'nosti mezhdunarodnykh dogovorov* (Moscow, 1957), pp. 60-2.
7 Korovin, *Sovremennoe mezhdunarodnoe publichnoe pravo* (Moscow/Leningrad, 1926), p. 93.
8 *Yearbook of the International Law Commission 1958,* vol. 2 (New York: United Nations, 1958), pp. 18, 20.
9 G. Dahm, *Völkerrecht* (Stuttgart: Kohlhammer, 1958-61), vol. 3, p. 150. G. H. Hackworth, *Digest of International Law* (Washington: Government Printing Office, 1940-4), vol. 5, pp. 60 et seq.; C. C. Hyde, *International Law,* 2nd edition (Boston: Little, Brown, 1945), vol. 2, p. 1528; M. O. Hudson, *Cases and Other Materials on International Law,* 3rd edition (St Paul: West Publishing Co., 1951), vol. 4, p. 2381.
10 J. B. Moore, *A Digest of International Law* (Washington: Government Printing Office, 1906), vol. 1, p. 249; cf. vol. 5, p. 341.
11 Dahm, *Völkerrecht,* vol. 3, p. 150.
12 (1870) 11 Wall. 164.
13 *Republic of Peru v Dreyfus Brothers & Co.* (1888), 38 Ch. D. 348.
14 *Reports of International Arbitral Awards,* vol. 1, p. 369.
15 (1927) 2 F (2d) 396. There may also be an obligation to continue an action lest a claim be prescripted: see *Guaranty Trust Co. v US* (1938) 304 US 126, where the United States government tried to be paid certain money as succeeding the Soviet Union in certain claims under the Litvinov treaty; the other party claimed prescription. The Court found that the Soviet government could not have gone to court in the United states before 1933 when it was recognized, but the Kerenski government could have done this.
16 BVfGE 6 336.
17 E. H. Feilchenfeld, *Public Debts and State Succession* (New York: Macmillan 1931), pp. 535 et seq.

18 D. P. O'Connell, 'Independence and the problems of state succession', in *The New Nations in International Law and Diplomacy* edited by W. V. O'Brien (New York: Praeger/ London: Stevens, 1965), p. 25. Cf. Quadri, *Diritto internazionale pubblico* (Palermo, 1968), p. 334.
19 Bobroy, 'Mezhdunarodnopravovoye priznaniye sovetskogo Soyuza', in *Ucheniye Zapiski Leningradskogo Gosudarstvennogo Universiteta* (Leningrad, 1948), p. 74.
20 Kozhevnikov, in *Soviet Yearbook of International Law 1949*, p. 98.
21 See Harvard draft, *American Journal of International Law* (1935) suppl. p. 1119.
22 USSR Academy of Sciences, *International Law* (1957), p. 257 (official textbook).
23 See further, infra, pp. 195 et seq.
24 I. Detter, *Essays on the Law of Treaties* (London: Sweet & Maxwell, 1967), p. 89.
25 Detter, 'The problem of unequal treaties', *International and Comparative Law Quaterly* (1966), p. 1073.
26 Detter, *Essays on the Law of Treaties*, p. 86.
27 Eek, 'Nya Stater och nya regimer', *Festskrift Reuterskiöld* (Stockholm, 1945), p. 79.
28 Article 74 *in toto* was added at the conference at the instigation of Chile—UN Doc. A/Conf.39/C/L.3.
29 Switzerland, Off. Reports, vol. 49 I 488.
30 Toynbee, *Survey of International Affairs*, 1924, p. 491.
31 Toynbee, *Survey of International Affairs*, 1924, pp. 491 et seq.
32 This declaration was quoted by the Court of Appeal of Paris as authoritative in *Renault v Roussy-Renault Co.*, Journal du Palais (1927), II, 1; Dalloz (1926) II, 196, note Niboyet.
33 *Lepeshkin v Gossweiler & Co.*, Federal Tribunal of Switzerland, Off. rep., vol. 49, I, p. 488. Cf. Ti-Chiang Chen, *The International Law of Recognition* (London: Stevens & Sons, 1951), p. 129.
34 Hjerner, *Främmande Valutalag och Internationell privaträtt* (Uppsala, 1956), p. 333.
35 Eek, in *Festskrift Reuterskiöld*, p. 78.
36 Eek, in *Festskrift Reuterskiöld*, p. 69 and Hjerner, *Främmande Valutalag och Internationell privaträtt*, p. 333.

37 Hjerner, *Främmande Valutalag och Internationell privaträtt*, p. 337.
38 Hjerner, *Främmande Valutalag och Internationell privaträtt*, pp. 334 et seq., also for the question of whether courts are at all competent to decide that recognition has taken place. Cf. Eek, in *Festskrift Reuterskiöld*, p. 72.
39 See, in particular, D. P. O'Connell, *State Succession in Municipal Law and International Law* (London: Cambridge University Press, 1967), Bibliography, for numerous other works by the same author. Note that Waldock claims that a 'majority of writers' would favour the 'clean slate' theory 'Commentary on the draft convention on succession' UN Doc. A/8710.
40 J. L. Brierly, *The Law of Nations*, 6th edition edited by Sir Humphrey Waldock (Oxford: Clarendon Press, 1963), p. 153.
41 Grotius, *De Jure Belli ac Pacis*, bk. 2, ch. 9, sec. 9.
42 O'Connell, *State Succession in Municipal Law and International Law*, vol. 2, p. 232 and vol. 1, pp. 8 et seq. for a discussion on doctrine.
43 For example, Zemanek, 'State succession after decolonization', *Académie de droit international. Recueil des cours* (1968), iii, p. 242.
44 O'Connell, *State Succession in Municipal Law and International Law*, vol. 2, p. 232.
45 O'Connell, *State Succession in Municipal Law and International Law*, vol. 2, pp. 352 et seq, and infra, pp. 172-5.
46 *Le Droit d'auteur* (1960), p. 336.
47 *Le Droit d'auteur* (1961), p. 257; *Le Droit d'auteur (Copyright)* (1962), p. 44; *Le Droit d'auteur* (1963), p. 114 and *Le Droit d'auteur (Copyright)* (1964), p. 9.
48 For example, Cambodia, Korea and Taiwan; see *Le Droit d'auteur* (1960), p. 338, p. 337 and (1961), p. 27.
49 *Le Droit d'auteur (Copyright)* (1965), p. 5 and (1917), p. 73.
50 Rapport du Conseil administratif de la cour, 1957.
51 *UNTS*, vol. 404, p. 322.
52 *UNTS*, vol. 470, p. 374.
53 *UNTS*, vol. 544, p. 286.
54 Declarations by Cameroon, Congo (Brazzaville), Congo (Léopoldville), Dahomey, Gabon and Ivory Coast.
55 See, for example, UN Doc. CN.4/200 and Add. 1 and 2. On the

ILO, where a 'declaration' is necessary for succession, see Handbook on State Succession, p. 234; cf. GATT, ibid., p. 237.
56 Ibid., p. 238.
57 See, for a division of previous practice according to the length of the treaty-making procedure, Detter, *Essays on the Law of Treaties,* pp. 15 et seq.
58 See Feilchenfeld, *Public Debts and State Succession,* for examples.
59 For example, the *Ottoman Debt* arbitration (1925), *Reports of International Arbitral Awards,* vol. 1, p. 571.
60 For example, article 254 of the Versailles treaty.
61 O'Connell, *State Succession in Municipal Law and International Law,* vol. 2, p. 372.
62 All ex-British territories have concluded such agreements except the East African and the Central African states, Gambia and Guyana: for reference, see, for example, agreements with Burma, Cmd. 7360; Malaya, *UNTS,* vol. 279, p. 287; Ghana, *UNTS,* vol. 287, p. 233. France has also concluded such agreements with Morocco, Laos, Cambodia and Vietnam, see, Documentation française, 1956, Nos. 0328 and 0363; ibid., 1953, No. 0811 and 1954, No. 067. Italy has concluded one similar agreement with Somalia, UN Doc. A/CN.4/150, annex 5 and the Netherlands one with Indonesia, *UNTS,* vol. 69, p. 3.
63 Cf. Report by ILC, 1972, A/8710, Commentary to article 7 of Draft Convention on State Succession, p. 41.
64 UN Doc. A/CN.4/150, p. 122.
65 Cf. A. D. McNair (Lord McNair), *The Law of Treaties* (Oxford: Clarendon Press, 1963), p. 650.
66 UN Doc. A/CN.4/200.
67 *Le droit d'auteur* (1959), p. 79.
68 UN Doc. A/CN.4/200, opinion of the Secretariat.
69 *Le droit d'auteur* (1959), p. 2, n. 12.
70 O'Connell, *State Succession in Municipal Law and International Law,* vol. 2, pp. 231 et seq.
71 See Sir Humphrey Waldock's commentary to article 30 of the Draft Convention on State Succession, A/8710, p. 197.
72 See, O'Connell, *State Succession in Municipal Law and International Law,* vol. 2, pp. 262 et seq., and Zemanek, in *RCADI*

(1968), iii, p. 242. But see, in particular, Herbst, *Staatensukzession und Staatsservituten* (Berlin 1962), p. 176 who denies that 'real' treaties are transmitted in state practice. On contracts *in rem*—for example, concession contracts—and the operation of a rule of presumption (also relevant for issues of nationality and state property), see I. Delupis, *Finance and Protection of Investments in Developing Countries* (Gower Press, 1973), pp. 111 et seq.

73 Cf. Sir Humphrey Waldock's commentary as quoted in note 71, at p. 197.
74 O'Connell, *State Succession in Municipal Law and International Law*, vol. 2, p. 252. Italics added.
75 Zemanek, in *RCADI* (1968), iii, p. 239, and A. J. Esgain, 'Military servitudes and the new nations', in *The New Nations in International Law and Diplomacy*, p. 97.
76 See I. Delupis, *Finance and Protection of Investments in Developing Countries* (Gower Press, 1973), pp. 105-13 for criticism of the theory of acquired rights.
77 F. A. Váli, *Servitudes of International Law*, 2nd edition (London: Stevens & Sons, 1958), p. 309; O'Connell, in *The New Nations in International Law and Diplomacy* and O'Connell, *State Succession in Municipal Law and International Law*, vol. 2, p. 232.
78 See, Brierly *The Law of Nations*, p. 193, and Rousseau, *Droit international approfondi* (Paris, 1971), p. 145.
79 Váli, *Servitudes of International Law*, p. 309.
80 O'Connell, *State Succession in Municipal Law and International Law*, vol. 2, p. 232.
81 *Free Zones of Upper Savoy and the District of Gex, Judgment, 1932, P.C.I.J.*, Series A/B, No. 46, p. 96.
82 O'Connell, *State Succession in Municipal Law and International Law*, vol. 2, p. 244; Váli, *Servitudes of International Law*, p. 161.
83 Váli, *Servitudes of International Law*, pp. 253 et seq.
84 O'Connell, *State Succession in Municipal Law and International Law*, vol. 2, p. 255.
85 Rousseau, *Droit international approfondi* (Paris, 1971), pp. 145, 146 and Brierly, *The Law of Nations*, p. 193.

86 Castrén, Suomen kansainvälinen oikeus, Borgå, 1959, pp. 122 et seq.
87 Paragraph of the Decision, League of Nations, *Journal Officiel* (1920) spec. supp., no. 3.
88 Finlands Överenskommelser med Främmande Makter 1922 no. 1, G. F. de Martens, *Nouveau Receuil général des traités* (3 ème série) (Leipzig/Greifswald: Theodor Weicher/Hans Buske/Julius Abel, 1908-44), vol. 12, p. 65.
89 Cf. Castrén, loc. cit.
90 Cf. Detter, in *ICLQ* (1966), pp. 1081 et seq.
91 See, Detter, *Essays on the Law of Treaties*, pp. 92-3 on acquiescence to a breach of a treaty and p. 76 on revision of a treaty by acquiescence.
92 For example, O'Connell, *State Succession in Municipal Law and International Law*, vol. 2, pp. 267 et seq.; Váli, *Servitudes of International Law*, pp. 264 et seq.
93 Wilson, Hague Arbitration Cases, p. 174; Travaux de la Cour d'Arbitration de la Haye, 147.
94 Cf. Brierly, *The Law of Nations*, p. 191.
95 *ICJ Reports 1960*, p. 6.
96 OAU Resolution of 1964, article 3. Only Somalia and Morocco made reservations.
97 *ICJ Reports 1962*, p. 6.
98 Cf. Sir Humphrey Waldock's commentary to the Draft Convention on State Succession, A/8710, at p. 200.
99 Sir Humphrey Waldock as quoted in note 98, at p. 203.
100 Sir Humphrey Waldock as quoted in note 98, at pp. 203-4.
101 For example, grazing rights may, in this way, be dependent on a frontier regime—see I. Brownlie, *Principles of International Law*, second edition (Oxford: Clarendon Press, 1973), p. 361 and Latham Brown, *International and Comparative Law Quarterly* (1956) on the Ethiopian Somali dispute on grazing rights. On grazing rights see also supra, pp. 22 and 141.
102 Sir Humphrey Waldock as quoted in note 98, for example, at pp. 205, 210.

Chapter 12

The Problem of Unequal Treaties

12:1 IDENTIFICATION OF UNEQUAL TREATIES

There has not been much written on the problem of unequal treaties, a relatively new subject of international law. It is not new in the sense that there have not previously been any unequal treaties but in the sense that international lawyers in the past have not attached much attention to the problem.

What then is an unequal treaty? Some writers[1] equate *unequal* treaties and *imposed* treaties; but then we might as well do without the term. As shown above (pp. 141-63) the possibility of a new state denouncing a treaty concluded under coercion is not very great. However, the *material* inequality of a treaty could perhaps furnish a new ground for invalidity. By 'unequal treaty' I mean an agreement which is concluded on unequal terms—that is, its contents are unequal for one of the parties. Therefore, the material contents of a treaty determine whether it qualifies as unequal rather than the way in which it was concluded. Some writers have suggested that such 'unjust', 'enslaving' treaties which lack reciprocity should be void. I have previously pointed out in an article[2] that such suggestions are too far-reaching and cannot be accepted without qualifications. To regard them all as void would merely endanger the rule *pacta sunt servanda* without which international law cannot survive.

It must be pointed out that nearly all treaties lack full reciprocity:

they are never quite 'equal'. It is unrealistic to demand that every treaty should be concluded on the basis of perfect equality in the sense that its provisions give equal rights to all parties. Many multilateral conventions give, it is true, equal rights and obligations to all parties. But few treaties of a more contractual character fulfil this requirement of reciprocity. Niboyet once suggested that

> ... il aurait lieu de creuser la question de savoir si la notion d'égalité entre les états est ou non compatible avec des traités ne stipulant pas la même chose au profit de chacun.[3]

but he then had only a limited type of treaty in mind: those relating to issues of conflict of laws—for example treaties which provide for the application of foreign law in a certain country. Such treaties ought, perhaps, to provide for reciprocity. Even for this limited category of treaties Niboyet's theory may have flaws: for does a state ever have any fundamental *interest* in having its own laws applied by a foreign court in a litigation where its own subjects are not involved?

To suggest, in general, that *all* treaties must give equal rights and duties to the parties, and that unless they do they are invalid, is not only unrealistic but also endangers the principle *pacta sunt servanda* as much as the claim that any form of pressure invalidates an international agreement.

It is becoming increasingly clear that most writers and most states have a particular type of treaty in mind when they talk about unequal treaties: many agree that the Bizerta agreement[4] was unequal, and the Évian agreement,[5] the Panama agreement[6] and the Cyprus agreement.[7] But what do these agreements have in common? No writer has so far perceived any common denominator. To me it appears that all these agreements concern:

1 A newly independent state.
2 Restrictions of territorial sovereignty.
3 The establishment of military bases, although in the case of Panama this is only incidental to the canal concession.

But does it help international law or, indeed, does it help new states to suggest that all such treaties are 'void'? Is not a state free to restrict its sovereignty as it pleases and, for that matter, does not every treaty restrict sovereignty? Any treaty certainly limits the independence of a state and this is not necessarily undesirable. By acceding to numerous technical conventions on international cooperation states do become dependent, and interdependent, and they become dependent not so much on each other as on the common system established for the common good.[8] Such intertwining of relations under present international law is inevitable and promotes cooperation between nations. It appears virtually impossible to claim that a state should be precluded by international law from restricting its own independence. It follows from the very essence of sovereignty that a state has the right to bind itself.

It is clear also that a state has the right to enter into bilateral treaties on, for example, military bases and international law cannot regard all such understandings as 'void'. In many cases it is abundantly clear that it is the new state that insists on the military bases; it is not invariably a great power which 'forces' the developing state to accept the bases. When, for example, Britain withdrew forces east of Suez many developing states requested Britain to keep the military bases in their own interest.

Thus, treaties on military bases can validly be concluded by developing states; they are not void under international law and, in some instances, such bases have been established in the interest of the developing nations.

12:2 AGREEMENTS RESTRICTING TERRITORIAL SOVEREIGNTY AND THE THEORY OF CONTINUOUS CONSENT

Certain treaties restricting territorial sovereignty could be called 'potentially unequal treaties' for they are only fair and just in so far, and for so long, as the host state gives its full and free consent to the territorial restrictions such treaties impose. Treaties of this kind involve a waiver of sovereignty, which by definition can only be temporary as the state must, at any time, with fair warning and compensation for incurred cost, be entitled to resume the sovereign functions or to recover possession and control of the portion of territory over which sovereignty has been restricted. These rights of denunciation follow from the rules of independence and self-determination (see p. 13).

It may be argued that such a thesis would offend the maxim *pacta sunt servanda;* but there is only a *pactum* on the understanding that the host state may be entitled, at some future date, to renounce, for example, a military base agreement when the host country has radically changed its foreign policy. For otherwise international law would allow a state to bind itself, in perpetuity to the same and one political course and what then would have happened to the conflicting rules of self-determination?

Therefore, it appears to be politically realistic to suggest that military base treaties and other treaties delegating sovereign functions of a state *in its own territory* are operative for as long as they achieve the consent of the host state—in other words, they are treaties which need *continuous consent* to be valid. To some it may be technically more attractive to pretend that there has been a fundamental change of circumstances after a change of foreign policy and that therefore the host state is entitled under international law to denounce the treaty under the principle *rebus sic stantibus*. But, as I have observed previously,[9] that principle, even though it is incorporated in the new Convention on the Law of Treaties,[10] is a great threat to the stability of international law as it entitles any state to repudiate an agreement after a change of circumstances which, according to the subjective test of that state, is 'fundamental'.

It seems preferable to limit the principle *rebus sic stantibus* to entail a right to revise a treaty, or a right to call for negotiation of revision of certain provisions. But there is nothing static or rigid about international law which would not make it possible to suggest a new rule, namely that military base treaties, or other treaties which allow for the exercise of sovereign functions by others in a state's own territory, require the continuous consent of the host state. This would mean that such treaties, which are not all that numerous, would be dealt with in a special way. Other treaties which delegate, to an organization, sovereign functions in a state's own territory are those of the European Communities, which delegate to the EEC, Euratom and the ECSC the right to enact laws which bind, in the members' own territory, individuals as if they were local laws. The consequence of my thesis would then be that any member state does have the right to leave the Communities although there are no provisions for this effect in the treaties. It appears that few have suggested that members do retain this right of withdrawal[11] as the majority claim that the states that have signed the treaties have forever forfeited this right of leaving. It is politically unrealistic to suggest that a state should not retain the right to withdraw from the Communities when its consent to waive that portion of its sovereignty is no longer present. In other words, the EEC treaties require the *continuous consent* of a member state in so far as they entail delegation, in the state's territory, of its sovereign functions. This does not mean that a state could decide to leave the Communities without fulfilling other contractual obligations to the other member states and to the Communities themselves, nor does it mean that a state in reality would find it easy to withdraw without far-reaching economic effects as the whole point of the European Communities has been to tighten cooperation between the member states, and to make them economically and politically interdependent to such an extent that they may encounter numerous difficulties should they wish to separate themselves from the other member states to which they have, by integration, become organically tied.[12]

Another group of treaties which would be affected by this thesis that treaties which allow for the exercise of sovereign functions by other states or organizations within the territory of a state require continuous consent, are the capitulation treaties with China concluded by the middle of the last century. These treaties, by which China renounced its sovereign right of jurisdiction to some extent, by allowing foreign consuls to adjudicate their nationals inside Chinese territory, have often been referred to as 'unequal'. I have previously elaborated my views on those treaties.[13] There are hardly any agreements of this type today.

The main bulk of 'potentially unequal treaties'—that is, agreements which may be unfair or *become* unfair when a state, for example, changes its foreign policy or when there is no longer any adequate quid pro quo—remain the numerous military base agreements. Such agreements are not 'void' under international law as military bases may even be in the interest of a particular developing state. But, apart from the legal theory developed above, it is politically unrealistic to suggest that such treaties should, in the absence of a time-limit, be valid *in aeternum*. Let us examine actual state practice to analyse what happens when a developing state no longer wishes to retain foreign military bases.

12:3 POTENTIALLY UNEQUAL TREATIES: AGREEMENTS ON MILITARY BASES

(a) Panama Bases
The Panama agreement and the way it was concluded are discussed on pp. 164-8, 182 and 214. By this agreement the Varilla government agreed not only to grant a concession to the United States for a canal but also to allow the stationing of military personnel incidental to the canal concession to 'safeguard' the interests of the United States in the Canal Zone. The agreement provides that

> The Republic of Panama grants to the United States in perpetuity the use, occupation and control of a zone of land under water for the construction, maintenance, operation, sanitation and protection of the said Canal. . . .
>
> The Republic of Panama grants to the United States all the rights, power and authority within the zone mentioned . . . which the United States would possess and exercise *if it were the sovereign* of the territory within which the said lands and waters are located to the entire exclusion of the exercise by the Republic of Panama of any such sovereign rights, power or authority.

The United States was given extensive rights to station troops in the Canal Zone to guarantee free navigation. Panama bound itself to 'sell' further land, if necessary, to the United States. The United States enjoys a monopoly under the agreement to build roads and railways; workers should preferably be Americans and they are exempt from taxes in Panama. For these privileges the United States agreed to pay an annual fee of $250,000 in gold coin.[14]

The agreement was revised in 1955 and in 1959. In 1955 the United States relinquished the monopoly to construct roads and railways but insisted on retaining a right to build a motorway between the oceans. Furthermore, workers would no longer, under the 1955 revision, be paid differently; there would be no discrimination between Americans and citizens of Panama. All employees in the Canal Zone would reenter the fiscal sovereignty of Panama. The annuity for the canal concession was raised in 1955 to $430,000 in gold coin. By the 1959 revision the annuity was raised to $1,930,000.[15]

(b) Military Bases in Cuba
In 1898 the United States declared:

> First that the people of Cuba are, and of right ought to be free and independent.
> Second, that it is the duty of the United States to demand, and the United States does hereby demand, that the government of Spain relinquish its authority and government in the island of Cuba and withdraw its land and naval forces from Cuba and Cuban waters at once.
> Third, that the President of the United States be, and hereby is, directed and empowered to use all United States land and naval forces and to call into active service the United States militia of the various states to such an extent as may be necessary to carry these resolutions into effect.
> Fourth, that the United States hereby disclaims disposition or intention to exercise sovereignty, jurisdiction or control over said island, except for the pacification thereof, and asserts its determination to leave the government and control of the island to its people when it is accomplished.[16]

By a treaty concluded later the same year with Spain, however, the United States reserved for itself the right to occupy the island when it was evacuated by Spain. The United States subsequently took an active part in the drafting of a constitution for Cuba and guaranteed for itself both in the so-called Platt Amendment passed by Congress in 1901 and in the Constitution of 1902, certain land in Cuba for coaling and naval purposes. The same provisions were included in a Treaty of 16 and 23 February 1903 between the United States and the newly independent Cuba. The United States would

> exercise complete jurisdiction and control over and within said areas and the right to acquire (under conditions to be hereafter agreed upon by the two governments) for the public purposes of the United States, any land or property therein by purchase or by exercise of eminent domain with full compensation to the owners thereof.

For the leasing of the naval and coaling stations the United States would, under a supplementary agreement of 2 July 1903, pay an annuity in gold coin as long as it retained the use of the lands. An agreement on relations between the two countries concluded in 1904 specified that

> Until the two contracting parties agree to the modification or abrogation of the stipulations of the agreement in regard to the lease of lands in Cuba to the United States of America for coaling and naval stations, signed by the President of the Republic of Cuba on 16 February 1903 and by the President of the United States of America on the 23rd day of the same month and year, stipulations of that agreement with regard to the naval station at Guantánamo shall continue in effect. The supplementary agreement in regard to naval or coaling stations signed between the two governments on 2 July 1903, shall also continue in effect in the same form and on the same conditions with respect to the naval stations at Guantánamo. So long as the United States of America shall not abandon said naval station at Guantánamo neither of the two governments shall agree to a modification of its present limits and the station shall continue to have the territorial area that it now has, with the limits that it has on the date of the signature of the present treaty.

Thus, by this latter agreement of 1904 the bases in Cuba were limited to the Guantánamo station; bases in northwestern Cuba, in Bahía Honda, would be discontinued.

The Guantánamo base is still in use by United States naval forces and the agreement is listed by the United States State Department as a treaty still in force. Some writers claim that it has not been repudiated by Cuba; in this context they have quoted Fidel Castro's speech of 6 January 1959 where he declared that 'all international commitments and agreements in force will be fulfilled'.[17]

On the other hand, according to a publication by the Ministry of Foreign Relations of Cuba, Castro has, in numerous other speeches, questioned the validity of the agreement although he repeatedly asserted that Cuba will not resort to force to 'solve the problem'. The agreement, he suggested, was not a real treaty validly concluded by the two parties. It was merely a unilateral decision by the United States Congress, by means of an amendment imposed on our Constitution after the Constitution had been imposed on us by the United States, by an Act of Congress, threatening Cuba with not leaving the country, if said amendment was not accepted.[18]

(c) Soviet Military Bases in Finland

The peace treaty of 1940 between the USSR and Finland provided that Finland agreed to rent to the Soviet Union, for thirty years, the Hangö peninsula and its surrounding waters for the establishment of a naval base. The base was taken by the Germans during the war and a new provision for a Finnish lease to the Soviet Union was embodied in the armistice agreement concluded in 1944 between the United Kingdom, the USSR and Finland.[19] The USSR was to be given a lease in Porkkala-Udd, and this time for fifty years. Right of transit to the base was also guaranteed for military personnel from the USSR across the territory of Finland.[20] This provision granting a lease in Porkkala-Udd was reiterated in the 1947 peace treaty (treaty of Paris) concluded between the Soviet Union and Finland.[21] But in 1955 the two parties agreed by a new treaty that the lease would lapse; it was discontinued the same year.

(d) Military Bases in Jordan

When Transjordan (now known as Jordan) became independent in 1946 an agreement on military bases was concluded between the new state and the UK. The agreement was embodied in the treaty of alliance which recognized Transjordan's independence and which provided for mutual assistance in case of attacks by third states. The provision on military bases entitled the UK to station armed forces in Transjordan in places where they were stationed upon the termination of the British mandate and 'in such other places as may be agreed upon'. Transjordan undertook to provide all facilities necessary for their accommodation and maintenance and the storage of ammunition and supplies, including the lease of any land required. And, the agreement stipulated, 'Any private sites on such land will, if necessary be expropriated.' The treaty with respect to the military bases was to be in force for 25 years; but the parties agreed in 1948 to replace it by a new 20-year Anglo-Jordanian agreement which, in turn, was terminated in 1957.[22]

(e) *British Bases in Libya*
British forces had been present in Libya since the Second World War: on 11 November 1943 when the Allies had forced Rommel to retreat Britain announced that the province of Cyrenaica was under British occupation. After the war, Britain—as well as the United States—maintained in the United Nations that it was necessary to retain their forces and their bases in Libya in order to preserve peace and security. On 21 November 1949, when the United Nations adopted a resolution recommending Libya's independence, British forces were already present in Cyrenaica; American forces were stationed near Tripoli and French forces in Fezzan.

In connection with Libya's independence on 24 September 1951 an agreement for financial aid from Britain was concluded; another agreement on British military bases concluded by the Amir before independence was recognized by the new government as binding upon Libya.[23] Both these agreements expired in 1953 when they were substituted by a 'permanent' agreement on friendship. This agreement contained provisions on mutual aid in the event of outside attack as well as detailed rules on the military bases similar to those laid down in the Jordan agreement (see p. 203). On 8 December 1969 Libya questioned the validity of the 1953 treaty and claimed that it had been concluded without the consent of the 'people'.[24] Britain agreed to withdraw its forces starting on 13 December, one week after the request and pledged itself to complete evacuation not later than 31 March 1971.[25]

(f) *Military Bases in the West Indies*
According to an agreement concluded in 1941 between the United Kingdom and the United States land would be leased by the United States for 99 years for the purpose of naval and air bases in the West Indies, Newfoundland, British Guiana and Bermuda.

The Federation of the West Indies, which had been set up in 1958, declared itself entitled to form its own alliances generally and to determine what military bases should be allowed. The West Indies was free to reject or to accept the 1941 agreement as basis for future negotiations. A new defence areas agreement was then signed between the United States and the Federation of the West Indies, the following year.[26]

When the Federation was dissolved in 1962 devolution agreements signed by Jamaica, and Trinidad and Tobago provided that the independent states would assume obligations arising from treaties concluded by the British government and by the government of the Federation of the West Indies. It has been argued that this instance proves that military base treaties are transmitted at state succession.[27] But the newly independent states had, only the previous year, given their collective consent in the form of a decision taken by the independent Federation of the West Indies, where in such matters they acted by unanimity.

(g) *The Sandbank Agreement*
By a treaty signed on 9 September 1952 between the United Kingdom and the Federal Republic of Germany the parties agreed on a practice bombing range near Cuxhaven in Germany, the 'Sandbank Range'. The United Kingdom would be entitled to use this range for practice bombing. The German government would bear the whole cost of the fixed installation for the bombing range. There is no provision, on the other hand, for any rent to be paid to Germany for the use of the bombing range.

The agreement stipulated that it was to be in force for five years. After this period it could be prolonged by mutual consent under a special clause.[28]

It is interesting to note that there is no evidence of a formal renewal of the agreement but it was 'considered to be in force' until 3 May 1958 when the United Kingdom ceased to use the base. If there was some understanding between the parties it was never formalized into a new treaty.

The agreement also raises the interesting question whether it, in fact, was a treaty properly so called within the constitutional provisions of West Germany. It was never transformed into internal German law as required under the German Constitution[29] and no decision to this effect ever appeared in the German *Gesetzblatt* during the relevant period.

(h) *Bizerta Agreement: Bases in Tunisia*
In 1881 the treaty of Bardo was concluded between France and the Bey of Tunis and under this agreement France established direct administration in Tunisia.[30] A further treaty, the treaty of La Marsa,

specified the details of the regime.[31] In 1955 France recognized the 'internal autonomy' of Tunisia excluding control of defence and foreign affairs, and the following year Tunisia was given independence.[32] Tunisia protested at the presence of French troops which remained in the country at the military base of Bizerta. Eventually, France agreed to conclude another agreement in 1958[33] but under this agreement France went no further than stating that only troops who were based in Tunis by virtue of earlier treaties would remain; negotiations would continue on a provisional regime for Bizerta, pending a definite agreement.

Since 1952 Tunisia had attempted in the United Nations, by invoking article 35(2) and article 1(2) of the UN Charter, to rid itself of French administration and rule.[34] In 1961 Tunisia claimed, by representations to the Security Council, that France by a mere promise of an agreement, a *pactum de contrahendo,* as in 1958, did not acquire any legal title for retaining troops in Bizerta.[35]

Open hostilities started in Tunisia on 19 July 1961 and the question of French military bases was discussed both by the Security Council and the General Assembly.[36] The General Assembly took a resolution on 21 August 1961, and it is interesting to note its wording:

> *The General Assembly* . . .
> 2. *Recognizes* the sovereign right of Tunisia to call for the withdrawal of all French armed troops in its territory without its consent;
> 3. *Calls upon* the governments of France and Tunisia to enter into immediate negotiations to devise peaceful and agreed measures in accordance with the principles of the Charter for the withdrawal of all French armed forces from Tunisian territory.[37]

Thus, the General Assembly did not even refer to the previous treaties which had granted France rights to maintain troops in Tunisia, nor did it refer to the question of state succession. It appears that previous treaties, at least in so far as they dealt with military bases, were held not to be transmitted to a newly independent state; and furthermore, the *consent* of that state is required for the presence of any military foreign forces.

(j) Évian Treaty: Bases in Algeria

According to an agreement of 18 March 1962 between France and the FLN government of Algeria, a new state of Algeria was to be established. The agreement provided[38] for measures to be taken to end strife in the area; there were provisions relating to the independence of the country and the organization of elections. There were also provisions which allowed France to use the Mers-el-Kebir base as a naval and air base for 15 years, and France would also have the right to use certain other airports and military bases. But it would be the obligation of Algeria to ensure that the bases had adequate water and electricity and Algeria also pledged itself to safeguard the security of the military bases. France was furthermore granted rights to the Saharan soil and subsoil, in particular certain rights of mining already acquired by France or French companies. For a period of six years French prospecting companies would be given priority to new sites.

In this case there was no previous treaty to be transmitted to a successor state. But a suceeding government declared itself entitled to repudiate, in 1965, the parts of the agreement which concerned military bases. All French troops left that same year.[39]

(k) Morocco Agreement

In 1950 France and the United States concluded an agreement for military bases in Morocco, which was then a French protectorate. The Sultan of Morocco protested at the time that France had not asked for the protectorate's consent. When Morocco became independent in 1956 a devolution agreement was signed between the new state and France. This agreement provided that Morocco would assume all obligations resulting from treaties concluded by France on behalf of Morocco and from such international instruments relating to Morocco as had not given rise to observations on its part. As the military base agreement had given rise to such observations it would not continue in operation.[40]

France admitted that the agreement on military bases in Morocco had been concluded in its own name and not in the name or on behalf of Morocco. The bases had been the 'property' of France and of the United States under the previous 1950 agreement.[41]

The United States attempted to negotiate a new agreement with the independent state on military bases in Morocco but for some reason the negotiations came to a halt. The United States decided to withdraw its forces from Morocco by the end of 1963 and made no demand for compensation for the $410,000,000 installations.[42]

(l) New Techniques: The Malta Agreements
If international lawyers have devoted comparatively little attention to military base treaties and their character, politicians have certainly not been unaware of the hazards of such agreements. In the case of Malta, the United Kingdom preferred not to conclude a straightforward lease agreement whereby the lessee would pay 'rent' for the base area. Instead, an agreement granting the right to station armed forces in peace and in war remained silent on this point; but under another agreement on 'financial assistance' large sums would be paid to Malta.

Recent events have shown that this technique has not been too successful and recent negotiations bear witness to the fact that a new state may well prefer a straightforward lease agreeement.

On the same day as Malta was given independence, 21 September 1964; it concluded an agreement with the government of the United Kingdom whereby the United Kingdom

> in peace and in war [was granted] the right to station armed forces and associated British personnel in Malta and to use facilities there for the purposes of mutual defence, the fulfilment of international or Commonwealth obligations, the assistance of other nations in maintaining their independence and stability or the protection of the citizens of the United Kingdom and Colonies or of Malta.[43]

Malta was bound not to allow any other forces to be stationed on the island. The agreement was concluded for a period of ten years and contained no clause allowing for premature denunciation.

Details on the stationing of forces were set out in an annex to the treaty.[44]

Another agreement dated the same day provided that

> Subject to provisions of the present agreement the government of the United Kingdom will during the three years ending on 31 March 1967 make available to the government of Malta

amounts not exceeding in total £18.8 million . . .

article 2. During the seven years beginning on 1 April 1967 but subject at all times to the continued operation of the agreement on mutual defence and assistance, the government of the United Kingdom will, subject to the provisions of the present agreement, make available to the government of Malta amounts not exceeding in total £31.2 million. . . .

But the 'assistance' given was not to be spent at the Maltese government's own discretion. 'As much as possible' should be spent on United Kingdom goods and services[45] and, furthermore, not all aid would be 'gifts': 25 per cent of aid up to 31 March 1969 would be 'loans bearing interest related to the current lending rates of the United Kingdom Exchequer'. However, there were no provisions on the modes of repayment. A further million pounds sterling was to be made available, also conditional on the continued application of agreement on mutual defence and assistance, over a ten-year period for the restoration of historic buildings by way of 'gift'. Some of the financial assistance to Malta would be granted in the form of loans made out to Bailey (Malta) Ltd, for the completion of improvements of a civil dockyard.[46] The company was guaranteed the continued concession of the dockyard by a separate exchange of letters dated 24 September 1964.[47]

Thus, the assistance which was to be given to Malta as 'gifts' was only given on condition that the agreement on military bases was still operative. Secondly, assistance in the form of 'loans' would indirectly benefit the donor, either in the form of payment for UK goods, or in the form of improvements to installations in Malta which the United Kingdom as military lessee could not find altogether uninteresting. But there was no compensation for the lease itself.

In spite of the fact that there was no denunciation clause, Mr Dom Mintoff, who became Prime Minister after general elections in June 1971, did denounce the military base agreement and issued an 'ultimatum' to the British to leave unless an increased offer for 'rent' was produced. British troops were to be allowed to 'pack' what they could. However, many forms of investment in military bases are such that they cannot be removed. There are airstrips and hangars on which a military lessee may have spent considerable sums, relying on the extended validity of a base agreement. If then the agreement is denounced prematurely the lessee could, in analogy with the rules on nationalization in international law, validly demand compensation.[48] On 26 March 1972 Mr Mintoff succeeded in concluding a new agreement with Britain for the military bases on the island. Under article 7 of this new agreement Britain will pay an annual 'rental' of £14 million in two instalments a year; although Britain has a separate agreement with NATO to offset the cost it is only Britain which is Malta's contracting partner. However, under the separate NATO agreement Britain is to receive £8.75 million from other NATO members for the Maltese bases and therefore Britain's own contribution under the new agreement of £5.25 million is not substantially higher than what it previously 'gave' as 'aid' to Malta: by a separate undertaking Malta has been promised a further £2,500,000 by Italy for Britain's continued use of the bases. In January 1973 Malta also obtained a pledge from NATO members—except Britain—to pay an additional 10 per cent to make up for losses through the floating of the pound.

According to the 1972 agreement Luqa airfield, which is Malta's base for military and civil air traffic, will have a 'single and undivided organization for the control and operation of essential airfield services'.[49] This organization will be provided by Britain although it is agreed that Maltese staff will be trained to operate Luqa as a civil airport to international standards.

Britain, and NATO, are granted the use of certain military facilities in the island; but Britain's approval is required *in casu* for the use of any facilities even if another NATO party should wish to make use of such facilities. However, Malta is free to grant any state the use of facilities in harbours other than those parts reserved for the exclusive use of Britain; those parts of Luqa airfield which are not occupied exclusively by Britain may also be used by other states without special permission from Britain. It may be surprising that although Malta may not, under article 2, allow any party to the Warsaw Pact such facilities, the forces of any other state may make use of the limited facilities: furthermore, any such other state may keep 'military missions' in Malta without Britain's approval being required. Even the Warsaw Pact members appear to be entitled to 'temporary' use of harbour facilities or of Luqa airfield should Malta so wish. Article 4 specifies that 'nothing in this agreement is intended or shall preclude the government of Malta from permitting *any foreign government mission* to make temporary use of the harbour facilities or the airfield at Luqa for the purpose of entering or leaving Malta.' However, the agreement does not define what is meant by a 'government mission': can it also be an armed squadron?

(m) Another New Type: the Cyprus Bases
A constitution for Cyprus was drafted at the Zürich and London conferences in 1959. The constitution was dated 6 April 1960 but the island was given formal independence four months later, on 16 August 1960. The same day a treaty concerning the establishment of the Republic of Cyprus was signed by Great Britain, Greece, Turkey and Cyprus itself. Under this treaty certain areas of the island would remain under the 'sovereignty' of the United Kingdom, namely the Akrotiri Sovereign Base Area and the Dhekelia Sovereign Base Area. Annex B, Part I,1, of the treaty further provides that the government of the United Kingdom shall have the right to:

> obtain after consultation with the government of the Republic of Cyprus, the use of such additional small sites as the United Kingdom may, from time to time, consider technically necessary for the efficient use of its base areas and installations in the island of Cyprus.[50]

By another annex Cyprus further agreed not to claim sovereignty over certain parts of its territorial waters.

Another treaty, called the treaty of guarantee, was also concluded on 15 August 1960 between Greece, Turkey, the United Kingdom and Cyprus. By this treaty Greece, Turkey and the United Kingdom undertake to guarantee the independence of Cyprus and Cyprus, on its part promises to

> respect the integrity of the areas retained under United Kingdom sovereignty at the time of the establishment of the independence of Cyprus.[51]

In the event of breach of this treaty, Greece, Turkey and the United Kingdom agree to 'consult' together with respect to the representations or measures that might prove necessary. But if common action should prove impossible, each of the three guaranteeing states reserves the right to take appropriate action.

A third treaty, the treaty of alliance,[52] concluded on the same day between Cyprus, Greece and Turkey, commits the parties to resist any attack on the independence or territorial integrity of the Republic of Cyprus, and provides for the stationing of mainland army contingents.

These two latter treaties are both enshrined in the Cyprus constitution. This constitution which was drafted by the guaranteeing states provides, in article 181, that

> The treaties guaranteeing the independence, territorial integrity and the constitution of the Republic concluded between the Republic and the Kingdom of Greece and the Republic of Turkey and the United Kingdom of Great Britain and Northern Ireland and the treaty of military alliance concluded between the Republic of Cyprus, the Kingdom of Greece and the Republic of Turkey, copies of which are annexed to the constitution as Annexes I and II shall have constitutional force.

Furthermore, two treaties are to be incorporated in the constitutional law of Cyprus but are to have an even higher rank than many provisions of the constitution itself. For article 181 is included among the articles which an annex to the constitution lists as *unamendable*. Such articles cannot in any way be amended, whether by way of variation, addition or repeal.

Although Archbishop Makarios, President of Cyprus since independence, has sometimes indicated that he is not 'happy' that the base areas are retained under British sovereignty, the validity of the treaty of establishment has never been questioned by the Cyprus government; in practice relations between the sovereign base areas and the Republic of Cyprus are very good.

The Cyprus government would certainly like to see the treaty of guarantee and the treaty of alliance abolished. In January 1964 Archbishop Makarios in fact announced that he had abrogated these agreements but, under international pressure, he subsequently conceded that his statement had been no more than a declaration of intent. However, on 4 April 1964 he notified the Turkish government that he had abrogated the treaty of alliance unilaterally. The British, as well as the Greek and Turkish governments regard the treaty as still in force. The General Assembly resolution on the 'sovereign equality' of Cyprus, taken on 18 December 1965, declared that

> The Republic of Cyprus, as an equal member of the United Nations is in accordance with the Charter, entitled to, and should enjoy, full sovereignty and complete independence without any foreign intervention or interference.[53]

This resolution has, by some Greek Cypriots been represented as invalidating the 1960 treaties. At any rate, one could safely say that the renegotiation of the two treaties is high on the Cyprus government's list of priorities. In practice, this is unlikely to happen until an intercommunal constitutional settlement has been reached. Because of the disturbances in Cyprus the United Nations forces in Cyprus—initially established by the Security Council with the consent of Cyprus on 4 March 1964—will remain in Cyprus at least until 15 December 1973, in the expectation that by then sufficient progress towards a final solution will make possible a withdrawal or substantial reduction of the force.[54]

In the complex network of international agreements and constitutional safeguards devised for Cyprus, let us for a while concentrate on the character of the sovereign base areas. The treaty under which these were established has not been questioned by the Cyprus government. Thus, the government continues to give its consent not only to the exclusion of its sovereignty from these areas but also to the presence of British forces. Does international law preclude a state from granting independence only to a part of a territory if it chooses to retain a portion of that territory for itself? The question would have been easier to answer if it referred to two neighbouring territories; then it appears to be quite in order for the metropolitan state to draw the borders as it wishes. But in the case of a far-off island it has been claimed that considerations of territorial integrity demand that no portion is retained at the time of independence: incomplete territorial devolution may not be in accordance with international law.[55] From this point of view the sovereign base areas would then really constitute leases, which technically could be discontinued. But no rent is paid for the 'leases'; but by another treaty the United Kingdom made available £12 million during a five-year period ending 31 March 1965 as 'financial assistance'[56]—a technique similar to that used in the case of Malta (see pp. 208-11). In addition to the assistance paid 'by way of grant' the United Kingdom also undertook to pay £500,000 towards the construction of a new civil air terminal at Nicosia airport, another £340,000 for the construction of roads for the purpose of bypassing the Ayios Nikolaos region of the Dhekelia Sovereign Base Area.[57]

12:4 'SOVEREIGN' RIGHTS OVER FOREIGN MILITARY BASES

In some cases a state may retain 'sovereignty' over military bases when it grants independence to a new state previously under its rule. This has been done, for example, in Cyprus. But is this real sovereignty? Sovereignty can be transferred: would it be possible for the United Kingdom to 'sell' its bases in Cyprus to someone else?

The same problem is presented by Panama: could the United States transfer its 'sovereignty' over the Canal Zone? If it were true sovereignty this would be possible. Conversely, could Panama transfer *its* 'sovereignty' over the Zone? It has been suggested that one way of defeating the rights of the United States under the treaty would be for Panama, which presumably retains the power of disposition, to transfer its 'residual sovereignty'; the treaty would then be a *res inter alios acta* not affecting a new 'residual sovereign'.[58] Panama might well, in such a case, be released from any obligations but it would also have lost the Zone altogether.

However, does the United States really enjoy *sovereignty* in the Canal Zone? The test could be whether the *actual territory* of the Zone *forms part* of the United States.

In one case the Supreme Court of the United States pronounced itself on this question. This was in *Canal Zone v Coulson*[59] where the Supreme Court held that

> It is apparent from an examination of the treaty that the United States is not the owner in fee of the Central Zone, but has the use, occupation and control of the same in perpetuity as long as they comply with the terms of the treaty and pay the $250,000 in gold coin of the United States to the Republic of

Panama. . . . We are therefore of the opinion that the Canal Zone . . . is not such territory that the Constitution would be legislative, and of its force carry its rights, privileges and limitations into it.

And, in *Luckenback Steamship Company v the United States*[60] the same Court held that ports in the Canal Zone are, in relation to the United States, to be regarded as 'foreign ports'. In *Re Cia. de Transportes des Gelabert*[61] the Supreme Court of Panama held that the airspace over the Canal Zone comes under the sovereignty of Panama. Also in *Re Burriel*[62] and in *Re Kenneth Robert Bartlett*[63] the Supreme Court of Panama held that the Canal Zone does not form part of the United States and that it is not foreign territory.

It does not seem to be necessary to use concepts such as 'parallel sovereignty' or 'residual sovereignty'[64] in the case of the Canal Zone. A careful analysis shows that there never was any transfer of a *totality* of sovereign functions but only of some—however far-reaching—sovereign rights. There is in fact little difference between the Canal Zone regime and that of other military bases although certain rights such as the right of jurisdiction may be more extensive than in most agreements (see pp. 105-7). The assumption that the United States enjoys some *sovereign rights* but not full sovereignty is supported by the fact that Panama's 'fiscal sovereignty' was 'reintroduced' into the Zone in 1955 (see p. 200).

The rights of the United States in Panama were not so extensive as to deprive Panama altogether of her sovereignty within the Canal Zone. In the Organization of American States Panama charged the United States with 'aggression' against Panama's civilian population within the Canal Zone in 1964. Such aggression amounted, claimed Panama, to a threat to peace in America. Panama asked for a meeting of consultation under the Rio treaty; article 6 of this agreement provides for deliberation of the Organ of Consultation in cases of aggression which are not armed attacks. Such meeting took place and a committee was established to investigate Panama's allegations. It was never suggested that the 'sovereign' rights of the United States in the Canal Zone would preclude such investigations.[65]

If the rights of the United States are so circumscribed in Panama where a treaty has granted 'sovereign' rights then the rights of states that have been granted a mere lease without such 'sovereign' privileges must be even more limited. In *Cornell et al. v Vermilya Browns Co.*[66] the Supreme Court of the United States held, with respect to a lease agreement with the United Kingdom, that the leased area in Bermuda was under the sovereignty of the lessor—that is, the United Kingdom—and that it was not the territory of the United States 'in a political sense, that is a part of its national domain'. Similarly, the same Court held in *Spelar v the United States*[67] that the United States did not have sovereignty over a leased air base in Newfoundland: it was a 'foreign country' within the meaning of the Federal Tort Claims Act. On the other hand, the lessee—in this case the United States—can, in a leased area, lay down regulations on fair labour standards providing for minimum wages and maximum hours for employees in such an area; for this purpose it would be considered as a 'territory or possession of the United States'.

The situation in Cyprus may be presumed to be similar; there, incomplete devolution (see p. 213) may have prevented Britain from retaining full sovereignty in the base areas.

12:5 LEGAL CHARACTERISTICS OF MILITARY BASE AGREEMENTS

From the above examples of military base agreements the following can be established:

1 Military base agreements are sometimes concluded in a less formal way than ordinary treaties, as for example the Sandbank agreement which because of its political nature was even exempt from the constitutional requirements of assent of the legislature and exempt from rules on a formal renewal or prolongation of the agreement.
2 Other agreements are concluded not only in solemn form but have even been included in a state's constitution (as in Cuba) or in a state's 'unamendable' constitution (as in Cyprus) to ensure stability of treaty regimes. But a state can always amend its constitution: a right of revision is incidental to the right of self-determination (see pp. 13 and 17).
3 In some cases states have been granted 'sovereignty' over base areas, as in Panama and Cyprus; but these agreements imply

a grant of only some 'sovereign functions' and are not, in essence, different from other treaties on military bases.

4 In other cases, states seek to guarantee the stability of a base treaty regime by relating it to economic aid. The fee for the lease is, in many cases, paid for in the form of 'economic aid' that is not, technically, paid in return for rights over a military base. For the base there is, in such cases, no quid pro quo.

5 Some states have granted leases 'in perpetuity', as in Panama, or for an indefinite period, as in Cuba.

6 Even if a military base agreement is concluded for an indefinite period, like the Évian agreement, or for long periods of twenty-five or fifty years like the Jordan or the Soviet-Finnish agreements, they have, in many cases, been discontinued, before they lapse.

7 The territorial state has invariably insisted on the necessity of continuous consent and, in numerous cases, denounced agreements when such consent was no longer present, as in Bizerta or in Algeria; such denunciations have never met any pronounced protest by the lessee. In the few cases where a claim for denunciation has not been accepted this has, as in Cuba, been due to lack of political strength.

As for the right to terminate an agreement on foreign military bases it appears that most states have claimed such a right by operation of the principle *rebus sic stantibus*: if the foreign policy changes the fundamental precondition for the agreement is absent and a state is therefore entitled to denounce it. The United Kingdom never questioned Malta's right (p. 208) to terminate the agreement during the recent negotiations on a British base on the island nor did it question the right of Jordan (p. 203) or Libya (p. 204) to break agreements in similar circumstances; and when Morocco indicated that it did not wish to continue the US military base it was dismantled (p. 207). Similarly, Algeria denounced the agreement providing for French military bases in the country and France never contested that it had such a right. In the few cases where a state has not been able to exercise such a 'right' it appears to have been for reasons of political force exercised by the lessee, and perhaps, to some extent, of military force or the threat of such force.[68]

However, I have previously examined the *rebus sic stantibus* doctrine[69] and advanced the view that this doctrine should only entitle a state to revise an existing treaty, not to denounce it unilaterally, as such unilateral denunciations threaten the very essence of binding international law. The International Law Commission, on the other hand, as well as a number of authorities[70] saw little risk in allowing this doctrine as a ground for denunciation and the Vienna Convention on Treaties included an article on the matter.[71] The only limit placed by this article on the application of the principle is that treaties establishing borders must not be affected by a denunciation.[72] However undesirable the doctrine may be, one could certainly claim that if it is to have any application at all it must entitle a state to denounce treaties on foreign military bases in its territory when its foreign policy, or perhaps entire economic system has changed.

But the matter can also be seen from another angle and then certain other rules can be suggested without invoking the *rebus sic stantibus* doctrine.

It is obvious that a foreign military base is an infringement on the territorial sovereignty of a state. For this reason many, particularly Soviet scholars, have suggested that agreements on such bases are 'unequal' and 'void'.[73] But it is also obvious that a state is entitled to allow such bases in its territory if it gives it free consent; such bases, as has been shown (p. 197), may not necessarily be a burden for the host country but may be entirely within its interest and perhaps even established on its request.[74] I suggest that since military base agreements provide for an important, but partial, delegation of sovereignty, this delegation is based exclusively on the host state's consent and is only operative as long as such consent is present. In other words, military base agreements are by their nature different from other international agreements and treaties, in that they, by necessity, require the *continuous consent of the territorial state* (see pp. 197-9).

On the other hand, denunciation of such a treaty cannot reduce rights under general international law—for example, the right of navigation through the Panama Canal could not be abolished even if the Zone treaty was denounced as the right exists under general international law irrespective of treaties (see p. 43).

In some cases a lessee of a military base may have incurred considerable expense in relation to the base. It might then be unfair if a host state could denounce a base treaty without compensation. Military base agreements are concluded between sovereign states whereas investment contracts are—at least normally[75]—concluded between a state on one side and a company on the other. Yet, if military base treaties are related to state investment contracts, use can be made of rules similar to those which apply in the case of nationalization of foreign property.[76] Military bases could then be denounced according to the mechanisms described above provided compensation was offered. The difference between denouncing military base treaties, or other territorial restrictions in this way, and traditional nationalization of foreign-owned property, would then be that in the case of military bases, compensation has, in practice, never been demanded, even if a foreign state, as in Morocco, has lost considerable sums by accepting the denunciation of a base treaty. Furthermore, the requirement that there must be no 'discrimination',[77] when foreign-owned property is nationalized has no counterpart in the case of military bases, as the rule implies that there must be no distinction between aliens and nationals, and that the nationalization law must be 'general'—questions which do not arise in the case of foreign military bases. A further difference is that in the case of military bases there are never any provisions for arbitration: this would be against the nature of the alliance and political friendship between the two nations concerned, an alliance reflected in the willingness to conclude a military base treaty.

In other words the rules of the eminent domain[78] by which a state can safeguard the interest of its community *in its own territory* operates not only in the case of nationalization of foreign-owned property but also in the case of denunciation of delegated sovereign functions, in conjunction with the rule of *continuous consent* required for potentially unequal treaties.

NOTES

1 For example, Nozari, *Unequal Treaties in International Law* (Stockholm, 1971), p. 119; Kozhcvnikov, in *Mezhdunarodnoe pravo,* ed. Korovin (Moscow, 1951), p. 379; Lukashuk, in *Soviet Yearbook of International Law, 1959,* pp. 18 et seq.; Zuyev, in

Soviet Yearbook of International Law, 1952, p. 61; Grzybowski, *Soviet Public International Law* (New York, 1970), p. 445. W. L. Tung, *China and the Foreign Powers: The Impact and Reaction to Unequal Treaties* (New York: Oceana, 1970), pp. 19 et seq.

2 See Detter, 'The problem of unequal treaties', *International and Comparative Law Quarterly* (1966), p. 1086.
3 Niboyet, 'La notion de reciprocité dans les traités diplomatiques de droit international privé', *Académie de droit international, Receuil des cours* (1935), ii, p. 281.
4 Lester, 'Bizerta and the unequal treaty theory', *International and Comparative Law Quarterly* (1962), p. 848.
5 Discussion in the Sixth Committee, A/C.6/S.R.784.
6 Ibid., A/C.6/S.R.790, cf. 189.
7 For example, Jacovides, *Treaties Conflicting with Peremptory Norms of International Law and the Zürich-London Agreements* (Nicosia, 1966), pp. 19 et seq.
8 I. Detter, *Law Making by International Organizations* (Stockholm: Norstedts, 1965), pp. 155 et seq.
9 I. Detter, *Essays on the Law of Treaties*, (London; Sweet & Maxwell 1967), pp. 95 et seq.
10 Article 62.
11 Detter, *Law Making by International Organizations*, pp. 216-17.
12 Detter, *Law Making by International Organizations*, pp. 216-17. Cf. supra, pp. 21 and 141.
13 Detter, in *ICLQ* (1966), pp. 1069 et seq. Cf. supra pp. 21 and 141.
14 Malloy ii, 1349.
15 *US Department of State Bulletin*, 32, No. 815, 2 February 1955, p. 237, and US, Treaties in Force, 1972.
16 See, *Guantánamo* (Havana, 1970).
17 D. P. O'Connell, 'Independence and the problems of state succession', in *The New Nations in International Law and Diplomacy* edited by W. V. O'Brien (New York: Praeger/ London: Stevens, 1965), p. 10. Cf. United States Naval Base; Guantánamo, US Dept. of Defense, 3rd ed., p. 1.
18 *Guantánamo*, p. 69.
19 M. O. Hudson, *Cases and Other Materials on International Law*, 3rd edition (St Paul: West Publishing Co., 1951), p. 144.

For the 1940 agreement see *American Journal of International Law* (1940), supp., p. 127.
20 Cf. supra, pp. 65 et seq.
21 *UNTS*, vol. 48, p. 203.
22 Cmd 6916 (1946); Cmd 7404 (1948).
23 Cf. supra, pp. 180 et seq. on consent in case of state succession. On the provisions of these agreements see, *On the Evacuation of British Forces* (Tripoli, 1970), p. 14.
24 Cf. supra, pp. 166 et seq. on democratic consent.
25 *On the Evacuation of British Forces*, pp. 33 and 37. Forces of the United States were present in Libya until 1971 when the Uqba Ben Nafa'e Air Base was evacuated; the Mallaha Base had been evacuated in 1970; see, *Evacuation Day of American Troops* (Tripoli, 1971), p. 5.
26 *TIAS*, No. 4734.
27 D. P. O'Connell, *State Succession in Municipal Law and International Law* (London: Cambridge University Press, 1967), vol. 2, p. 260. Canada declared that it was willing to continue the 1941 agreement with respect to Newfoundland after its cession in 1949 by exchange of notes on 13 February and 19 March 1952. O'Connell claims that one must not draw the conclusion from this consent that military base treaties are 'personal' and thus not commonly transmitted under the alleged rules of state succession (p. 262). But it does not seem to be state practice to transmit such treaties without such consent, see, supra pp. 180 et seq.
28 *UNTS*, vol. 151, p. 217.
29 On this question, see articles 73 and 32 of the German constitution and also, Detter, *Law Making by International Organizations*, pp. 274 et seq.
30 BFSP 72, 247.
31 BFSP 72, 743.
32 For text, see, *Revue égyptienne de droit international* (1957), p. 222.
33 UN Doc. S/4869, 21 July 1961.
34 See, further, M. S. Rajan, *United Nations and Domestic Jurisdiction*, 2nd edition (London: Asia Publishing House, 1961), p. 165.
35 UN Doc. A/PV 996, 21 August 1961, p. 32.

36　UN Doc. S/PV 961, 966, 21-29 July 1961; A/PV 996, 1006, 21-25 August 1961. On United Nations constitutional law see Lester, in *ICLQ* (1962), p. 848.
37　UN Doc. A/L/351.
38　France, *Journal officiel*, 20 mars 1962, pp. 3015 et seq.
39　Other parts of the treaty were renegotiated, see, further, I. Delupis, *Finance and Protection of Investments in Developing Countries* (Gower Press, 1973), pp. 160 et seq.
40　M. M. Whiteman, *Digest of International Law* (Washington: Government Printing Office, 1963-5), vol. 2, p. 984; Zemanek, 'State succession after decolonization', *Académie de droit international. Recueil des Cours* (1968), iii, p. 240; Flory, *Annuaire français de droit international* (1955), p. 28.
41　*Annuaire français de droit international* 1956, p. 834.
42　*New York Times*, 28 May 1956.
43　*UNTS*, vol. 588, p. 55.
44　This agreement was revised by an exchange of letters on 8 July 1966 but the revision merely concerned certain errors on a map and did not in substance alter the agreement.
45　Article 4.
46　*UNTS*, vol. 588, p. 109.
47　*UNTS*, vol. 588, p. 109.
48　See, further, Delupis, *Finance and Protection of Investments in Developing Countries,* pp. 78 et seq. and infra p. 219.
49　*The Times*, 30 March 1972
50　*UNTS*, vol. 382, p. 10.
51　*UNTS*, vol. 382, p. 3.
52　Cmnd. 1093 (1960).
53　Resolution adopted at the 1102nd mtg. 4 March 1964.
54　S/10441, 11 December 1971 and decision of 15 June 1973.
55　Cf. Bedjaoui, Report on Succession of States, *Yearbook of the International Law Commission 1968,* vol. 2 (New York: United Nations, 1969), p. 114.
56　*UNTS*, vol. 382, p. 231. The agreement was renewed in 1965.
57　*UNTS*, vol. 382, p. 232.
58　Brownlie, *Principles of International Law,* second edition (Oxford: Clarendon Press, 1973), p. 105.
59　Hudson, Cases, 1929, 397.
60　*AD 1929-1930* 80.

61 *AD 1938-1940* 180.
62 *AD 1931-1932* 111.
63 *AD 1929-1930* 81.
64 Brownlie, *Principles of Public International Law*, p. 117.
65 OAS Council, 31 January and 4 February 1964; cf. Fenwick, 'Legal aspects of the Panama case', *American Journal of International Law* (1964), p. 436.
66 *AD 1947* 49.
67 *AD 1948* 64.
68 For example, Cuba, which sought to denounce the Guantánamo Base Agreement, cf. supra, p. 203.
69 I. Detter, *Essays on the Law of Treaties* (London: Sweet & Maxwell, 1967), pp. 95 et seq. Cf. also supra, pp. 155 and 198.
70 Cf. comments by the special rapporteurs in the International Law Commission, see *Yearbook of the International Law Commission 1957*, vol. 2 (New York: United Nations, 1957), pp. 56-65 (Sir Gerald Fitzmaurice) and *Yearbook of the International Law Commission 1963*, vol. 2 (New York: United Nations, 1965).
71 Article 62 of the Vienna Convention.
72 Article 62(2).
73 Talalayev-Boyarshinov, 'Unequal treaties as a mode of prolonging the colonial dependence of the new states of Asia and Africa,' in *Soviet Yearbook of International Law, 1961*, pp. 169-70.
74 Cf. consent to UN forces, Detter, *Law Making by International Organizations*, pp. 61 et seq. On enforcement action see supra. p. 22.
75 But see the Évian treaty, Delupis, *Finance and Protection of Investments in Developing Countries*, pp. 85 and 158.
76 See further, Delupis, *Finance and Protection of Investments in Developing Countries*, pp. 67 et seq.
77 Delupis, *Finance and Protection of Investments in Developing Countries* pp. 68 et seq.
78 Delupis, *Finance and Protection of Investments in Developing Countries*, pp. 61 et seq.

PART FIVE

CONCLUSIONS

Conclusions

Independence implies the right to remain free from foreign interference. However, a state can never cut itself off from all relations with other states in the modern international community. There will always be states exposed to military, political and economic pressure from other countries. But modern international law is taking increasing notice of what smaller, or newer, states face in this respect. There are now rules to protect states from being exposed to undue pressure during treaty negotiations. These safeguards guarantee that an agreement concluded under, primarily, military force, does not take effect in international law; it is void. This new rule will undoubtedly be of great importance to developing nations although economic or political force has sometimes been as compelling to these nations as military power. However, in order to preserve a certain stability of treaty relations it has, so far, proved impossible to declare all treaties concluded under economic or political force void, as there are presumably no treaties, even among equal partners, which were not concluded subject to some form of pressure.

If independence then implies the negative state of remaining free from foreign interference, self-determination, as a concept, may be used to designate the positive elements of the same rule: the right to secede from colonial rule, the right to be the supreme power within the territory of the state and the right to a representative government. It has been shown how these rights have been secured to varying degrees under modern international law, concentrating upon the practical implications of independence and self-determination on the power of peoples in their own territory.

A state has freedom to act within its borders without any interference by other states. But there are certain exceptions to this power. Such exceptions fall into two groups: those relating to the territory itself and those relating to individuals and property in that territory.

Exceptions relating to the territory include restrictions imposed by general international law concerning innocent passage through territorial waters and international rivers; rules concerning access to ports; and rules concerning pollution.

Nearly all states are also bound by international conventions to allow for transit overland; and even apart from such conventions it could be argued that a landlocked state must have some minimum right to reach the sea; if it were denied this right the 'freedom' of the high seas would become meaningless. Similarly, a state, which, because of its geographical position, is cut off from international trade routes, is probably entitled to some minimum form of overland transit if such a right is necessary for its survival.

Concerning air transit it must be emphasized that now nearly all states have joined the International Civil Aviation Organization whose constitution ensures certain transit rights for nonscheduled flights; a great majority of states have also adhered to the transit agreement which covers rights for transit of scheduled flights. There exists today a quasi-universal right of transit for civil aircraft under international treaty law.

A state's sovereignty over aliens is restricted by rules on the immunity of state agents. There is now extensive treaty regulation of the immunity of diplomats and consuls but, even outside such conventions, state agents enjoy certain immunity under traditional international law. However, new rules on the immunity of agents other than diplomats seem to indicate that immunity is only allowed when 'official acts' are involved. Territorial sovereignty thus covers jurisdiction over trade delegations, public ships engaged in trade and acts *de jure gestionis* of a foreign state; even immunity of diplomats is, outside the treaty framework, increasingly reduced and probably no longer covers all private acts. Diplomats do not, it seems, enjoy immunity if they abuse their rights.

Territorial sovereignty over individuals has also important limitations in so far as international law imposes rules on human rights and, sometimes, on extraterritorial asylum to be respected by the territorial state whether or not it has acceded to treaties and conventions on these matters.

For any further restrictions of territorial sovereignty specific consent is required. A treaty concluded under armed force is nowadays invalid under international law, although it is submitted that an exception must be made in the case of boundary treaties. A change of government does not affect the validity of treaties which bind the state and the people after such changes. But if there is a *coup d'état* treaties may, in some cases, be suspended.

Consent to further territorial restrictions, beyond what general international law demands, requires absence of coercion and full and free consent of a state. Such consent must not be construed as following automatically from state succession, even if treaties concern the land itself, and thus, technically, are *in rem*.

There are no servitudes in international law: such 'servitudes' could only be put to the test at state succession; and at state succession no obligations are 'inherited' unless consent is given. Thus no 'dispositive' or 'real' treaties are automatically transmitted to a successor state. But numerous treaties, multilateral or bilateral, dispositive or personal, are transmitted to successor states for *convenience,* as a new method of adhering to treaties. The only difference between accession by state succession and accession by specific declaration (as in traditional international law) is then that in the first case the declaration has retroactive effect as from the date of independence; but in no case does this occur without the actual consent of the new state.

Thus, there are no 'servitudes' which survive state succession, and it is unrealistic to claim that a state should be bound by its predecessor's agreements on military bases. Furthermore, any treaty delegating to others the exercise of sovereign functions in a state's territory can be denounced *on certain conditions*. Such power of denunciation is incidental to the rule of self-determination; a people cannot, against its will, bind itself in perpetuity to restrictions of sovereignty in its own territory when the contents of a treaty has become *unequal*.

This power of denunciation—which entails lesser hazards than the accepted principle of *rebus sic stantibus*—only concerns certain restrictions by *treaty* of a state's sovereignty in its own territory. Treaties which may have this effect do appear to require the *con-*

tinuous consent of the territorial state. It appears that, for example, military base treaties may be denounced in certain cases, even if they have been validly concluded and even if they are not the fruit of coercion. I have previously put forward the view that the principle *rebus sic stantibus* presents great danger to the international legal system as it leaves a state free to rid itself of international obligations under treaties merely by claiming that circumstances that applied when the treaties were concluded have, in the opinion of that state, undergone a fundamental change. Such subjective assessment of 'fundamental change' is bound to contribute to insecurity and the undermining of international treaty relations. But if we allow for the principle of continuous consent in the case of treaties which delegate to others sovereign functions *within a state's own territory,* and submit such denunciation to certain conditions, we deal with a certain *group* of treaties, and limit the power of denunciation to certain cases.

Some of the treaties in this group concern military bases; these treaties may be denounced if they become burdensome, or unequal —for example, if a state has changed its foreign policy or considers there is no adequate quid pro quo. But when treaties of this kind are denounced—and state practice shows that such denunciation is usually 'accepted' without protest—the lessee of a base may have to leave behind installations worth considerable sums. Many facilities are necessarily abandoned, such as buildings, airstrips, etc., and they can normally be put to some profitable use by the territorial state. In cases like these it appears fair to allow for a rule of compensation.

Treaties on military bases can then be compared with state investment contracts and use can be made of rules similar to those which apply to nationalization. Treaties on military bases, and perhaps certain other agreements *in rem,* could be denounced only on condition that adequate compensation is offered. Technically, the same rules for compensation should apply as for nationalization but, in practice, compensation has never been demanded, even when a state has lost considerable sums by accepting the denunciation of a base treaty. The requirement of nondiscrimination has no practical counterpart in the case of military base treaties. Finally, unlike many investment contracts, military base treaties never provide for arbitration. Two nations that conclude a military base agreement are not likely to foresee any future dispute that could be adequately

Conclusions

settled by arbitration.

By virtue of the eminent domain a state can thus rid itself of certain territorial restrictions under treaties. The most common types of such restrictions in modern international law are the numerous military base agreements. But there are also other restrictions of a state's self-determination in its own territory not necessarily *in rem* to which similar rules on denunciation may apply and to which I have also referred: the capitulation treaties in China could be validly terminated once such termination was deemed to be in the 'public interest'; similarly the legislative functions delegated to the EEC can be terminated in so far as a member, by leaving the organization, may resume its full legislative power in its own territory; it is another matter that vast economic problems would be involved if a member attempted to leave such an integrated community as the EEC. However, the right to withdraw from this organization subsists, even in the silence of the treaties of Rome, if such withdrawal was in the public interest of a country.

The group of treaties which a state could denounce according to the mechanisms I have described are thus certain agreements which restrict the sovereignty of a state in its own territory, and, more precisely, *those which allow for the exercise of sovereign functions by another state, or by an organization, within the territory of the state.* Such functions may either be judicial—as in the case of the capitulation treaties with China under which consuls of the great powers were given right to adjudicate in cases involving their own nationals in China. Other sovereign functions may be of legislative nature, like the power of lawmaking exercised by the European Communities within the territory of the member states. The third type of sovereign functions which may be exercised by another country within the territory of a sovereign state are functions relating to the armed forces, as laid down in military base agreements. All these types of treaties by which states delegate their own sovereignty in their own territory may be denounced according to the principles of independence and self-determination when there is no longer any consent to tolerate such infringements upon the sovereign rights of the state. In other words, all such treaties require, unlike other types of agreements in international law, not only the *initial* consent of a state but its *continuous consent.*

Writers who claim that all treaties are invariably binding, lest the principle *rebus sic stantibus* furnish its dubious ground for denunciation, have never discussed the mechanisms of the eminent domain as applied to treaties. A state cannot rid itself of any treaty; it can denounce a specific *group of treaties*: those of which the material contents have *become unequal*. But should such inequality subsist international law cannot demand that the interests of the people of that state are forsaken to uphold the principle *pacta sunt servanda,* the rule of independence and self-determination, as safeguarded by the eminent domain and the rule of continuous consent, has priority.

A matter regulated by treaty may not remain 'essentially' within a state's 'domestic jurisdiction' as understood in article 2(7) of the United Nations Charter. However, the question whether the powers of the eminent domain shall be exercised rests exclusively with the territorial state: no other state may intervene in such a matter which lies within the reserved domain, in other words a matter which is *internal* to that state.

On the other hand, other matters no longer form part of the reserved domain; there are general rules of international law operating within a state's territory as described in Part One of this book. For example, certain questions relating to transit to the sea, pollution or human rights are now of paramount importance to the international community as a whole and can no longer be sheltered behind the walls of a national state by a plea of domestic jurisdiction or by the arguments of the reserved domain that such matters are 'internal' to that state alone.

Index of Cases

Albissola, The (Italy)   47 n81
Amand, *Re* (UK)   141 n2
Ambatielos claim (arbitration) (Commission of Arbitration: Greece & UK)   126 n10
Amkor Corporation v Bank of Korea (USA)   102 n13
Anglo-Norwegian Fisheries case— *see* Fisheries case
Arantzazu Mendi, The (UK)   102 n6, 108 n40
Archimedes, The (Sweden)   30
Asylum case (ICJ)   24, 135 n42

Baccus S.R.L. v Servicio Nacional del Trigo (UK)   102 n1
Balloni v Chilean Ambassador (Italy)   117 n9
Balmaceda case (France)   116 n6
Banco Nacional de Cuba v Sabbatino (USA)   158 n64
Barbuit's case (UK)   120 n19
Barcelona Traction, Light and Power Co. Ltd, Second Phase (ICJ)   129
Bartlett, Kenneth Robert, *Re* (Panama)   215
Berizzi Bros v SS Pesaro (USA)   104
Bigelow v Princess Zizianoff (France)   120
Brown (Robert E.) claim (British–US Arbitration Claims Tribunal)   126 n11
Brunswick (Duke) v Hanover (King) (UK)   103 n14

Burriel, *Re* (Panama)   215

Canal Zone v Coulson (USA)   214
Canevaro case (Permanent Court of Arbitration)   125 n3, 128 n23
Carl Zeiss Stiftung v Rayner & Keeler Ltd (No. 2) (UK)   102 n2
Chung Chi Cheung v R. (UK)   103 n23
Comina v Kite (Italy)   117 n8
Compania de Transportes de Gelabert, *Re* (Panama)   215
Compania Naviera Vascongado v SS Cristina (UK)   102 n6, 108 n40
Concordat case (Germany)   169
Corfu Channel case (Merits) (ICJ)   41-2, 93
Cornell *et al* v Vermilya Browns Co (USA)   216
Customs Regime between Germany and Austria (PCIJ)   143 n7

Daimler Co. Ltd v Continental Tyre & Rubber Co. (Great Britain) Ltd (UK)   128 n24 & n25
Delagoa Bay Railway Co. case (international arbitration)   129 n26
Dexter & Carpenter v Kungl. Järnvägsstyrelsen (USA)   102 n1
Dickinson v Del Solar (UK)

Dickinson *continued*
  116 n6, 117 n12
Dralle v Czechoslovakia (Austria)
  102 n11

Egyptian Delta Rice Mills Co. v
  Comisarí General de Madrid
  (Egypt)   108 n46
Emperor Maximilian's Heirs v
  Lemaître (France)   103
Engelke v Musmann (UK)   120 n20
Exchange, The Schooner v
  M'Faddon (USA)   103 n21, 105

Faber, The (Arbitration between
  Germany and Venezuela)   47
Fallois, de (France)   117 n13
Farouk (King) v Christian Dior
  (France)   103
Fisheries case (ICJ)   31, 45
Fisheries Jurisdiction (UK v
  Iceland) (ICJ, interim
  protection)   35
Fisheries Jurisdiction cases,
  Jurisdiction of the Court
  (ICJ)   35
Flack claim (British-Mexican
  Claims Commission)   128 n23
Fong Yue Ting v US (USA)   73 n48
Franconia, The—*see* R. v Keyn
Freeborn v Fou Pei Kouo (France)
  117 n15
Free Zones of Upper Savoy and the
  District of Gex (PCIJ)   5 n4,
  143 n7, 181-2

General Accident Fire & Life Ass.
  Comp. (Eire)   117 n12
Genocide case (ICJ)   133
Gilbert case   106 n32
Girard case (USA)   105
Guaranty Trust Co. v US (USA)
  169 n15

Hamspon v Bey of Tunis (Italy)
  108 n41

Iceland v UK (ICJ)   34-5
Interpretation of Peace Treaties
  with Bulgaria, Hungary and
  Romania (ICJ)   143 n7

Island of Palmas (Permanent Court
  of Arbitration)   5-6, 152

Japan v Smith & Stinner   106 n32
Juan Ysmael & Co. Inc. v
  Government of the Republic
  of Indonesia (UK)   108
Jurisdiction of the European
  Commission of the Danube
  (PCIJ)   48

Krajina v Tass Agency (UK)
  102 n1, 102

Lake Lanoux case (France-Spain
  Arbitral Tribunal)   96
Landreau claim (arbitration
  between USA & Peru)   130 n21
Legal Consequences for States of the
  continued Presence of South
  Africa in Namibia (South-
  West Africa) notwithstanding
  Security Council Resolution
  276 (1970) (ICJ, advisory
  opinion)   15
Legal Status of Eastern Greenland
  (PCIJ)   5 n4
Lehigh Valley Railroad Co. v State
  of Russia (USA)   169
Lepeshkin v Gossweiler & Co.
  (Switzerland)   171, 172 n33
Lorentzen v Lydden & Co. Ltd
  (UK)   141 n2
Lotus, The SS (PCIJ)   23, 24
Luckenback Steamship Co. v US
  (USA)   215

Machel case (France)   103 n24
Magdalena Steam Navigation
  Company v Martin (UK)   117
Missouri v Illinois (USA)   93 n4
Mosul case—*see* Treaty of Lausanne
Musgrove v Chun Teeong Toy
  (UK)   73

Namibia case—*see* Legal
  Consequences for States, etc.
Nederlands Beheers Institut v
  Nimwegen (Netherlands)   155-6
Neer's claim (Mexican Claims
  Commission)   125 n2

New Jersey v City of New York (USA)   93 n4
Newton, The (France)   47, 105 n28
Nishimura Ekiu v US (USA)   73
North American Dredging Co. Claim (US-Mexico Claims Commission)   128 n17
North Atlantic Fisheries arbitration (Permanent Court of Arbitration)   182
North Sea Continental Shelf cases (ICJ)   38

Orinoco Steamship Co. (Permanent Court of Arbitration)   128 n19
Oscar Chinn (PCIJ)   48
Ottoman Debt arbitration (Arbitration under the Treaty of Lausanne 1925)   176 n59

Pan American Tankers Corporation v Republic of Viet-Nam (USA)   102 n13
Panevezys-Saldutiskis Railway (PCIJ)   126 n9, 128 n21
Parkinson v Potter (UK)   120 n20
Parlement belge, The   104
Perruchetti v Puig y Casauranc (Italy)   117
Peter Pázmány University (PCIJ)   128 n22
Porto Alexandre, The (UK)   105 n27, 108 n39
Prince Danilo of Montenegro (Italy)   103 n15
Prince of Monaco in the United States   103 n20

Queen Mary of Rumania   103 n19

R. v A.B. (UK)   117
R. v Kent—see R. v A.B.
R. v Keyn (The Franconia) (UK)   30
R. v Lunan (Canada)   119 n17
R. v Turnbull   119 n17
Renault v Roussy-Renault Co. (France)   172 n32
Republic of Bolivia Exploration Syndicate Ltd, Re (UK)   116 n6

Republic of Peru v Dreyfus Brothers & Co. (UK)   169 n13
Reservations to the Convention on the Prevention and Punishment of the Crime of Genocide (ICJ, advisory opinion)   133
Respublica v De Longchamps (USA)   116 n3
Right of Passage over Indian Territory (ICJ)   24, 24 n8, 72, 180, 186
Rinaldi case (Italy)   117
Rose v R. (Canada)   119 n17
Ruden's case (Peruvian-US Claims Commission)   128 n22, 129 n26
Rumania v Trutta (Italy)   102 n7, 108 n41, 108 n47

SA des chemins fer liègeois-luxembourgeois v Netherlands (Belgium)   102 n8
Sabbatino case—see Banco Nacional de Cuba v Sabbatino
Sally, The (France)   47, 105 n28
Sapphire, The (USA)   169
Savarkar case (Permanent Court of Arbitration)   5 n3
Soc. Le Gostrog et l'URSS v Ass. France-Export (France)   102 n10
Socobelge v Greece (Belgium)   108 n44
Spelar v US (USA)   216

Tani v USSR Trade Delegation (Italy)   102 n4
Temple of Preah Vihear (ICJ)   187
Trail Smelter arbitration (US v Canada)   92-3, 94, 96
Treaty of Lausanne (Mosul case) (PCIJ)   143 n7
Treaty of Neuilly (PCIJ)   143 n7

USSR Trade Delegation v Borga (Italy)   102
US v Deutsches Kalisyndikat Gesellschaft (USA)   102 n13

Wimbledon, The SS (PCIJ)   44, 143 n7

Index of Treaties

1659	France & Spain (Peace of the Pyrénées) 72 n42	1899	The Hague Convention I 175
1774	France & Spain (customs limits) 31	1901	USA & UK (Panama Canal: Hay–Pauncefote treaty) 43
1815	Treaty of Turin 181-2		
1821	Treaty of Dresden 44	1903	Panama & USA (Hay–Bunau–Varilla treaty) 43, 165-6, 168, 182-3, 196
1831	Treaty of Mainz 44		
1839	Treaty of London 44		
1842	Belgium & Holland (boundaries) 72 n42	1903	USA & Cuba (lease of land) 201
1856	Peace treaty (Crimean War) 183-4	1904	International Agreement for the Suppression of the White Slave Traffic 130
1856	Treaty of Paris 44		
1861	Italy & Switzerland (Campione) 72 n42	1904	USA & Cuba 202
		1905	Sweden & Norway (dissolution of union) 63
1866	France & Spain (Llivia) 72 n42	1905	The Hague Convention on civil procedure 171
1868	Convention of Mannheim 44		
1878	Treaty of Berlin 44	1907	The Hague Convention I (Convention for the Pacific Settlement of International Disputes) 175
1881	Treaty of Bardo (France & Tunisia) 205-6		
1881	Treaty of La Marsa (France & Tunisia) 205-6		
		1910	International Convention for the Suppression of the White Slave Traffic 130
1883	Treaty relative to the Navigation of the Danube (treaty of London) 44		
		1913	Germany & France (air transit) 79
1885	General Act of the Conference at Berlin 44	1919	Convention for the Regulation of Aerial Navigation (Paris) 79-80, 82-3
1885	Treaty between Portugal & Spain 31		
1886	Berne convention 174-5, 178	1919	Covenant of the League of Nations 143, 144-5 art. 23 58
1888	Convention of Constantinople (Suez Canal) 43		
1895	Germany & Switzerland (Railway traffic and boundaries) 61 n6, 72 n42	1919	Minorities treaty with Czechoslovakia 131

Index of Treaties

1919 Minorities treaty with Poland 131
1919 Minorities treaty with Romania 131
1919 Minorities treaty with the Serb-Croat-Slovene State (Yugoslavia) 131
1919 Sweden & Norway (grazing) 141 n1
1919 Treaty of Neuilly (Peace with Bulgaria) 131, 143 n7
1919 Treaty of St-Germain-en-Laye (Peace with Austria) 131, 143 n7
1919 Treaty of Versailles (Peace with Germany) 44, 131, 143, 143 n7
    art. 254 176 n60
    art. 380 44
    art. 435 182
1920 Minorities treaty with Greece 131 n31
1920 Treaty of Brünn 131 n31
1920 Treaty of Dorpat 131 n31
1920 Treaty of Riga 131 n31
1920 Treaty of Trianon (Peace with Hungary) 131
1921 Belgium & UK (Belbase agreement) 48–9
1921 Convention and Statute on Freedom of Transit (Barcelona) 60
1921 Convention and Statute on the Regime of Navigable Waterways of International Concern (Barcelona) 45, 60
1921 Convention Respecting the Nonfortification and Neutralization of the Åland Islands 184–5
1921 Declaration Recognizing the Right to a Flag of States having no Sea-coast (Barcelona) 60
1921 International Convention for the Suppression of Traffic in Women and Children 130
1921 Turkey & USSR 145
1922 Treaty of Upper Silesia 131 n31
1923 Convention and Statute on the International Regime of Maritime Ports (Geneva) 50
1923 Convention and Statute on the International Regime of Railways (Geneva) 60, 63
1923 Italy & Switzerland (Campione) 72 n42
1923 Treaty of Lausanne (Peace with Turkey) 131, 143 n7
1924 Minorities Treaty 131
1926 Brussels agreement 104
1926 International Convention with the Object of Securing the Abolition of Slavery and the Slave Trade 130
1928 Havana Convention on Diplomatic Officers 121
1928 International Treaty for the Renunciation of War as an Instrument of International Policy (Pact of Paris) 143, 144–5
1929 Nile Waters Agreement (UK & Egypt) 93, 182
1930 International Labour Convention concerning Forced or Compulsory Labour 131
1936 UK & Egypt (immunities and privileges of British forces in Egypt) 107 n37
1938 Munich agreement 151-2, 154-6
1940 Montevideo Treaty on International Sea Trade 104
1940 USSR & Finland (peace treaty) 203
1941 UK & USA (bases in West Indies) 204
1944 Armistice agreement (with Finland) 203
1944 Convention on International Civil Aviation (Chicago) 80–2, 84–5
    art. 5 80–1
1944 International Air Services Transit Agreement 81, 85
1944 International Air Transport Agreement 81
1945 Charter of the United Nations 13, 14–15, 130, 146
    art. 1 16
    art. 1(2) 7
    art. 2(4) 145, 147, 148, 149
    art. 2(7) passim
    art. 55 7, 131

Index of Treaties

1945 Charter *continued*
    art. 73 7–8
    art. 76 8
1946 UK & Transjordan (alliance) 203
1946 USA & UK (Bermuda agreement on air services) 80 n11
1947 General Agreement on Tariffs and Trade 66–7, 68, 69
    art. 5 66–7, 72
1947 Treaty of peace with Bulgaria 131, 143 n7
1947 Treaty of peace with Finland 131, 203
1947 Treaty of peace with Hungary 131, 143 n7
1947 Treaty of peace with Italy 131, 153
1947 Treaty of peace with Romania 131, 143 n7
1947 UK & Burma (devolution) 176 n62
1948 Convention on the Prevention and Punishment of the Crime of Genocide 130, 133
1948 International Labour Convention concerning Freedom of Association and Protection of the Right to Organize 131
1948 Treaty of Economic, Social and Cultural Collaboration and Collective Self-defence (Brussels) 106
1948 UK & Transjordan (Alliance) 203
1949 Convention on Road Traffic (Geneva) 68
1949 Conventions for the Protection of War Victims (Red Cross) 175, 176
1949 International Labour Convention concerning the Application of the Principles of the Right to Organize and to Bargain Collectively 131
1949 North Atlantic Treaty 106
1950 European Convention on Human Rights 126, 131, 132
1950 France & USA (military bases in Morocco) 207
1951 Convention for the Establishment of the European and Mediterranean Plant Protection Organization 91
1951 Convention relating to the Status of Refugees 130
1951 International Labour Convention concerning Equal Remuneration for Men and Women Workers for Work of Equal Value 131
1951 Treaty Establishing the European Coal and Steel Community 198
1951 UK & Libya (temporary financial agreement) 204
1953 Convention on Political Rights of Women 130
1953 UK & Libya (friendship and alliance) 204
1954 Convention relating to the Status of Stateless Persons 130
1954 Geneva Agreement on Indo-China 131 n3
1954 International Convention for the Prevention of Pollution of the Sea by Oil 91
1955 Afghanistan & USSR (transit) 68
1955 State Treaty for the Reestablishment of an Independent and Democratic Austria 131
1955 Treaty of Friendship, Cooperation and Mutual Assistance (Warsaw Pact) 106, 210
1955 USSR & Finland (military bases) 203
1956 Convention on the Abolition of Slavery, the Slave Trade and Institutions and Practices similar to Slavery 130
1956 Multilateral Agreement on Commercial Rights of Non-Scheduled Air Services in Europe 81–2
1957 Chile & Bolivia (construction of a pipeline) 64–5

1957 International Labour
 Convention concerning the
 Abolition of Forced
 Labour 131
1957 Treaty establishing the EEC
 (Rome) 137, 198-9
 art. 238 71
1957 Treaty establishing the
 European Atomic Energy
 Community (Euratom) 198
1957 UK & Federation of Malaya
 (devolution) 176 n62
1957 UK & Ghana (devolution)
 176 n62
1957 UK & Jordan (Exchange of
 notes terminating treaty of
 alliance) 203
1957 USSR & Poland (visiting
 forces) 106 n34
1958 Convention on the
 Continental Shelf 37-8
1958 Convention on the High Seas
 35, 74, 104
 art. 3 69
 art. 9 104
1958 Convention on the Territorial
 Sea and the Contiguous
 Zone 29-32, 104
 art. 1 29
 art. 4 31-2, 46
 art. 5(2) 46
 art. 7 45
 art. 14 39-41
 art.16(4) 42 n63
 art. 18 39 n47
 art. 19 105 n28
 art. 20 105 n29
 art. 21 104
 art. 23 103 n22
 art. 24 32
1958 Discrimination (Employment
 and Occupation) 131
1958 Pakistan & Afghanistan
 (transit) 68
1959 Sudan & Egypt (Nile waters)
 95
1960 Convention against
 Discrimination in
 Education 131
1960 Cyprus, Greece & Turkey
 (treaty of alliance) 212-13
1960 India & Pakistan (use of
 Indus river) 95
1960 UK & Cyprus (financial
 assistance) 213-14

1960 UK, Greece, Turkey &
 Cyprus (establishment of
 republic of Cyprus) 211,
 213
1960 UK, Greece, Turkey &
 Cyprus (treaty of
 guarantee) 211-13
1961 Convention on the Reduction
 of Statelessness 130
1961 European Social Charter 131
1961 Exchange of Notes Settling
 the Fisheries Dispute
 between Iceland and the
 UK 32
1961 USA & Federation of the
 West Indies (defence areas
 agreement) 204
1961 Vienna Convention on
 Diplomatic Relations 116,
 118, 119
 art. 31 116-17
 art. 32 116 n6
 art. 37 116 n7
 art. 39 116 n6
1962 Equality of Treatment
 (Social Security) 131
1962 Évian agreement 196, 207,
 217
1962 Social Policy (Basic Aims
 and Standards) 131
1962 UK & Jamaica (devolution)
 205
1962 UK & Trinidad and Tobago
 (devolution) 205
1963 Convention on Consuls 119,
 121
1963 Treaty banning Nuclear
 Weapon Tests in the
 Atmosphere, in Outer
 Space and Under Water
 91
1963 USA & Japan (consuls)
 121 n22
1963 USA & South Korea (consuls)
 121 n22
1964 European Fisheries
 Convention 32 n19
1964 International Labour
 Convention concerning
 Employment Policy 131
1964 UK & Malta (aid) 208-9
1964 UK & Malta (military bases)
 208
1964 USA & USSR (consuls)
 121 n22

Index of Treaties

1965 UK & Cyprus (renewal of 1960 agreement) 213 n56
1965 UK & The Netherlands (continental shelf) 38 n43, 38 n44
1965 UK & Norway (continental shelf) 38 n43
1966 Convention on the Elimination of all Forms of Racial Discrimination 130
1966 International Covenant on Civil and Political Rights 12–13, 15, 16, 130
1966 International Covenant on Economic, Social and Cultural Rights 12–13, 15, 16, 130
1966 UK & Denmark (continental shelf) 38 n43, 38 n45
1967 Convention on the Elimination of all Forms of Religious Intolerance 130
1967 Convention on Fishing in the North Atlantic 32 n19
1967 European Convention on Consular Functions 121
1967 Treaty on Principles governing the Activities of States in the Exploration and Use of Outer Space 83
1967 Treaty for the Prohibition of Nuclear Weapons in Latin America 91
1968 African Convention on Conservation of Natural Resources 91
1968 Agreement on the Rescue of Astronauts, the Return of Astronauts and the Return of Objects launched into Outer Space 83
1968 Convention on Road Traffic 68
1968 Sweden & Norway (continental shelf) 38 n43
1968 Treaty on the Non-proliferation of Nuclear Weapons 91
1968 USSR & Czechoslovakia (visiting forces) 106 n34
1969 American Convention on Human Rights 131
1969 Convention on Intervention on the High Seas in case of Oil Pollution Damage 91
1969 Convention on Special Missions 119
1969 International Convention on Civil Liability for Oil Pollution Damage 91
1969 Vienna Convention on the Law of Treaties 142, 146, 152, 188
    art. 52 149, 150, 152, 153, 155
    art. 62 155, 198, 218 n71, 218 n72
    art. 63 171
    art. 64 133
    art. 74 171
    art. 84 149
1970 Convention for the Suppression of Unlawful Seizure of Aircraft 119
1971 Convention for the Suppression of Unlawful Acts against the Safety of Civil Aviation 119
1971 Scandinavian Convention on Cooperation to Prevent Oil Pollution of the Sea 91
1971 Treaty on the Prohibition of the Emplacement of Nuclear Weapons and Other Weapons of Mass Destruction on the Seabed and the Ocean Floor and in the Subsoil thereof 91
1971 UK & Germany (continental shelf) 38 n43, 38 n44
1971 UK, USSR, USA & France (West Berlin) 73 n45
1972 Convention on International Liability for Damage caused by Space Objects 83
1972 Sweden & Finland (continental shelf) 38 n43
1972 Sweden & Norway (grazing) 141 n1
1972 UK & Malta (military bases) 210-11
1972 UK & NATO (bases in Malta) 210-11
1973 Convention on Prevention of Marine Pollution 91

Subject Index

Aerial Navigation Act 1911 (UK) 79
Afghanistan
  proposals for a transit convention 69
Air defence identification zones 82
Airspace
  extent of 82-4
  passage through 79-87
Åland islands 16, 183-6
Albania
  and ICAO 85
  minorities 131
Algeria
  French bases 207
  human rights 132
  independence 8
  Yaoundé recommendations 33
Aliens, treatment of 6, 101, 125-9
  power to admit to a state 73
Amazonas river 44
Andorra
  and ICAO 85
Angola
  rail transit 61-2
Archipelagic principles 34, 42
Arctic Waters Pollution Prevention Act 1970 (Canada) 93
Argentina
  claims to territorial waters 31, 33, 34 n25, 37 n38
  Montevideo and Lima declarations 31 n16
  patrimonial sea 33
Asylum, right of 24
  extraterritorial 134

Australia
  and French nuclear tests 93-94, 118
  Permanent Court of Arbitration 175
  proposals on privileges of coastal states 33
Austria
  minorities 131
  and Paris agreement 152
  and South Tirol 152-3

Baarle-Duc 72
Baarle-Nassau 72
Bangladesh 16
Bays, access to 45-6
Belgian Congo—*see* Congo, Republic of the
Belgium
  and port facilities in Tanzania 48-9
  and rail transit in Belgian Congo 61-2
Benguela railway 61-2
Berne Union 174-5
Bodin, Jean 3
Bolivia
  dispute with Chile over Lauca river 97
  pipelines in Brazil 64
  pipelines in Chile 64
  proposals for a transit convention 69
Boundary treaties 155-6, 187-8
Brandt, Willy 154

Brazil
 Bolivian pipelines in 64
 claims to territorial waters 31, 33
 Montevideo and Lima declarations
  31 n16
 patrimonial sea 33
Bulgaria
 air transit agreement 85
 minorities 131
 shooting-down of Israeli plane
  85–6
Burundi (formerly Ruanda-Urundi)
 and port facilities in Tanzania
  48–9
Büsingen 72

Calvo, Carlos 127
Calvo clause 127–8
Cambodia
 Berne convention 174 n48
 Permanent Court of Arbitration
  175
Cameroon
 Berne convention 174
 Red Cross 175 n54
 Yaoundé recommendations 33
Campione 72
Canada
 air defence identification zones
  82
 oil protection zone and prevention
  of pollution 34, 93
 patrimonial sea 33
 Permanent Court of Arbitration
  175
 US pipelines through 65
Canals
 right of passage through 43–4
Castro, Fidel 202
Catatumbo river 47
Ceylon
 Permanent Court of Arbitration
  175
 see also Sri Lanka
Chile
 Bolivian pipelines in 64
 claims to territorial sea 31, 34 n25
 dispute with Bolivia over Lauca
  river 97
 Montevideo and Lima
  declarations 31 n16
 patrimonial sea 33
China
 capitulation treaties 23, 141, 170,

China continued
  199, 231
 Coercion 141–63
  historical background 143–7
  types of illegal force 148–59
  see also Consent
Colombia
 Lima declaration 31 n16
 and Panama Canal 165–6
 Santo Domingo declaration 33
Commission internationale de la
  navigation aérienne (CINA)
  80
Companhia do Caminho de Ferro
  de Benguela 62
Congo, Republic of the (formerly
  Belgian Congo)
 Berne convention 174
 and port facilities in Tanzania
  48–9
 rail transit 61–2
 Red Cross 175 n54
 see also Zaïre
Congo, Republic of the (formerly
  Middle Congo)
 Berne convention 174
 Red Cross 175 n54
Congo river 44
Consent to treaties
 and change of government 168–72
 continuous, theory of 197–8,
  218–19
 expression of 165–94
 need for, by newly independent
  states 173–88
 by the people 166–8, 204
 see also Coercion
Consuls
 in China 141
 immunity 119–21
Contiguous zone 5, 32–7
Continental shelf 37–9
 exploitation of 33, 37
 passage over 39
Continuous consent 197–9, 218–19
Corinth canal 43
Costa Rica
 fishery zone 34
 Santo Domingo declaration 33
Cuba
 nationalization of American
  property 158
 US bases 183, 201–3
Cyprus
 Berne convention 174
 British bases 211–14, 216

Cyrus *continued*
  independence 8
Czechoslovakia
  air transit agreement 85
  minorities 131
  and Munich agreement 151-2, 154-6

Dahomey
  Berne convention 174
  human rights 132
  Red Cross 175 n54
  Yaoundé recommendations 33
Danube river 44, 48
DDR
  and West Berlin 73
Declaration on the Granting of Independence to Colonial Countries and Peoples 9-10, 131
Denmark
  Åland islands 184
Developing countries
  need for safeguards on treaties 141-3
Devolution agreements 176-8
Diplomatic Immunities Restriction Act 1955 (UK) 117
Diplomatic immunity 115-24
  of consuls 119-21
  historical background 115-16
  of international civil servants 121-2
  specific rights and privileges 116-19
Dispositive treaties and agreements 173-4, 179-80
Domestic jurisdiction *passim*
  see also Reserved domain
Dominican Republic
  Lima declaration 31 n16
  Santo Domingo declaration 33

EEC—*see* European Economic Community
Ecuador
  claims to territorial sea 31, 36
  Montevideo and Lima declarations 31 n16
Eden, Anthony 154
Egypt
  Nile 95-6
  Suez Canal 43
  Yaoundé recommendations 33

Elbe river 44
Electricity transmission 63
  convention on 60
El Salvador
  claims to territorial sea 31
  Montevideo and Lima declarations 31 n16
Enclaves 24, 59, 72, 86
Equality between states, right of 3, 10
Equatorial Guinea
  Yaoundé recommendations 33
Escaut river 44
Estonia
  and Åland islands 184
  minorities 131
Ethiopia
  human rights 132
  Yaoundé recommendations 33
European Communities 21, 141
  withdrawal of member states 198-9, 231
European Economic Community 4-5
  association agreements 70-1
  delegation of legislative power 4, 22, 141, 198, 231
  right of withdrawal 199, 231
Extraterritoriality 5, 115, 116, 117, 134-5

Feilchenfeld, E. H. 170
Fiji
  archipelagic principles 42
Finland
  and Åland islands 16, 183-6
  Soviet military bases 203
Fishery Limits Act 1964 (UK) 32 n19
Fishing zones 32, 33-7
Fitzmaurice, Sir Gerald 146, 167
Force
  definition of illegal force 148-50
  economic and political 148-50, 156-9
  military 151-6
  see also Coercion
France
  and Åland islands 184
  and Algeria 158, 207
  and Libya 204
  and Morocco 207-8
  bases in Tunisia 205-6
  declaration by National Assembly

France *continued*
  19 Nov. 1792 6–7
  nuclear tests 93–4, 118

Gabon
  Berne convention 174
  human rights 132
  Red Cross 175 n54
General Assembly of the United Nations
  binding force of resolutions 13–14
  and colonial crises 8
  Commission on Human Rights 11–12
  and Cyprus 212–13
  Declaration on the Elimination of Discrimination against Women 131
  Declaration on the Granting of Independence to Colonial Countries and Peoples 9–10, 131
  Declaration on the Rights of the Child 131
  Economic and Social Council 11
  Fourth Committee 10
  and French bases in Tunisia 206
  and law of the sea 37
  resolutions on self-determination 8–11
  Sixth Committee 148, 158
  Universal Declaration of Human Rights 8, 11, 13, 126, 131, 132, 133
Germany
  and Åland islands 184
  Munich agreement 151–2, 154–6
  Sandbank range 205, 216
Gestionis, acta de jure 100, 102, 106–7, 228
Ghana
  claims to territorial waters 31
Grazing rights 22, 141, 159 n1, 188, 194 n101
Greece
  association with EEC 70, 71
  Corinth canal 43
  minorities 131
Gromyko, Mr 156–7
Grotius, Hugo (Huigh de Groot) 59
Guantánamo Base 183
Guatemala
  Lima declaration 31 n16
  Santo Domingo declaration 33

Guinea
  claims to territorial waters 31
  human rights 132

Haiti
  Santo Domingo declaration 33
Heads of state
  immunity for private affairs 103
Helsinki rules 96–7
High seas
  and continental shelf 37–8
  and internal waters 46
  jurisdiction over ships on 23
  and territorial waters 34
Honduras
  Lima declaration 31 n16
  Santo Domingo declaration 33
Huber, Max 5–6, 156
Human rights 6, 101, 123–5, 129–34
  economic, social and cultural 11–12
  fundamental 14, 126, 129–30
  political and civil 11–12
  Universal Declaration 8, 11, 13, 126, 131, 132, 133
Hungary
  minorities 131
Hyde, C. C. 166

Iceland
  claims to territorial waters 31
  dispute with United Kingdom 34–5
  patrimonial sea 33
  Permanent Court of Arbitration 175
Immunity
  of diplomats and consuls 114–22
  for foreign state property 107–9
  for private affairs of foreign heads of state 103
  for state-owned ships 103–5
Imperii, acta de jure 100, 106–7
Imposed treaties—*see* Coercion
Independence, right of *passim*, 3, 4, 8, 10, 197, 227, 232
  and consent to treaties 197
  legal value of the rule 13–18
  territorial 4–13
  and territorial devolution 213, 216
  see also Self-determination
India

Subject Index

India *continued*
  dispute with Portugal 24, 70
  patrimonial sea 33
  Permanent Court of Arbitration 175
  use of Indus river 95
Indonesia
  and archipelagic principles 34, 42
  Berne convention 178
  independence 8
  patrimonial sea 33
  and Straits of Malacca and Singapore 42
Innocent passage
  through airspace 80, 85
  through territorial sea 39–41
International Civil Aviation Organization (ICAO) 80–2, 84–5
International control commissions 141
International Law Commission, drafts of conventions
  on the law of treaties 133, 142, 145–6, 148, 152, 153, 218
  on prevention of crimes against diplomats 119, 121–2
  on representation in international organizations 121
  on succession 188
  on territorial sea and contiguous zone 40
International organizations
  contrasted with states 4
  immunity of civil servants 116, 119, 121–2
International servitudes—*see* Servitudes
International Tin Council 176
Intertemporality
  and Vienna convention on law of treaties 156
Intervention 14, 21, 108, 126–9, 130, 213, 227, 232
Investment guarantee agreements 71
Iraq
  minorities 131
Israel
  El Al plane shot down by Bulgaria 85–6
  Jordan Basin dispute 97
  Shooting-down of Libyan plane 86
Italy
  and Åland islands 184

Italy *continued*
  devolution agreement with Somalia 176 n62
Ivory Coast
  Berne convention 174
  human rights 132
  Red Cross 175 n54
  Yaoundé recommendations 33

Jordan
  British military bases 203, 217
Jurisdiction
  of consuls 120
  over ships on the high seas 23
  over ships in port 47–8
  over state-owned ships 103–5
  over visiting forces 105–7
  over warships 47, 103
  in territorial waters 23, 30, 34
  waiver of 22
  see also Immunity
Jus cogens 133–4

Kenya
  association with EEC 70
  human rights 132
  patrimonial sea 33
  Red Cross 175
  trans-African highway 70
  Yaoundé recommendations 33
Kiel canal 43–4
Korea
  Berne convention 174 n48

Landlocked states
  access to the sea 47, 59–60
  convention on 69–70
  right to flags of ships of 60
  right of transit 72–5, 86–7
Laos
  Permanent Court of Arbitration 175
  proposals for a transit convention 69
Latvia
  and Åland islands 184
  minorities 131
Lauca river 97
League of Nations 131
  and Åland islands dispute 16, 183–6
  and coercion 144–5
Libya
  British bases 204, 217

Libya *continued*
  human rights 132
  nationalization 159
  plane shot down by Israel 86
Liechtenstein
  and ICAO 85
Lima declaration 31, 34 n26
Lithuania
  and Åland islands 184
  minorities 131
Llivia 72
Luossavaara-Kiirunavaara AB 63

McNair, Lord 146
Majority rule, right to 14, 17-18
Makarios, Archbishop 212
Malagasy Republic
  Berne convention 174
  human rights 132
Malaysia
  and Straits of Malacca and Singapore 42
Mali
  Berne convention 174
  human rights 132
Malta
  association with EEC 70
  military bases 208-11, 217
Masaryk, Jan 154
Mauritania
  claims to territorial waters 31
  human rights 132
Mauritius
  archipelagic principles 42
  Yaoundé recommendations 33
Meuse river 44
Mexico
  Lima declaration 31 n16
  patrimonial sea 33
  Santo Domingo declaration 33
Military bases 141-2
  jurisdiction 105-7
  sovereignty over 214-17
  treaties concerning 180, 196-7, 198, 199, 200-14
Mintoff, Dom 209-10
Moçambique
  rail transit 62
Monaco
  and ICAO 85
Montevideo declaration 31, 34 n26
Morocco
  Berne convention 174
  independence 8
  US bases 207-8, 217, 219

Namibia 15
Nationality of business enterprises 128-9
Nationalization
  analogy for denunciation of military base treaties 219, 230-1
  and immunity 109
  motives 158-9
Nepal
  proposals for a transit convention 69
Netherlands
  devolution agreement with Indonesia 176 n62, 178
New York group 33-4
New Zealand
  and French nuclear tests 93-4
  patrimonial sea 33
  Permanent Court of Arbitration 175
Nicaragua
  Montevideo and Lima declarations 31 n16
  Santo Domingo declaration 33
Niger
  Berne convention 174
  human rights 132
Nigeria
  association with EEC 70
  claims to territorial waters 31
  human rights 132
  Red Cross 175
  trans-African highway 70
  Yaoundé recommendations 33
Niger river 44
Nile river 95-6, 182
Northern Rhodesia—*see* Zambia
North Sea
  continental shelf 38-9
  fishing 32 n26
Norway
  patrimonial sea 33
  protection of continental shelf 37
  rail transit rights 62-3
Nuclear tests 93-4, 118
Nürnberg trials 6, 130, 132, 133

O'Connell, D.P. 170
Oil protection zones 34

Pacta sunt servanda, principle of 148, 168, 195, 196, 198
Pakistan

Pakistan *continued*
 and Bangladesh 16
 Permanent Court of Arbitration 175
 use of Indus river 95
Panama
 claims to territorial waters 31
 Montevideo and Lima declarations 31 n16
 and Panama canal 43, 165-6, 168, 182-3, 200, 214-17
Panama canal 43, 165-6, 168, 182-3, 200, 214-17, 219
Paraguay river 44
Paraná river 44
Passage over land—*see* Transit
Passage through air 79-90
Passage through water, right of 29-50
 definition of innocent passage 39-41
 internal waters 45-50
 international rivers 44-5
 straits and artificial canals 41-4
 territorial sea 29-41
 by warships 39-41, 47
Patrimonial sea 33-4
Peace treaties 152-3
People's Republic of the Congo— *see* Congo, Republic of the (formerly Middle Congo)
Permanent Court of Arbitration 175
Persian Gulf
 continental shelf 38
Personal treaties 173
Peru
 claims to territorial waters 31, 36
 Montevideo and Lima declarations 31 n16
 patrimonial sea 33
Philippines
 air defence identification zones 82
 archipelagic principles 42
 off-coast islands 46 n77
 Permanent Court of Arbitration 175
Pipelines 63-5
Plata, Río de la 44
Poland
 air transit agreement 85
 and Åland islands 184
 minorities 131
Pollution 91-5
Ports

Ports *continued*
 access to 47-50
Portugal
 and rail transit from Belgian Congo 61-2
 right of passage over Indian territory 24, 72
Protection zones 31 n15

Quid pro quo 185, 217

Rail transport
 agreements on 60-3
 convention on 60
'Real' treaties 179-80
Rebus sic stantibus, doctrine of 155, 198, 217, 218, 229-30, 232
Recognition of new governments 172
Reserved domain *passim*, 129, 232
 see also Domestic jurisdiction; Intervention
Rhine river 44
Rhodesia 168
 border closure (1965) 65
 border closure (1973) 62, 74, 86-7
 and rail transit 62
 'will of the people' 18, 168
Right of establishment 71
Río de la Plata—*see* Plata, Río de la
Rio Grande 44
Rivers
 equitable use of international 95-7
 national 46-7
 rights of navigation on international 44-5, 48
Road transit 65-70
 conventions on 68
 GATT regulations 66-7, 72
Romania
 minorities 131
Ruanda-Urundi—*see* Rwanda and Burundi
Rwanda (formerly Ruanda-Urundi)
 human rights 132
 and port facilities in Tanzania 48-9

St Lawrence river 44
Saltwater colonialism 16

Sanctions, economic 158
Santiago declaration 31
Santo Domingo declaration 31, 33, 34 n26
Seabed, exploitation of 33, 37, 38
Self-determination, right to passim, 3, 4
  and consent to treaties 168, 188, 197, 229
  historical background to 6–8
  and human rights 130
  instruments dealing with 8–13
  international conventions on 11–13
  legal value of the rule 13–18
  and restrictions of sovereignty 197
  and right to amend own constitution 216
  right to free elections 14
  right of succession 14, 15–17
  and sovereignty 3–18
  and state succession 188
  see also Independence
Senegal
  Berne convention 174
  human rights 132
Servtitudes 180–6
  cases on 181–6
  and military bases 180
  and territorial waters 29, 30
  theory of 180–1
Sierra Leone
  claims to territorial waters 31
  human rights 132
  Red Cross 175
  Yaoundé recommendations 33
Singapore
  and Straits of Malacca and Singapore 42
Six livres de la république (Jean Bodin) 3
Somalia
  human rights 132
South Africa
  and Namibia 15
South America
  extent of territorial sea 35–7
Southern Rhodesia—see Rhodesia
South Tirol 152–3
South-West Africa—see Namibia
Sovereignty 3–4
  delegation of 21–2
  over airspace 82–4
  over internal waters 45–7
  over military bases 214–19

Sovereignty continued
  over ports 47, 48
  restrictions of 21–3
  over territorial waters 29, 30, 34
  residual 214–15
  and self-determination 3–18
Spain
  and Cuba 201
Sri Lanka
  patrimonial sea 33
State succession 48, 143, 168–88, 205, 206
Stimson, Henry Lewis 144
Stimson doctrine 144–5
Straits
  right of passage through 41–3
Sudan
  Nile waters 95–6, 182
Suez canal 43
Sweden
  and Åland islands 16, 184–5
  jurisdiction in territorial waters 30
  and rail transit through Norway 62–3
Syria
  reservations on Vienna Convention on Law of Treaties 150

Taiwan
  Berne convention 174 n48
Tanganyika
  Red Cross 175
  see also Tanzania
Tanganyika Concessions Ltd 62
Tanzania
  association with EEC 70
  pipeline 65
  sites at Dar es Salaam and Kigoma 48–9
  Yaoundé recommendations 33
Territorial sea
  definition of innocent passage 39–41
  extent of 31–9
  and internal waters 46
  right of passage through 29–41
Territorial waters—see Territorial sea
Territorial Waters Jurisdiction Act 1878 (UK) 30
Togo
  Yaoundé recommendations 33
Torrey Canyon 93
Trans-African Highway 70

Transit overland, right of 24, 59–75
  of electricity 63
  general 71–5
  of military equipment 72, 74
  by pipeline 63–5
  by rail 60–3
  by road 65–70
  under bilateral agreements 68–9
  under EEC association agreements 70–1
  under GATT 66–7
  under international conventions 68
  under investment guarantee agreements 71
Treaties
  coercion to conclude 141–63
  consent to 165–94
  personal and dispositive 173–6
  unequal 195–223
Trinidad and Tobago
  patrimonial sea 33
  Santo Domingo declaration 33
Tunisia
  Berne convention 174
  French bases 205–6
  independence 8
  patrimonial sea 33
Turkey
  association with EEC 70, 71
  minorities 131

Uganda
  association with EEC 70
  human rights 132
  Red Cross 175
Unequal treaties 195–223, 229
  identification 195–7
  potentially 197, 199, 200–14
  theory of continuous consent 197–9, 229–30
Union minière du haut Katanga 61–2
USSR
  and Åland islands 183–6
  and ICAO 85
  military bases in Finland 203
  state succession 169–72
  and West Berlin 73
United Kingdom
  attitude to immunity 102, 103, 105, 107
  bases east of Suez 197
  bases in Jordan 203, 215

United Kingdom *continued*
  bases in Libya 204, 217
  and Belgian port facilities in Tanzania 48–9
  and Cyprus 211–14, 216
  devolution agreements 176–7
  dispute with Iceland 34–5
  jurisdiction in territorial waters 30
  and Malta 208–11, 217
  and Panama canal 43
  proposals on seabed exploitation 37
  Sandbank base in Germany 205, 216
  sovereignty over airspace 79
  three-mile limit 31
  twelve-mile limit 32 n19
United Nations
  conference on the law of the sea 1973 33
  Economic Commission for Europe 68
  and Namibia 15
  and self-determination 7–8
  and treaties procured by force 145–7
  see also General Assembly
United States of America
  air defence identification zones 82
  bases in Morocco 207–8, 217
  bases in West Indies 204–5
  and Cuba 158–9, 201–3
  fishing vessels seized by Ecuador 36, 158
  and Indonesia 158
  and International Covenants on Human Rights 12
  and Laos 158
  and Libya 204
  and Panama Canal 43, 165–6, 168, 182–3, 200, 214–16
  pipelines in Canada 65
  protests about extensions of territorial sea 35–6
  and right of transit to Alaska 59
  and Stimson doctrine 144
  three-mile limit 31
Universal Declaration of Human Rights 8, 11, 13, 126, 131, 132, 133
Upper Volta
  Berne convention 174
  human rights 132
Uruguay

Uruguay *continued*
  claims to territorial waters 31, 37 n38
  Montevideo and Lima declarations 31 n16

Venezuela
  patrimonial sea 33
  Santo Domingo declaration 33

Waldock, Sir Humphrey 146
Warships
  jurisdiction over 47, 103
West Berlin 71
Williams, Sir Robert 62

Yacimientos Petroliferos Fiscales Bolivianos (YPFB) 64

Yaoundé declaration/recommendations 31, 33, 34 n26, 74
Yugoslavia
  association with EEC 70
  minorities 131

Zaïre (formerly Republic of the Congo)
  human rights 132
  rail transit 61–2
  Yaoundé recommendations 33
Zambia (formerly Northern Rhodesia)
  Berne convention 174
  border closure (1965) 65
  border closure (1973) 62, 74, 86–7
  pipeline 65
  and rail transit 62
  Red Cross 175
Zulia river 47